LAW AND THE BIBLE

Volume One

– A Collective Genesis –

by George P. Fletcher

Richard V. Meyer, Editor

Responses and Contributions
Herbert Morris, Joel S. Baden, Arthur J. Jacobson,
Katharina de la Durantaye, and Richard V. Meyer

Introduction
Suzanne Last Stone

Mazo Publishers

Law And The Bible: A Collective Genesis

ISBN: 978-1-94612411-1
Copyright © 2017

Contact
George P. Fletcher: GeoPFletcher@aol.com
Richard V. Meyer: meyer@mc.edu

I\/I

Mazo Publishers
P.O. Box 10474
Jacksonville, FL 32247 USA

www.mazopublishers.com
mazopublishers@gmail.com

I dedicate this volume to the two women and two men who have exhibited the patience and perseverance to see beyond my many failings and continue providing me the encouragement to attempt the next great challenge in life.

To my beautiful wife of twenty-eight years, Melissa

To my loving and eternally supportive mother, Mary Anna

To my comrade in arms and law, Mark "Max" Maxwell

To the man who served as the "genesis" for this project, my teacher, mentor and friend, George Fletcher.

Contents

Foreword

Richard V. Meyer

In the fall of 2006, I met George Fletcher for the first time. It was an event that would forever change the direction of my life. I was an active duty Judge Advocate in the United States Army fresh from a tour in Alaska. I was pursuing a graduate legal degree at Columbia Law in preparation for a follow on assignment teaching at the United States Military Academy at West Point. At the time I headed into my studies viewing them as a rest break from an incredibly tasking military career. I was so wrong.

My first class at Columbia was George's "Jurisprudence of War." Though that first session lasted just 75 minutes, for me it was paradigm shifting. I had been studying and practicing the laws of war for over a decade and had been taught and led by some leading scholars in the field. Yet in George's classroom I felt like a Roman being introduced to the Arabic concept of zero.

George exhibited himself as the epitome of the creative thinker ... a presumptively square peg in the highly derivative field of law. He flexed the magical ability to consider all the thoughts and rules that have gone before and yet not be constrained by them. His questions in class somehow managed to both challenge and simultaneously support the pillars of the laws of war. Next to him I felt like an intellectual infant in need of swaddling.

I left that classroom and immediately changed my academic schedule, taking all four of the classes that George taught that semester, paying only passing attention to the topics. Just over seven hours later I was in a seminar room for a class labeled "Biblical Jurisprudence"; a class co-taught by George and a visiting Professor from Cardozo Law, Suzanne Last Stone.

George & Suzanne started class with some quick introductions and we soon realized that we were quite the eclectic group in terms of religion and nationality. Of the nine students, we had two American Mormons, one Israeli atheist, one Israeli Jew, one Canadian Muslim, one American born again Baptist, one American atheist, one Chinese Buddhist and finally me, an American Roman Catholic.

It was déjà vu for me as my prior knowledge of the topic was quickly marginalized by George's original thoughts. George took the most familiar text on the globe and converted it into something fascinating and new. However this time his questions were countered by Suzanne's simple and yet perfect explanations based on Jewish law and tradition. We nine were caught up by the momentum of George's poignant and expository questions before being bolted back down by Professor Stone's millennia deep wisdom. Back and forth we were born by the waves of thought until our minds were completely frazzled.

Two hours later, George and Suzanne ended class, got up and left the room. None of the rest of us moved. After a brief silence the conversations started ... each of us finding a unique way to express how our minds had just been blown asunder. It set the standard for the entire semester, and my wife learned to never expect me home before midnight on Tuesdays.

Almost a decade later when I was teaching law, thanks to George's career redirection, I learned of a project to collect George's writings on Biblical Jurisprudence and publish them along with reactions from a variety of contributors. I was elated when given the opportunity to have a role in it. I want to be clear that though I bear the title of editor, most of the credit for this work belongs to George's then research assistant Lee Cooper. Lee helped seek out and secure the contributions and put up with my ever changing views about the organization of this volume. Without him, the book would have remained a concept rather than a reality. He should be proud, as I am, of the august list of contributors to this work. Take a look at the bios at the end of this volume and you will see why I am more than humbled to appear beside them. Further, I can think of no better nor more appropriate scholar to introduce this intellectual journey than the aforementioned Suzanne Last Stone.

I have three pieces of advice as you enter into this philosophical wonderland. As you read the ten chapters in this volume, I advise that you experience them with others, stopping frequently to discuss the ideas presented. Have a copy of the Bible handy at all times; any version will do. In class we each used the version supported by our respective faiths, so we often spent time exploring the significance of the wording differences.

I also advise that those of you of faith try reading through a secular lens as well. Faith is not a necessary attribute for this discussion. One need only understand that the drafters of all of the foundational legal codes in the Western world were schooled using these stories. Like the facts in a seminal Supreme Court case, the stories of the Bible provide the context necessary to fully comprehend the values these men adhered to and incorporated into the law. Further, like the facts of a case, the veracity of a Biblical story is irrelevant to its role of adding depth to a legal rule or axiom.

Finally and perhaps most importantly, I advise you to read the articles as George would, simultaneously looking to accept and reject each assertion therein all the while identifying what new thought you have to add to the discussion.

I will end this foreword with the words of my Canadian Muslim friend and classmate, Hanif Nori, who described this topic and class as the "... only one that makes you sit back every now and then and just say Wow!" I sincerely hope this happens for you.

Introduction

Suzanne Last Stone

The remarkable renascence of intellectual interest in the Bible and Hebraic thought has produced some of the most intriguing challenges today to the standard story of the "great separation" between religion and politics. From Eric Nelson's *The Hebrew Republic*,[1] which argued that several central modern political ideals including religious toleration had their roots in religious convictions drawn from a reading of the Hebrew Bible, to Paul Kahn's *Out of Eden*,[2] which presents a political theology of liberalism traced back to the story of Adam and Eve in the garden, writers have newly sought to understand our modern world through its engagement with the Hebrew Bible just as much as with the pagan world of Greece and Rome.

George Fletcher was a very early pioneer of this intellectual project. His insistence that the ideal of equality that we moderns have come to embrace so thoroughly could not be philosophically justified without an acknowledgment of its roots in the Hebrew Bible and most especially in the story of the creation of humans

---

1 Eric Nelson, *The Hebrew Republic: Jewish Sources and the Transformation of European Political Thought* (Cambridge: Harvard University Press, 2010).

2 Paul W. Kahn, *Out of Eden: Adam and Eve and the Problem of Evil* (Princeton: Princeton University Press, 2006).

in God's image since it long predated these and other studies.[3] But an etiology of our modern concepts is not the driving force of Fletcher's scholarship. Rather, he is concerned to let the Hebrew Bible speak to us "as it was." And no one has paid the sort of meticulous attention to the language of the Hebrew Bible, to the ways even Genesis reflects the lawyer's art, and to the moral emotions explored in Genesis that underlie our most basic conceptions of justice, than has George Fletcher.

Fletcher is, of course, uniquely qualified for this task. He brings to his close reading of the Hebrew Bible a remarkable array of talents. He is a prodigious master of the nuances of the Hebrew language, a mastery honed by his astonishing command of multiple languages, which also has allowed him to access exceptional German scholarship unavailable to most English readers, such as Claus Westerman's lengthy and comprehensive commentary on Genesis 1-11. He is equally at home in philosophy and easily locates for the modern reader the crucial differences between biblical and Kantian conceptions of free will, biblical and modern accounts of the origins of language, and biblical and modern accounts of guilt.

Yet, George Fletcher is, first and foremost, a lawyer. And his deep understanding of the intellectual grammar of law, the subject of Fletcher's provocative book, *Basic Concepts of Legal Thought*,[4] thoroughly infuses his essays on the Book of Genesis. In *Basic Concepts of Legal Thought*, Fletcher aimed to introduce students not only to some of the central problems of jurisprudence but also, and importantly, to the structure of legal argumentation and legal reasoning. Law exists 'in the mind,' and not only in books or social interaction. Legal thought is a distinctive way of grasping the universe. And it is this distinctive way of grasping the universe that the Book of Genesis most especially provides us, George Fletcher declares, if only we let it speak to us as it was.

As the consummate teacher he is, Fletcher invites his

---

3 Supra George Fletcher, "In God's Image: The Religious Imperative of Equality Under Law" published as Chapter Nine in this volume. Part II of that article emphasizes the foundational role of Genesis in our current concepts of equality.

4 George Fletcher, *Basic Concepts of Legal Thought* (New York: Oxford University Press, 1996).

colleagues and students to debate with him and extend his work. In this initial volume, five colleagues (several of whom were former students) have taken up this invitation. The result is a lively conversation about the meaning and generative power of two central images in Genesis: Adam and Eve's eating from the tree of knowledge of good and bad and the creation of humans in the image of God. These two central images orient the volume, which is divided into two parts: the first, Rethinking the Fall of Man and the second, The Collective Human Identity. The volume's editor, Richard V. Meyer, has chosen the titles carefully and perspicuously. They immediately orient the reader to two central contentions that animate Fletcher's essays: First, if we wish Genesis to 'speak to us as it was,' we must retrieve the meaning of the Garden of Eden story before the idea of original sin bequeathed by Christian theology obscured its import. Second, we must re-learn the meaning of collective understandings of human identity and, even more importantly, human responsibility.

Part One begins the conversation with two essays by George Fletcher analyzing the Garden of Eden story. In these two essays, Fletcher offers a new way of understanding the consequences of the first humans eating of the forbidden fruit. Genesis narrates that eating the fruit will enable humans to become like God. But what precise attribute of God will humans acquire? Fletcher eschews the usual answers – immortality or procreative powers – and asks us, instead, to focus more closely on the nature of divine activity revealed in the creation narrative. "The divine mind stands for organizing the world in sets of bilateral distinctions," he writes. The thrust of the narrative is that distinction is "good," even "very good," as the biblical text tells us. The divine activity of creation is an ever-increasing process of separation: light and darkness, night and day, earth and heaven, water and land, species distinguished into kinds, man and woman, creation and rest. The opposite of distinction is chaos. The "biblical way of seeing the world" Fletcher concludes, is antithetical to the modern replacement of categorical distinctions with admixtures."

Fletcher argues persuasively that this divine capacity to distinguish is also the key to unraveling the meaning of humans acquiring "knowledge of good and evil" by eating the forbidden fruit. As he writes: "The important point for understanding the 'knowledge of good and evil' is not the moral question of equality but the very existence of distinctions as a way of perceiving and organizing reality. The 'good' is that which stands in opposition to something else – light as opposed to darkness, humans as opposed to animals. The 'bad' is that which has no contrast, no sense of being paired with an alternative."

This is, of course, a deeply Hebraic reading of the Bible, one that will be especially familiar to those steeped in the sources of the Jewish rabbinic tradition, the closest inheritors of the biblical worldview. Looked at through the lens of the early rabbinic tradition, the Bible is a drama of ever-increasing distinction and particularity. Not only are humans separated from animals, but humans themselves are divided into distinct collectivities, each with its own language. And Israel is divided from the "other nations." Even biblical messianic visions preserve allegiance to the drama of distinction, imagining a great reign of peace when the lion shall lie down with the lamb, a time when great and powerful nations will co-exist in peace with smaller ones, yet remain separate collectivities. Paul's alternative, cosmopolitan vision of utopian community, outlined in Galatians 3:28: "There is neither Jew nor Gentile, neither slave nor free, there is neither male and female, for you are all one in Christ Jesus," marks the end of a worldview still uninflected with Greek thought.

The distinctive intellectual grammar Fletcher describes is also a prominent feature of early rabbinic discourse.[5] Isadore Twersky's description of rabbinic thought as a "coincidence of opposites" vividly captures the rabbinic style of juxtaposing opposites without attempting to dissolve the tension between them or to achieve any sort of synthesis. In this respect, the rabbis continued the biblical way of seeing the world, applying it to ever more binary categories and pairs of oppositions.

The rabbis were first and foremost jurists and so we should not be surprised by this intellectual grammar. For this way of ordering the world, Fletcher argues, "intersects with the inculcated habits of those trained in law." It is the traditional lawyer who has continued the biblical mode of thought, Fletcher tells us. In the

---

5 See Suzanne Last Stone, *In Pursuit of the Countertext: The Turn to the Jewish Legal Model in American Legal Theory*, 106 Harv. L. Rev. 813 (1993).

modern world, with its rejection of sharp differences, traditional legal approaches have given way occasionally to matters of degree, such as comparative fault. The traditional legal mindset, Patrick Glenn argued by contrast, tends to bridge differences by multiplying categories, by bringing back the 'excluded middle.' [6] We can see this tendency in the rabbinic tradition, too, which, over time, developed intermediate categories bridging the binary distinction between Jews and the rest of the nations, such as Noahides or "nations constrained by the ways of religion." But these bridging techniques are parasitic on first apprehending the world through a set of binary distinctions.

Fletcher's comparison of the world of legal thought and the world of biblical thought sheds new light on the overall place and function of Genesis in the Torah corpus. For, Fletcher is implicitly claiming that Genesis, too, and not only the remaining four books of the Pentateuch that explicitly set forth laws, is a legal document. Genesis emerges as a necessary introduction to what follows: in a sense, a primer in how to think legally when later confronting the more explicit legal sections of the Hebrew Bible.

This is an extremely interesting contribution to the traditional rabbinic understanding of the Book of Genesis. Although the rabbis may have perpetuated the biblical mode of thought, the rabbis usually understood Genesis as history and not law and often questioned why the Torah, as a work of law, began with the story of creation and not with the chapter on laws in Exodus ("Elu HaMishpatim" or "These are the laws."). With rare exceptions, traditional commentators did not approach Genesis as law. These rare exceptions were concentrated around the rabbinic concept of Noahide law, the set of commandments God gave to all humanity. Genesis certainly described a world full of laws but was this merely history, a recounting of the way of life at the time, or a record of God's commands, the Talmudic rabbis asked. And, if these laws could be retrieved from Genesis, what precisely are the most basic laws humans must obey, given the narrative of divine creation? The reader of George Fletcher's fascinating essays on the creation story may not be surprised to discover that at least one astute minority

---

6 See Patrick H. Glenn, *Legal Traditions of the World,* 5th Ed. (New York: Oxford University Press, 2014).

opinion singles out a prohibition on admixtures. [7]

Fletcher's important point that becoming like God through eating the forbidden fruit refers to acquiring divine attributes other than immortality, is also taken up by his beloved teacher and colleague, Herbert Morris. In his contribution to the conversation about Rethinking the Fall, Morris analyzes Poussin's painting, Spring or Earthly Paradise. The serpent is conspicuously (and intentionally, per Morris) absent from Poussin's depiction of Adam and Eve in the garden. Morris links this absence with the painting's title, Spring, implying a rebirth. That rebirth is achieved not by eating from the Tree of Life, which Poussin paints in dark and ominous tones, but, rather, by eating from the Tree of Knowledge of Good and Bad, which is rendered in luminous tones. In choosing knowledge over immortality, Adam and Eve become creatures worthy of God's respect. In the final essay of Part One, Richard V. Meyer experiments with Fletcher's insight that Genesis is a text about law and legal reasoning. Meyer tests Fletcher's assertions about the meaning of the stories by reading the text in light of the canons of statutory interpretation. While largely confirming Fletcher's conclusions, Meyer challenges Fletcher's central contention that a close reading of Genesis 'as it was' does not support the later Catholic account of man's fall.

If the creation story presents an occasion for reflection on the intellectual grammar common to biblical and legal thought, the Joseph cycle of stories presents an occasion for reflection on the moral emotions that underlie our modern conceptions of justice, most especially in the arena of criminal law, the field George Fletcher reigned over for decades.

In his two essays introducing Part Two, Fletcher contrasts two understandings of guilt: Guilt as objective, a form of pollution creating a collective stain that can only be expunged through expiation or cleansing; and guilt as an interior feeling state. We moderns are prone to tell a story of moral progressivism, from primitive collectivism to modern individualism, and therefore identify the sense of guilt as consciousness as a uniquely modern concept, born with the emergence of the individual. Fletcher shows us that both senses of guilt appear in Genesis and both senses of

---

7 See Babylonian Talmud, Tractate Sanhedrin 59a.

guilt are still with us today. Retributive punishment – the belief that a guilty act requires punishment reflects the belief that "crime pollutes the moral order and the punishment serves to restore the...world as it ought to be." And so-called modern, interior guilt is precisely what Joseph's brothers experience when they encounter Joseph long after they left him to die. Here, guilt is a second-order failure to resist base impulses.

The modern story of moral progressivism is a myth. We moderns are still very much in the grips of a collectivist imagination. Witness the contemporary resurgence of collective forms of punishment in response to terrorism, which is often perceived as an act made possible by a group. What is wrong with this picture, Fletcher persuasively argues, is not the notion of collective guilt, which is entirely coherent. Rather, there is no necessary connection between collective guilt and collective punishment. The collective may bear some responsibility for the acts of members of their group but this does not justify collective punishment in response. Here again, remarkably, Fletcher has teased out of the biblical sources an ideational schema that seems to reappear in the texts of the Bible's earliest readers: the rabbis. Rabbinic tradition preserves the Bible's emphasis on collective forms of responsibility and, at the very same time, restricts the courts' right to punish on a collective basis. Fletcher thus has not only illuminated modern law, he has illuminated the roots of the rabbinic tradition by recovering biblical concepts too long encrusted over by layers of intervening interpretation.

These different senses of guilt and collectivist notions of responsibility and punishment are pursued further in Joel Baden and Katharina de la Durantaye's responses. Baden offers a meticulous analysis of the schema of sin offerings stipulated by Leviticus 4-5. Here, as elsewhere in the Hebrew Bible, unwitting sinning is distinguished from brazen or presumptuous sinning. Only intentional sinning, in theory, merits the death penalty but the sin can be absolved by bringing a sin offering essentially identical to the one an unwitting sinner must bring. Baden sets out to solve why the two different categories of sinners are seemingly treated identically. The unwitting sinner, Baden argues, is objectively guilty: a stain has been committed that must be removed. While individuals may not feel an interior sense of guilt for unwitting sins, they are still responsible as individual members of a collective to repair the breach that objective sin potentially creates between God and Israel and hence must bring an offering. The intentional sinner, though he brings the same sin offering, must also recite a confession. The confession signals awareness of individual responsibility. Fletcher's challenge to take collectivism seriously is the focus of Katharina de la Durantaye's extended case study of the "laws of soccer." Drawing on German case law, Durantaye points out that stadium bans issued by club owners against fans amount to the imposition of liability on fans for the bad behavior of other fans – a contemporary reincarnation of collective punishment.

The volume closes with a remarkable exchange between George Fletcher and Arthur Jacobson that returns us to the story of the creation of humans in the image of God. The principle of equality, particularly as developed in the American legal and political context, should be understood, Fletcher argues, in holistic rather than strictly analytic terms. Its roots are in an inextricable combination of biblical imagery and Kantian philosophy that cannot be separated and have implications for constitutional law. Fletcher's reading relies on the first account of creation. Jacobson turns to the second version of the creation story and offers a fascinating counter-interpretation. The second story is about freedom, not equality, Jacobson argues. What is at stake is primarily God's freedom, which emerges only when God has another being with which to interact. God's interactions are deeply personal, not abstractly equal. God punishes inequitably and God loves, often favoring certain humans over others, such as Abel over Cain. God's evolution through the two creation stories shows the deep tension between equality and freedom.

⌘ ⌘ ⌘

For many years, George Fletcher's students have been charmed and delighted by his thought-provoking reading of the Bible. His class on Biblical Jurisprudence, which I had the privilege of co-teaching with him on occasion, was for many the intellectual highlight of their legal education. Readers of this wide-ranging, thoughtful, and iconoclastic collection of essays can now share their experience.

A Collective Genesis

In 1978 George P. Fletcher vaulted to the top of his field when he published the landmark volume *Rethinking Criminal Law.* Unlike most young scholars entering the world of serious legal scholarship, Fletcher did not need to find a new and developing issue in order to make a significant addition to the existing literature. Instead, Fletcher first eviscerated and then resurrected one of the most sacred cows of jurisprudence... the fundamentals of the criminal law. In *Rethinking*, Fletcher looked at well-settled legal concepts from a variety of perspectives ranging from moral philosophy to political philosophy, history, international law and comparative law.[1] The result was the most-cited book on criminal law in the world and one that even has the rare honor of being the subject of its own symposium.[2] Ultimately, Fletcher's original manner of exploring old and familiar concepts caused a paradigm shift in the world's criminal law scholarship.

Starting in 1999, Fletcher tackled the most sacred of cows imaginable when he began his reanalysis of the Torah (referred to as the Pentateuch by Christians). No body of literature has been more read, analyzed and deconstructed than the first five books of the Bible. Somehow, however, Fletcher still found new ways to think about and analyze the stories and lessons contained therein. Fletcher used his love of and skill with languages to unearth arcana and breathe new life into age old lessons. Unlike *Rethinking*, these works were published in a series of articles in various law reviews

1 Russell L. Christopher, Symposium Forward, 39 Tulsa L. Rev. 737 (2004).

2 Id.

and journals. This volume (and its successor) operates as both an assembly of these works as well as a reactive symposium about them.

This first volume is broken into two parts. The first will have four total articles, two of which were drafted by Fletcher and two are reactions to those articles by two other scholars. These articles focus on analyzing the two creation stories in the book of Genesis. They explore the obvert legal and moral messages as well as the (linguistically) covert messages within the text. This first section is aptly title "Rethinking the 'Fall' of Man."

Part II of the volume contains three more Fletcher articles and three responses that further explore the meaning of the ancient text, but this section also evaluates the effect these concepts may have had on Western moral and legal philosophy. For reasons that become evident in that section, it is titled: The Collective Human Identity."

The title of this volume reflects both the shared role that the first book of the Bible has had for Judaism, Christianity & Islam, but also the role Fletcher's writings have had in reinvigorating the field of biblical jurisprudence.

PART I

Rethinking The "Fall" Of Man

The story of Eden is perhaps the most universally recognized story in the Western world. Jews, Christians, Muslims and even atheists have heard the story of how Adam and Eve ate the forbidden fruit and were subsequently banished from the Garden. However, it is a comparatively modern and primarily Christian practice to label this tale as the "Fall of Man." Whether one evaluates Adam and Eve's actions as sinful under the Christian tradition, or as a necessary maturing event of the Jewish teaching has a tectonic effect on the moral and legal lessons gleaned from the text.

In the first piece in this section, "The Jurisprudence of Genesis", Fletcher challenges the Catholic and Muslim interpretations of creation and the origins of man. It is a linguistic based (re)interpretation of the book of Genesis. Focusing on the original Hebraic wording, Fletcher walks through the mechanics of creation to demonstrate the significance of those stories for considering moral questions through the lens of Genesis.

Fletcher begins by explaining how the creative acts of the first Genesis story happen via performative speech. Adam, too, uses language to name the animals. But, language is a social phenomenon for communicating across individuals, which adds some mystery to the story when we consider that God and Adam are also described as being alone initially. Similarly, God is described as a judge, presumably of some pre-existing system of justice.

Abraham, too, later suggests the ontological priority of justice over God's conduct, suggesting that God was not a sole actor operating in complete vacuum. Fletcher then builds on these two broad areas of thought by rolling them into the question of whether "goodness" is an intrinsic property, or merely a relative (or, instrumental) property. Fletcher brings this high stakes question back down to the story of Eden, arguing that when Adam and Eve obtain "knowledge of good and evil" they are not necessarily obtaining some sort of omniscient moral sense. Rather, they are able to take on the role of judges, discerning and organizing reality with their words, exercising a mode of thought that is most commonly exemplified in legal thinking in modern society. This power of language itself is embedded with a sort of tension: language liberates and empowers humans to think and act independently, and yet language only has power insofar as it is a social tool.

The piece's closing section returns to the necessity and limitations of language, particularly in the context of interpreting authoritative texts. These texts, Fletcher argues, contain many tensions and do not always contain easy moral solutions, but they are the inspiration and starting point for reflection.

This leads directly into the second piece, "Thinking about Eden", in which Fletcher emphasizes the importance – and challenge – of translation for key passages in the story of Adam and Eve in Eden. Fletcher uses his own translation and modern rules of judicial interpretation to take on two major and often unchallenged aspects of Genesis: (1) the gender of the divinity and the first human, and (2) the idea of the eating from the Tree of Knowledge as original sin.

Fletcher identifies the role of gendered pronouns as key to analyzing the gender of God and Adam. Different translations of neuter pronouns (or, masculine pronouns that can be used for the neuter) can lead to divergent interpretations of the text. Fletcher argues that God is often assumed to be either masculine or androgynous (having no gender). However, he proposes that the correct translation leads the reader to conclude that both God and Adam (in the "first" creation within Genesis) possessed both the male and the female gender.

Continuing his attack on the Christian doctrine of human guilt arising out of original sin (and related religious ideas arising out of the Eden story), Fletcher contends that the Genesis narrative reveals shows no sign of guilt. Rather, the story could be read as revealing shame, not guilt, and even this is contestable depending on interpretation. Fletcher provides an alternative reading of the Tree of Knowledge, which he calls the "separation thesis." The separation thesis provides that eating of the fruit was a necessary step in the evolution of humans becoming independent actors, able to distinguish their separateness from God, as well as distinctions all around them. Knowledge of opposites and distinctions is the foundation for analytical thought and laws to organize society. The separation thesis, Fletcher concludes, is also appealing because it does not engage in the "anti-humanistic errors of original sin, misogyny, or sexual repression."

The first contributor response comes from the man who may have had the most important role in motivating Fletcher to dedicate himself to biblical jurisprudence and to whom the second Fletcher article is a tribute. Fletcher mentions spending countless hours with Professor Herbert Morris exploring the mysteries contained within the Torah. In "The Absent and Present Serpent" in Nicholas Poussin's "Spring", Professor Herbert Morris analyzes Poussin's painting, "Spring or Earthly Paradise", as a vehicle to uncover a radical alternative to traditional interpretations of the story of the eating from the Tree of Knowledge. Morris notes the conspicuous absence of a key element in Poussin's painting of what is clearly Adam and Eve in the Garden of Eden: the serpent. Because the serpent is so central to most readings and artistic depictions of Genesis 3 (and a motif in other Poussin paintings), it was clearly an intentional omission. Morris dismisses a few potential explanations, including that this is simply the scene just before the serpent enters the story, noting that Poussin's omission demands a heightened awareness of the details of the painting and, by extension, the story of Adam and Eve. Such awareness can transform the story to one of "rebirth" – hence the title, Spring – as these human beings elevate human life.

Morris walks the reader through the painter's works to elaborate on this theory, noting that the tree which we presume to be the Tree of Knowledge is, in fact, beautiful and alluring, while the Tree of Life is dark and foreboding, with the undesirability and uncertainty of eternal life. The Tree of Life is depicted in a "serpentine" manner, suggesting that the serpent actually lurked in the Tree of Life, but that Eve and Adam determined to seek the light of Knowledge over the potential darkness of eternal Life without knowledge. Morris supports his argument with other observations about the painting, and concludes that Eve and Adam may be fairly described as stoic heroes for their "veneration of knowledge, reason, and nature." With knowledge, and God's approval of their choice, the humans have become "creatures capable of dignity and worthy of respect."

The final article of this section is a response by Fletcher's former student, Professor Richard V. Meyer. Meyer accepts Fletcher's translations as well as most of his reinterpretations and analysis and yet differs on the ultimate conclusion about the "Fall of Man."

Meyer uses the legal case brief method and accepted axioms of statutory interpretation to expand upon Fletcher's reinterpretation of the creation stories. Meyer argues that the term "day" as it is used in the two creation stories does not describe a unit of time but rather an event. Specifically, Meyer argues that the text mandates that the word day means "when God acts." Further, he argues that the essential descriptive aspect of Eve was not her gender but that she was a product of Man as opposed to coming directly from God.

Meyer uses these two concepts to show that guilt is not a necessary aspect of Original sin. He argues that the Jewish tradition of a maturing event and the Christian concept of a fall are not in conflict. Rather than debunk this Catholic dogma, Meyer proposes that Fletcher's reinterpretation and his resultant separation thesis provide an excellent foundation for Christian creation ideology.

CHAPTER ONE

The Jurisprudence Of Genesis

George P. Fletcher

Genesis is both the supreme text of Western culture and yet underappreciated in its original language and integrity. The story of creation has informed artists of word and image from Dante and Michelangelo to John Steinbeck and Mark Twain. Adam, Eve, Cain, Abel, the serpent – we could hardly think about good and evil, free will and determinism, crime and punishment without them. Though its influence makes it the supreme text, Genesis in the words of the original Hebrew has been virtually lost to modern readers.

Genesis: The Original

The original text of the Hebrew Bible inspired theological and literary imagination at the expense of the words themselves. Jewish teachings took off in many directions with the elaboration of *Midrashim* or legends surrounding the text. Reading *Midrash* has the effect, in the metaphor of one of my teachers, of throwing you out to sea like a swimmer without a life preserver. The swimmer is cut off from the text and he must find his way back, and sometimes the return to the text requires great leaps of association.

Preferring systematic theology, the Catholic Church found

it important to implant architectonic doctrines in the text without much regard for whether these were supported by more than a *midrashic* hint. The serpent in the Garden became the devil.[1] Adam and Eve's eating of the forbidden fruit became the "original sin" by which humanity fell into a state that requires redemption. Original sin became a dogma of the Catholic literature and generated literary reflections on the Fall by Dante, Milton, and scores of others. It did not matter much whether the original text supported this reading or not. In the idiom of lawyers, the Supreme Court (namely the Church) had spoken and no one cared that much about what the Constitution (namely, the Bible) actually said.

Islam had its own way of undermining the original stories of Genesis. Though it accepts both the Hebrew and Christian Bibles, the Islamic tradition changes some of the stories of Genesis to fit the preconceptions of the religion. For example, in retelling the binding and intended sacrifice of Isaac, the tradition substitutes Ishmael – Isaac's half-brother and the reputed progenitor of the Arab peoples – for Isaac.[2] The guiding assumption must have been that being sacrificed to God was an honor that should be reserved for one of Islam's own.

The Reformation glorified the text but at the same time camouflaged the original Hebrew version. Calvin, Luther, and their movements claimed to have returned to the original words, but they did so in multiple vernacular versions that supposedly brought the divine revelation closer to the people. As Benedict Anderson insightfully points out, the Protestant movement correlates with the rise of the printing press and the commercialization of the holy text.[3] A bestseller was born – in all the languages of the world. Bringing the text to the vernacular meant that the original texts disappeared even more from public consciousness.

In the American experience, fundamentalists recite their indigenous version by heart and they believe that their text – e.g., the transient King James version – is the revealed word of

1 See Elaine Pagels, *The Origin of Satan* (New York, 1995).

2 While the Koran does not explicitly name which son of Abraham was designated for sacrifice, Islamic tradition holds that it was Ishmael. The relevant passage is *Sura* 37: 99-112.

3 Benedict Anderson, *Imaginary Communities: Reflections on the Origin and Spread of Nationalism* (London, 1983).

God. The literalists overlook the simple fact that the process of translation itself implicitly endorses an orientation and a school of interpretation. We will have occasion to look at some of these issues of translation that bear an ideological imprint.

According to some, the final blow to the integrity of the Hebrew text came in the nineteenth century with the emergence of scientific biblical criticism.[4] Scholars noted certain word patterns that indicated the probability of different authorship. The four primary texts came to be called the "E" or *Elohim*, the "J" or *Jehovist*, the "P" or *Priestly*, and the "D" or *Deuteronomic* source – the designation of God being one of the factors distinguishing the first two sources. *Elohim* as the sole name of God typically signals the "E" text; the joint name *Adonai Elohim* (= *Jehovah Elohim*)[5] marks the "J" text. This process of identification is a little tricky, however, for the "P" text also uses the single word for God – *Elohim* – as opposed to the double word *Adonai Elohim*.

In Genesis 1:1 through 2:3, the name of God is *Elohim*. This name returns in Genesis 5: 1. I shall refer to this as the first story of creation. The familiar hallmark of the first story is the recitation of the seven days of creation in Genesis 1. The intervening material from 2:4 to the end of chapter 4 constitutes the second story, which, because it contains the Garden of Eden, is of primary interest to us. It turns out that although the first story relies on *Elohim* as the name of God, it is thought to be of the later Priestly and not of the "E" source.[6] The second story, the "J" source, is considered the older of the two versions of creation.[7]

---

4 Julius Wellhausen, *Prolegomena to the History of Ancient Israel* (Gloucester, Mass., 1973) (originally published in 1883).

5 The Hebrew here rendered as *Adonai* or *Jehovah* is the Tetragrammaton – *Yud-Heh-Vav-Heh*. Orthodox Jews do not pronounce this name and therefore use a euphemism that means "Lord." Thus the translation in English text of this name is typically "Lord God," which represents an attempt to render the Tetragrammaton Y-H-V-H, often written as Y-H-W-H in English.

6 Samuel R. Driver, *An Introduction to the Literature of the Old Testament* (Edinburgh, 1891); Robert B. Coote, *In the Beginning: Creation and the Priestly History* (Minneapolis, 1991).

7 The Book of Genesis 2-5, 15-19 (H.C.O. Lanchester trans., Cambridge,

Some people regard this mode of source criticism as threatening to their faith that God delivered the entire text to Moses on Mount Sinai. The alternative, more appealing view holds that the canonization of a single text in the tradition requires us to ponder and reconcile contradictions and divergent views that might derive from these distinct sources. The text retains its integrity and is enriched by its readers having believed for centuries that the different approaches represent compatible visions of a single truth.

My inquiries are directed, therefore, to the Hebrew text as accepted as the authoritative version for over a thousand years. The best place to begin is with the first line: "In the beginning God created the Heavens and the Earth." *Breshit Elohim et haShamaim v-et Haaretz.* A long tradition of interpretation supports the reading of the verb *barah*, or "created," as implying creation *ex nihilo* – out of nothing. The same verb shows up later to explain the miraculous creation of human beings – as a quantum leap compared to every that had gone before. The second story of creation takes a more modest view of the human condition. Adam, the first being, is made from the earth, a fact that prompts theologian Phyllis Trible to refer to him as the "earth creature."[8] Why all of this matters will become clear in due course when we turn to the events in the Garden and the moral problem of gender equality.

But there is some preliminary work to be done, and much of it centers on two themes that emerge early in the book. The first is the phenomenon of speech and its impact on the world, and the second is the concept of the "good," or *tov*, which is the way God describes the product of creation.

The Genesis Of Language

The first creative act is expressed in Genesis 1:3: "God said, "Let there be light" and there was light." This is a classic case

---

1923); Stephen Mitchell, Genesis: *A New Translation and Commentary,* xxviii (New York, 1996).

8 Phyllis Trible, "Not a Jot, Not a Tittle: Genesis 2-3 After Twenty Years," in Kristen Kvam, Linda Shearing, and Valerie Ziegler (eds), *Eve and Adam: Jewish, Christian, and Muslim Readings on* Genesis *and Gender* (Bloomington, Indiana, 1999),439.

of the performative use of speech. Speaking in itself produces an external effect. More modest examples of performative speech in our daily life are contextualized statements like, "I do," spoken with a partner facing a minister, or handing someone a physical object and saying, "This is yours." These are performatives that produce a change in legal relationships – for example, bringing about a marriage or a change in ownership.[9] God's performative changes the external world by creating light. The closest we can come to this phenomenon in human experience is the way speech acts impact upon the external world by changing legal relationships.

Performatives like using language to get married conform to John Searle's model for constitutive rules: X counts as Y in C. That is, saying "I do" in the circumstances C – namely, standing before a judge or cleric – counts as an act of Y, or getting married. Thus speech changes the world. The circumstances are essential for this transformation or constitutive act to occur. Social convention enables the formula to work. "X counts as Y in C" implies that the speech act X can change the world because we understand the circumstances C to include the possibility that a speech act will have external consequences.[10]

But God appears to create without being bound by circumstances or convention. And this is puzzling, for how can God use language – even have language – without a community of speakers? How can anyone acquire language without engaging in interaction with other speakers? This is the problem that Wittgenstein dubbed the puzzle of private language.[11] It is no accident, perhaps, that in the early passages of Genesis, God is described as surrounded by a heavenly court. The word *Elohim* is plural, even though it is used with the single form of the verb. More significantly, when God decides to create Adam in Genesis 1:26, God begins the process of creation with the famous line, "Let

---

9 The leading work on performatives in the law is H. L. A. Hart, "The Ascription of Responsibilities and Rights," (1949) 49 *Proceedings of the Aristotelian Society* 171.

10 For an elaboration of Searle's view, see G. Fletcher, "Law," in Barry Smith (ed.), *John Searle* (Cambridge, 2003).

11 See Saul Kripke, *Wittgenstein on Rules and Private Language* (Cambridge, Mass., 1982).

us make Adam in our own image." There is no consensus on how best to read this line, but surely one possibility is that God was speaking to other divine figures.

Genesis's view on the nature of language becomes more poignant in the example of Adam's naming the animals as they come before him:

And out of the ground God formed every beast of the field and every bird of the air and brought them to Adam to see what he would call them, and whatever Adam called every living creature that was its name. (Genesis 2: 19)

There is something tempting about the view that words mean whatever each individual wants them to mean. John Locke fell sway to the view of language conveyed in Genesis: "Words in their primary or immediate signification stand for nothing but the ideas in the mind of him that uses them."[12] Thus, if Adam wanted a certain set of sounds to stand for a lion or tiger, he had the choice.[13]

The basic problem with this analysis of language acquisition becomes clear as soon as we reflect on the problem of consistency over time. In our biblical example, how would Adam know that a new image is the same one that came before and provided the basis for the supposed naming? And how would Adam know, acting alone, that the sound articulated the second time was the same as the first time?

Ludwig Wittgenstein developed this critique of the naive view expressed in Genesis by stressing the place of following rules in this conception of language. Using words was not the practice of recurrently naming some inner image of an object or an event but of following rules implicit in the language itself. A certain sound comes to mean lion or tiger because speakers consistently use the same sound to refer to the particular animal. That is, they must follow the rule about what the word means – even as

12 As quoted in Norman Malcolm, "Wittgenstein, Ludwig Josef Johann," 8 *Encyclopedia of Philosophy* 327, 338 (Paul Edwards, ed. New York, London 1967).

13   I surrender to the convention of using of masculine pronoun in this context, although it is my firm view – not developed in this article, that at the stage of the text in which Adam names the animals he/she/it cannot be identified by gender. See G. Fletcher, "Thinking About Eden: A Tribute to Herbert Morris," *Quinnipiac Law Review* (forthcoming).

they collectively develop the meaning by a series of interacting communications. As Norman Malcolm captures the argument: "You might believe that you have always called the same thing by that name." Yet nothing could determine whether this belief was right or wrong.[14]

The point is that languages are learned in a process of constant reinforcement, and that presupposes a group of people and that someone else knows the language well enough to correct the learner. There is a phenomenon of twinspeak – two children living apart from the world developing a language together. But the notion of single-speak seems to be philosophically untenable, and all our experience with mute "wolf children" supports this philosophical argument.[15]

The rejection of private language has important significance for understanding the way individuals are embedded in social arrangements. The myth of an individual – a single Adam – standing alone with God encourages the liberal faith in individuals as self-contained entities. Once we recognize the irreducibly social nature of language, however, we can no longer conceive of individuals as standing wholly outside a network of human interactions that enable them to speak.

Interestingly, the problem of solitary existence might be more significant for Adam than it is for God, who in all the earlier passages of the creation story is surrounded by a heavenly court. Contrary to the long tradition of monotheism, God might in fact have had companions in the divine sphere. But Adam stands alone – admittedly, with God listening. It is not surprising that in the passage immediately prior to the naming of the animals God says, "It is not good for Adam to be alone." As we know, among all the animals named, Adam found no counterpart – no "helper against himself." The proper match was within him all along, and thus the story turns to the separation of the male and female within Adam

---

14 N. 12 above, 339.

15 The most famous case in Europe is Caspar Hauser, who was found in 1828 in Nuremberg. Under the care of a physician he learned to speak and related his experience of being imprisoned alone in a cellar from childhood. See Paul Johann Anselm Feuerbach, *Einige wichtige Actkenstücke den unglücklichen Findling Caspar Hauser betreffend* (Berlin, 1831).

and the birth of Eve, whom Adam recognizes immediately as "bone of my bones, flesh of my flesh."

It is worth mentioning a contrary reading of the second story, however, which begins with a recognition of God's loneliness and his need for Adam to till the ground. Arguably, God needs a "helper against himself," precisely as does Adam.

In the theory of language, however, there is a problem with either God or Adam being alone when they acquire language. Adam was with God when he started to name the animals, but there is no sign that God taught him to speak. On the contrary, the text emphasizes Adam's choice of labels for the animals that pass before him. Though this is problematic in the theory of language, there may great moral significance in the idea that a single God creates a single Adam in God's own image, both whole in themselves (though perhaps lonely). The moral significance of this myth will be of concern at the end of this paper.

God And The Good

There is much more to be said about the line after the creation of light: "And God saw the light, that it was good." The phrase "that it was good" renders two words in the Hebrew text – *ki tov*. God saw the light *ki tov*. *Ki* could be rendered as "because," or "like," or "as." The word also appears in the famous expression, "Love thy neighbor as thyself," which originally appears in Leviticus 19:18 and is then adopted by Jesus in Matthew 18. This famous teaching could be rendered differently as "Love thy neighbor because he or she is like you." Similarly, the critical logical connective *ki* in *ki tov* could be translated as "because" rather than "as" or "that." Thus the proper translation could be "God saw the light because it was good."

The philosophical issue now becomes clear. Was the goodness of the light ontologically prior to God's creation of the light? Or did the process of God's looking upon the light make it good? To paraphrase a famous paradox from Plato's *Theaetetus*:[16] Did God see the light because it was good? Of was it good because God gazed upon it?

---

16 Plato, *The Theaetetus* (John McDowell trans., New York, 1973).

It may come as a surprise to some readers to think of a value system predating God's act of creation or independently of God's will, but in fact this idea is entrenched in Genesis. The most dramatic example comes in Abraham's argument with God about the destruction of Sodom and Gomorrah. As will be remembered, God suggests to Abraham that the sin of Sodom and Gomorrah is great, and that God should go down to investigate and determine whether the entire city should be destroyed. Abraham confronts God about the justice of destroying "the righteous with the wicked." And in the process of debating how many righteous souls would be sufficient to save the city, Abraham utters the famous challenge: "Will not the judge of the entire universe do right?" (Genesis 18:25) The implication is that there is a standard of right or just conduct that is independent of God's will. While this view is questioned later in the "binding" of Isaac (Genesis 22:1, *et seq.*), the text remains ambiguous: Abraham's challenging God supports the ontological priority of the right as a standard for judging God's conduct. If this is true, it is not surprising that the text also supports an independent standard of goodness, which God can recognize but which is not dependent on divine definition.

Good And Evil

It is not easy to understand what goodness means in the context of Genesis. God approves of every stage of creation by proclaiming it "good" and, after the creation of Adam, that it was all "very good." But what does this mean? There are some clues in the juxtaposition of good and evil in the famous expression, "tree of the knowledge of good and evil" (Genesis 2:9). There is a sound basis for thinking of goodness, at least in the latter context, as intrinsic rather than instrumental. Prior to the eating of the fruit, Eve notices that the "tree was good for food" (Genesis 3:6).[17] It had instrumental value also to make her "wise" or "to enlighten her." But the knowledge of goodness and its opposite appears to be intrinsic, a value in itself apart from the advantages of being wise. This much seems correct, but we still have to probe the meaning of this intrinsic quality of goodness.

---

17 Note that this passage also uses the expression *ki tov*, which supports the translation "that it was good" in Genesis 1:3.

Problems arise when we try to pin down the opposite of *tov* or good. The Hebrew word *ra* could be translated as either "bad" or "evil." As in French and other Romance languages, there is no distinction in Hebrew between these two ideas that seem so strongly defined in English and German (*schlecht*, bad, and *böse*, evil). The word "evil" has become entrenched as the opposite of goodness in the scheme of Genesis, and one wonders why? The Hebrew could as easily be translated as "bad," but the English and German translations typically opt for the stronger term.

What did the couple learn by eating of the fruit that was either good or evil? The text is not clear. As soon as they eat, their eyes are opened and they realize that they are naked, and they cover themselves with fig leaves. They appear to be ashamed of their nakedness,[18] and this shame is presumably connected to the knowledge of "bad" or "evil" that they have acquired. But nakedness takes on a negative association only so far as it carries sexual overtones. The Christian reading of the text, as evidenced in Augustine's reference to Adam and Eve's "disobedient flesh," had made much of this dark side of nakedness.[19]

An adequate account of the knowledge acquired by eating of the forbidden fruit, however, must explain the positive side of the action, which consists in their becoming "like gods." The serpent predicts that this will happen (Genesis 3:5), and God confirms that by virtue of their having dared to eat, "Adam has become like one of us, knowing good and evil" (Genesis 3:25). In light of this elevation in status, it is hard to understand the deeply entrenched Christian reading of "disobedience" in the Garden as the symbolic fall of humanity, the roots of an original sin that passes forever from generation to generation. Paul made a great leap from the text when he wrote, "(B)y one man sin entered into the world, and death by sin."[20] Whatever one thinks about the doctrine of original

---

18 The connection between "shame" and "nakedness" is borne out in Genesis 2:25, which informs us that before their eyes were open they were naked but not ashamed. On the significance of "nakedness" in the text, see the article cited in n. 13 above.

19 Not these exact words but the substance is found in Augustine, *City of God* (John O'Meara trans., London, 1972), 523.

20 Romans 5:12.

sin, it certainly represents a rather imaginative extension of the text as we have read it for thousands of years.

An adequate reading of the eating of the forbidden fruit and its aftermath would have to account for the mixed sentiments of shame and glory that arise from Eve's and Adam's venturing forth on their lives as human beings. They become aware of their biological differences in genitalia and they become like gods in ways yet to be explored. This complex sentiment of being both animal and divine hardly resonates with the idea of original sin, or with the view that they have acquired knowledge of evil.

The concept of evil as we understand it today has a long history, and it has undergone a transformation from the time that Europeans regarded the Lisbon earthquake of 1755 as an evil event[21] to the current sentiment that evil flows from a perverted human will. It is hard to imagine how anyone could regard the great gift of sexuality as evil and conclude that this was the evil of which Adam and Eve acquired knowledge.

Man And Woman

These reflections leave unspecified the meaning of the first couple's becoming "like gods" as a result of eating the forbidden fruit. The Hebrew in this context actually permits the translation that they have become "like God," for the word *Elohim* used in this context is plural and is translated into the singular when referring to God the creator, but as plural when the transformation of Adam and Eve is described.

Some suggest that they become like gods in a way connected to their discovery of sexuality – namely, by becoming capable of procreation. The most that could be said, however, is that they became aware of their procreative abilities. They are supposed to die as a result of eating the fruit, and eventually they do, but it is hard to fathom the connection between this attribute of humanity and the ability to procreate.

I want to suggest another interpretation of their becoming like gods, one that has nothing to do with sexuality, procreation, or death. If we go back over the preceding passages and we inquire

---

21 See Susan Neiman, *Evil in Modern Thought: An Alternative History of Philosophy* (Princeton, NJ, 2003).

into the attributes of God revealed in the narrative, two qualities stand out. The most obvious is the creative ability to bring forth the heavens and the earth. But underlying this ability is another quality, one that seems to have gone unnoticed in the long history of commentary on Genesis.

The divine mind stands for organizing the world in sets of bilateral distinctions. We see this at the very beginning in the separation of light and darkness, then of night from day, the earth from the heavens, the water from the land, the living from the inert, and finally on the sixth day, the separation of humans, made in the image of God, from all other creatures. The one distinction that is not fully worked out by the time God rests on the seventh day is that between male and female. Although the terms "male" and "female" do appear in Genesis 1:27, the concepts of man and woman do not appear until the second creation story in Genesis 2:22. The male and female are best understood – and this was the standard rabbinic reading for hundreds of years – as aspects of a single being called Adam.[22]

The central theme of the second story of creation is to elicit the distinction between man and woman as distinct and separate beings as the ultimate achievement of the creation story. The prologue to the separation of Adam into two halves is God's concession, after Adam could not find a partner in the animal kingdom, that "it is not good (*tov*) that Adam should be alone." Interestingly, God does not say that it is "bad" or "evil" for Adam to be alone, rather that the single being's aloneness was "not good." Adam did not partake of the qualities that God perceived as good when God contemplated the light, the separation of the earth from the heavens, and all the other distinctions God brought forth in creating the world. "Not good" apparently means not embedded in the architectonic distinctions that constitute our world.

To remedy the fact that it was not good for Adam to be alone, God brought a deep sleep upon the single being and separated it into two halves. Most people, schooled on the King James translation of the Bible, expect to hear a story here about God's taking one of Adam's ribs and fashioning it into a woman later named Eve – the mother of all living beings. Although the Hebrew word *tsela* could

---

22 See the collection of materials cited n. 8 above.

be translated as "rib," there are alternatives, and indeed some of these alternatives are better supported by parallel usage in the Bible. In all subsequent uses of the word, the connotation of *tsela* is not "rib," but "side" – as in the side of the holy ark.[23] The better understanding of the fashioning of Eve is, therefore, that God makes her from one side of Adam. There are obvious implications of this translation for favoring the equality of men and women, as opposed to the traditional reading supporting the subordination of Eve's half of the species.

The important point for understanding the "knowledge of good and evil" is not the moral question of equality but the very existence of distinctions as a way of perceiving and organizing reality. The "good" is that which stands in opposition to something else – light as opposed to darkness, humans as opposed to animals. The "bad" is that which has no contrast, no sense of being paired with an alternative. Call this the biblical way of seeing the world.

The alternative to the biblical way of seeing the world is to replace categorical distinctions with the gradual spectrum from one pole to the other. This is indeed a popular way of thinking in the contemporary West. There is no division between light and darkness. Everything comes in shades of grey. There is no clear difference between humans and animals. Intelligence and "humanity" are supposedly a matter of degree. There is no sharp divide between male and female. We are all said to be a mixture of yin and yang, heterosexual and homosexual impulses. It is not an exaggeration to say that skepticism of this sort – the rejection of sharp distinctions – is one of the conditions of modernity.

The biblical view stands for an ordering of the world that has much to commend it. It is God's way of creation. To acquire wisdom in this world is to understand the opposites that constitute the world. The goodness that God perceives in the light and in all subsequent forms of creation is precisely its form – its being organized into sets of opposition categories. Sometimes these opposites are hierarchical (light, darkness), sometime equal (land, water). This is the knowledge that Adam and Eve acquire, I submit, when they dare to disappoint God and take the step toward becoming like gods themselves. They acquire knowledge of the good, namely the world of distinctions, and of the bad, those areas

---

23 Exodus 36: 31-32.

of life that are still, in the words of Genesis 1:2, without form and function.

And Legal Thinking

This is the juncture at which the biblical way of seeing the world intersects with the inculcated habits of those trained in law. Among professionals and scholars, the lawyers are the primary exponents of the biblical mode of thought. They shun the evasion of arguing that good and bad are just poles on a spectrum. They are skeptical about incremental changes on a continuous range and favor instead a break with sharp edges.

The traditional concepts of the legal culture are set up very much on the model of light and darkness. Property exists or it does not. Those who have property have the right to exclude those who don't have it. The same is true of torts, crimes, and contract. If a tort or crime is committed, or a contract breached, a hierarchical relationship comes into force, between the promisee on the contract and the right-holder and the duty-holder, between the victim of the tort or crime and the perpetrator. There is no room in this system of rigid alternatives for shades of grey, for continua ranging by degrees from a little to a lot.[24]

The modern style of legal thought, however, is amenable to ideas of which there may sometimes be more, sometimes less. Two notable examples are discretion and comparative fault. The way the concept of discretion is used, judges have a lot of discretion under vague rules and less discretion under relatively precise rules. This is at least the conventional way of talking about discretion. Not that everyone agrees. Ronald Dworkin began his career in legal philosophy by defending the traditional conception of rights against the contemporary understanding of judicial discretion.[25] Though he never articulated the problem in this language, it is clear that his purpose was to defend a conception of law that recognized sharp conceptual cleavages, such as that between principles and policies[26]

---

24 For an elaboration of these themes, see Gunther Teubner, *Law as an Autopoietic System* (Oxford, 1993), ch. 3.

25 Ronald Dworkin, *Taking Rights Seriously* (London, 1977), ch. 2.

26 Ibid. And see also R. Dworkin, *Law's Empire* (London, 1986).

– a dichotomy that lies at the foundation of this theory of law.

The doctrine of comparative negligence comes into legal thought with a slightly different agenda. The traditional approach to liability for accidents has always favored an on/off system of negligence and contributory negligence. Either you were liable for the full amount of damage caused, or you were not liable at all. The principle of comparative fault holds that the plaintiff and defendant must share responsibility for an accident to which they both contribute. In the United States, the jury must determine the degree of each party's share according to their relative fault in bringing about the injury. The idea remains that each pays for the amount of damage caused, but the standard that is measured in degrees is not typically causation but rather negligence or fault.[27]

Some elements of the traditional mode of legal thinking have held fast. For example, there is no adjustment of liability based upon the degree of proof. There is no possibility of a little bit of liability based on a little bit of proof. Either the proof is sufficient, or it is not; either you cross the line, or you do not. This way of thinking recalls the importance of sharp distinctions in the biblical mode of thought.

It would be too much to claim that when Eve and Adam ate of the forbidden fruit, their eyes were opened and they became like ... lawyers. No one dares equate lawyers with gods. The devil is a more likely object of comparison. Yet there seems to be a common foundation to legal thought and to the mode of thinking that we have come to call the "knowledge of good and evil."

Free Will

The eating of the forbidden fruit is generally regarded as the first act of "free will," which turns out to be a critical theological premise in the doctrine of the Fall. Eve and then Adam choose to disobey God, and through this original sin all of humanity is corrupted. As Augustine concluded, "The deliberate sin of the First man is the cause of original sin."[28] Jews, Muslims, and many

---

27 See, e.g., *Li v Yellow Cab*, 532 F.2d 1226 (1975).

28 Augustine, *De nuptiis et concupiscentia* (On Marriage and Concupiscence), II, xxvi, 43 (420), in 5 *A Select Library of the Nicene and*

Protestant sects reject the doctrine of original sin, but so far as I can tell they retain the idea that Eve and Adam acted freely in eating of the fruit.

The thesis of free will serves two functions in theological thought. First, it provides a basis for blaming human beings for their sin, and thus blaming humanity for its corrupted condition and, for those who accept the doctrine of original sin, for the stain that passes from generation to generation. Further, the "free will" of human beings reconciles God's supposed omnipotence and omniscience with disobedience by Adam and Eve. Their free will renders them a force independent of God's control over the universe.

I can understand the theological appeal of "free will," but it is harder to grasp the philosophical possibility of uncaused freedom in human beings. This is not freedom in the Kantian sense, which is not uncaused but rather caused by submission of the will to the moral law.[29] Indeed from a Kantian point of view, Eve's eating the fruit is not free at all. She is drawn to the fruit because "it was good for food and pleasant to the eyes." In the suggestive title of Aviva Zornberg's book, this was "The Beginning of Desire."[30] Eve's eating was a textbook example of heteronomous action shaped by sensual impulses. That is, it was not induced by reason, as required for free and autonomous action, but rather by desire and sensual input. Also, her decision is induced, in part, by the cunning of the serpent. It appears in fact that the serpent engages in a fraudulent misrepresentation to convince Eve to touch and then eat of the fruit ("surely you shall not die"). Those whose actions are shaped by fraud are not generally said to act freely.

Still, I am able to understand that they were able to reflect on what they were doing and they could have resisted the temptation. In this limited sense they – and all of us – are relatively

---

Post-Nicene Fathers of the Christian Church: Saint Augustine: Anti-Pelagian Writings 257, 300 (Philip Schaff ed. and Peter Holmes *et al.* trans., 1971).

29   See Immanuel Kant, *Fundamental Principles of the Metaphysics of Morals* 18 (Thomas Abbott trans., Indianapolis, Indiana 1949) ("Duty is the necessity of acting from respect for the law").

30   Avivah Gottlieb Zornberg, *The Beginning of Desire: Reflections on Genesis* (Philadelphia, 1996).

free in our actions.

The more dramatic example of freedom in the story, however, is the depiction of language and how it functions. Adam is presented as totally free in picking the names of the animals. Though, as I have suggested earlier, this depiction exaggerates the private as opposed to the social nature of language, we nonetheless enjoy an element of freedom in speaking that remains in doubt with regard to our actions.

Our freedom in using language is expressed in several ways. For one, our capacity to formulate complex syntax is not subject to replication in a computer program. In one of his early works, *Syntactic Structures*, Noam Chomsky demonstrated that human language could not be reduced to a finite set of algorithms.[31] This proposition is critical for the purposes of demonstrating that computers – which rely on a finite set of algorithms – could not be programmed to replicate the infinite variety of human conversation. Further, when we speak we are free not only to make our sentences as long and complex as we like, but also to invent new words and to play with words in a way that baffles the finite imagination of computer programs. Speaking is not like playing chess – which, after all, only poses a complicated though finite set of logical alternatives. On the basis of Chomsky's argument one can safely predict that there will be no "Deep Jaw" – by analogy with "Deep Blue" – that will be able to speak with us with the same originality as we find in human communication.

The pursuit of freedom is strongly connected with our quest for that which is human about us. If we attribute "free will" to Adam and Eve, we affirm their humanity and emphasize the seemingly primary characteristic that makes them different from animals. (Their humanity is affirmed, paradoxically, at the same time that it is corrupted by original sin.) I find it odd, however, that we are inclined to see the distinctively human in their action of rebellion rather than in speech. Chomsky's thesis is so striking because he directs our attention to an unexplored source for understanding what it means to be human.

The intriguing characteristic of speech is that we are both free and socially dependent. We cannot learn to speak except

---

31 Noam Chomsky, *Syntactic Structures* (The Hague, 1965).

in interaction with others, but we once we learn we are free to improvise, write poetry, tell jokes, compose lectures about Genesis and untold other original things for which we take credit as our own. Speech is a social product and yet we can secure copyright for our property in our original uses of written language.

Whether our actions are free is much more troubling. In order to make the case for freedom, we tend to think of the individual atomistic ally – acting free of sensual impulses (Kant's sense) and free of the influence, coercion, and deception that undermine voluntary commitments. Only if the individual is abstracted from the environment can we think of him or her as acting freely. We are incessantly troubled by the thesis that criminal conduct is a product of genes and circumstances, but no one offers a parallel account of speech. The conflict between nature and nurture arising in thinking about what we do, not about what we say.

The Authority Of The Word

The key to understanding both law and theology is to grasp both the necessity and the limitations of the written word. In both disciplines we begin with authoritative texts. We are socialized into accepting these texts as our guides for thinking about the issues they address. Americans have an instinctive attachment to the U.S. Constitution. They take the authority of its words for granted. Just like religions, American and English law have their holy texts. The French have their *Code civil* and the Germans, their *Grundgesetz* and their civil code.

As lawyers think in the language of their constitutions, civil codes, and leading cases, the adherents to the three biblical religions – Jews, Christians, and Muslims – all accept the words of Genesis as authoritative. Both in law and in religion, however, the authoritative words go only so far. They are the starting point but not the final point of reflection.

Even if we penetrate through to those words in the Hebrew original, and even if we understand them properly in context, the guidance of the words cannot resolve our moral quandaries. We cannot decide what is ultimately right or wrong simply by consulting a holy text of either the legal or religious community.

The tension between the words and moral vision is no more

acute than in the first two chapters of Genesis, and particularly on the issue of equality between men and women. Any serious reader of the text will notice striking differences between the two accounts of creation, the first detailed in Genesis 1 and the second beginning in Genesis 2:4. Here are some of the differences (I shall refer to the stories as one and two):

In one, creation last seven days; in two, only one day, and there is no mention of a Sabbath on which God rested.

In one, the name of God is Elohim, typically translated as God; in two, it is JHWE or Jehovah Elohim, translated as "Lord God."

In one, human beings are created in God's image; in two, human beings are made from the earth.

In one, human beings have no purpose other than to celebrate their existence; in two, human beings have a necessary function in the scheme of creation; nothing could grow because "there was no Adam to till the ground."

In one, the origin of humanity lies in a single being called Adam; in two, Adam is bifurcated into male and females halves.

Historically, the difference between these two texts is that the first story has been a powerful stimulus to egalitarian thrust of politics, at least since the late eighteenth century. The idea that all human beings are created in the image of God enabled Thomas Jefferson to coin the unforgettable phrase: All men are created equal.[32] Abraham Lincoln gave this phrase new currency in the Gettysburg Address in 1863.[33] And Martin Luther King, Jr., had a dream that the vision of Jefferson and Lincoln would soon be realized in the United States.[34] The aspiration of moral equality – of universal human dignity – provided the bedrock for the movement to abolish slavery, the drive toward the equality of men and women, and the critique of unequal treatment of homosexuals[35]

---

32 Declaration of Independence, 4 July 1776.

33 For a detailed analysis of the Gettysburg Address, see G. Fletcher, *Our Secret Constitution: How Lincoln Redefined American Democracy* (New York, 2001), ch. 2.

34 Martin Luther King, *"I have a Dream" – 40th Anniversary Edition: Writings and Speeches that Changed the World* (San Francisco, 2003).

35 The equal treatment of homosexuals finally triumphed in *Lawrence v Texas*, decided by the Supreme Court on 26 June 2003. See Linda

and children born out of wedlock.[36] It is difficult to image modern egalitarian politics without recourse to rhetoric of *Imago Dei*. Even the secular Israeli human rights organization calls itself *Btselem*, which is direct invocation of the principle *btselem Elohim*, or "the image of God."

At the same time, the second story of Genesis has functioned as a primary prop for the subordination of woman. The Christian reading of the text has furthered this view, as related in 1 Timothy 2:13:

For Adam was formed first, then Eve. And Adam was not the one deceived; it was woman who was deceived and became a sinner.

In *Paradise Lost*, Milton adopts this line of thought for subordinating women:

> For contemplation hee and valour formed,
> For softness shee and sweet attractive Grace,
> Hee for God only, shee for God in him.[37]

Obviously the first story resonates more with modern sensibilities than does the second. Shall we say that Genesis 1, with its emphasis on creation in the image of God, is right and Genesis 2, with its subordination of women, is wrong? Well, one could do that, but then one calls into doubt the relevance of the biblical text as supporting authority. It is difficult both to take the text seriously and to read it in a way that supports our preferred positions on human dignity and equality.

I have no easy answer or solution to this problem of

Greenhouse, "The Supreme Court: Homosexual Rights," *The New York Times*, 27 June 2003, AI.

36 In *Mathews v Lucas*, 427 US 495 (1976), the majority of the Court upheld a distinction in the social security law, which allowed children born in wedlock more favorable terms for receiving benefits than children born out of wedlock. Dissenting, Justice John Paul Stephens made a passionate appeal for equality (at 516): "The reason that the United States Government should not add to the burdens illegitimates inevitably acquire at birth is radiantly clear: We are committed to the proposition that all persons are created equal."

37 John Milton, *Paradise Lost*, Book IV, lines 296-98 (London, 2000).

exegesis. But there is clearly a difference between confronting a contradiction in the biblical text and a straightforward rejection of a passage simply because it seems "wrong." It is very tempting to argue that it was clearly wrong for God to command Abraham to sacrifice his son Isaac, and that Abraham should have resisted and argued with God.[38] But this wholesale rejection of the text implies the superiority of one's own moral judgment. This is much different from wrestling with a contradiction in the text by bringing to bear our moral sensibilities.

I also find some solace in the multiple functions of the biblical text. The words of Genesis both teach us normative standards and document our wayward impulse to deviate from these standards. Genesis 1 teaches us a principle of equality that flies in the face of the inequality seemingly endorsed in other chapters of Genesis and in the interpretive tradition that reads words like "rib" into the text and assumes that Eve was created from Adam. A similar bias has entered the reading of the story of Sodom and Gomorrah, which takes it for granted that the sin of the local residents was their desire to engage in homosexual *sodomy* (even our language incorporates the bias). In fact the text never says this clearly, and there other readings that are more faithful to the details of the story, for example, the view that the sin was attempting sex with angels, or infringing the hospitality that Lot had extended to the visitors.

The problem of interpreting the biblical text is, of course, similar to that which lawyers and judges encounter all the time in confronting a historic legal text that lends itself to conflicting understandings. In legal cultures there is a point to retaining, and indeed cultivating, tensions among legal sources. In my view, documented in a recent book, the American constitutional culture embodies ongoing contradictions, for example, between the freedoms enshrined in the Bill of Rights and the commitment to equality expressed in the post-Civil War Fourteenth Amendment.[39]

---

38 See Alan M. Dershowitz, *The* Genesis *of Justice* (New York, 2001) ("No one today would justify killing a child because God commanded it." at 110). See more particularly Carol Delaney, *Abraham on Trial* (Princeton, NJ, 1998).

39 See n. 33 above.

The advantage of conflicts in principle is that the legal culture retains its flexibility and adaptability.

I am not sure that this is the value of the contradiction between the first and second stories of creation. The biblical text may represent rather a conflict between a normative and an anthropological approach to equality. While equality remains the ideal, we encountered then and we witness now widespread social discrimination. The text of Genesis reminds us simultaneously of our ideals and our weaknesses. If we resolve the contradiction in favor of egalitarian principles, if we follow the American Declaration of Independence and the Gettysburg Address, we can do so in the conviction that we are still honoring the text as we seek to bring our tradition into harmony with our contemporary values.

CHAPTER TWO

Thinking About Eden:
A Tribute To Herbert Morris

George P. Fletcher

For lawyers, nothing could be more natural than confronting a text. This is what we do every day – we read and interpret statutes and judicial opinions. The task in approaching these respected texts is to pay careful attention to the details of language and then to make sense of the text as a whole. There is much debate these days about conflicting canons of interpretation – about literalism and originalism, and other "isms" – but none of these schools has impressed me as much as the simple need to stand before a text and to construe its parts as an integrated whole.[1]

Genesis is the supreme text of Western culture. The story of creation has informed artists of word and image, from Dante and Michelangelo to John Steinbeck and Mark Twain. Adam, Eve, Cain, Abel, the serpent – we could hardly think about good and evil, free will and determinism, or crime and punishment without them.

Yet there is another side to the story of this revered text. In the words of the original Hebrew, Genesis has been virtually lost

---

1 For a model of this form of interpretation, see John Hart Ely, Democracy And Distrust: A Theory Of Judicial Review (1980).

to modern readers. The original text of the Hebrew Bible inspired theological and literary imagination at the expense of the words themselves. Jewish teachings took off in many directions, with the elaboration of legends and imaginative stories called *Midrashim.* The *Midrash* recreates the experience, in the metaphor of one of my teachers, of a swimmer thrown out to sea with a life preserver. The swimmer is cut-off from the text and must find his or her way back. Sometimes, the return to the text requires great leaps of association.

Preferring systematic theology, the Catholic Church found it important to implant architectonic doctrines in the text with little regard for whether these doctrines were supported by more than a *Midrashic* hint. The serpent in the Garden became the devil.[2] Adam and Eve's eating of the forbidden fruit became the "original sin" by which humanity fell into a state that requires redemption. Original sin became a dogma of the Catholic literature, and generated literary reflections on the Fall by Dante, Milton, and scores of others. It did not matter much whether the original text supported this reading or not. In the idiom of lawyers, the Supreme Court (namely, the Church) had spoken, and no one cared that much about what the Constitution (namely, the Bible) actually said.

Islam had its own way of undermining the original stories of Genesis. Though it accepts both the Hebrew and Christian Bibles, the Koran changes some of the stories of Genesis to fit the preconceptions of that religion. For example, in retelling the binding and intended sacrifice of Isaac, the Koran substitutes Ishmael – Isaac's half-brother, and the reputed progenitor of the Arab peoples – for Isaac.[3] The guiding assumption must have been that being sacrificed to God was an honor that should be reserved for one of Islam's own.

The Reformation glorified, but at the same time camouflaged, the original Hebrew text. Calvin, Luther, and their movement claimed to have returned to the original words, but they did so in multiple vernacular versions that supposedly brought the divine

---

2 See Elaine Pagels, *The Origin Of Satan* (1995).

3 While the Koran does not explicitly name which son of Abraham was designated for sacrifice, Islamic tradition holds that it was Ishmael. The relevant passage is *Sura* 37:99-112.

revelation closer to the people. As Benedict Anderson insightfully pointed out, the Protestant movement coincides with the rise of the printing press and the commercialization of the holy text.[4] A bestseller was born – in all the languages of the world. Bringing the text to the vernacular meant that the original texts faded even more from public consciousness.

In the American experience, fundamentalists recite their indigenous version by heart, and they believe that their text – e.g., the time-bound King James version – is the revealed word of God. The literalists overlook the simple fact that the process of translation itself implicitly endorses an orientation and school of interpretation. Just to take one critical example, Western readers have come to assume that Eve was created from Adam's rib. In fact, the Hebrew word for "rib" – *tsela* – is at least as appropriately translated as "side."[5] Obviously, whether Eve represents merely a body part or an entire half of Adam has great significance in thinking about whether women should be treated as subordinate or as equal partners with men. This is but one example of disputed translation, though with vast moral and legal consequences.

According to some, the final blow to the integrity of the Hebrew text came in the nineteenth century with the emergence of scientific biblical criticism.[6] Scholars noted certain word patterns that indicated the probability of different authorship. The three primary texts came to be called the "E," or *Elohim*; the "J," or *Jehovah*; and the "P," or *Priestly* sources, the designation of God being one of the factors signaling the source. *Elohim*, as the sole name of God, typically signals the "E" text; the joint name *Adonai Elohim* (or *Jehovah Elohim*)[7] marks the "J" text.

In Genesis 1:1 through 2:3, the name of God is *Elohim*. This

---

4 Benedict Anderson, Imagined Communities: Reflections On The Origin And Spread Of Nationalism (1983).

5 Exodus 26:26-27, 36:31-32 (referring in both cases to a "side of the tabernacle.").

6 S. R. Driver, Modern Research As Illustrating The Bible (1909); Julius Wellhausen, Prolegomena To The History Of Ancient Israel (Peter Smith, ed., Times Mirror 1973) (1883).

7 The Hebrew here rendered as "Adonai" or "Jehovah" is the Tetragrammaton *Yud-Heh-Vav-Heh*. Orthodox Jews do not pronounce this

name returns in Genesis 5:1. I shall refer to this as the first story of creation. The familiar hallmark of the first story is the recitation of the seven days of creation in Genesis 1. The intervening material from 2:4 to the end of chapter 4 constitutes the second story which, because it contains the Garden of Eden, is of primary interest to us. Although the first story relies on *Elohim* as the name of God, it is thought to be of the Priestly, and not of the "E," source.[8] The second story, the "J" source, is considered the older of the two versions of creation.[9]

Some people regard this mode of source criticism as threatening to their faith that God delivered the entire text to Moses on Mount Sinai. The alternative, more appealing view holds that the canonization of a single text in the tradition requires us to ponder and reconcile contradictions and divergent views which might be derived from these distinct sources. The text retains its integrity, and enriches its readers who have believed for centuries that the different approaches represent compatible visions of a single truth.

The importance of the Hebrew text of Genesis is only confirmed by all these multiple reactions. *Midrashic* flights of fancy, implanted doctrines like the Fall, the rewriting of a basic story in Islam, the recurrent efforts at correct translation, the survival of a single object of study – all these testify to the power of the Hebrew text.

This essay, then, is an exercise in interpreting a revered, but neglected, text. I take as my object of study the story of Adam and Eve in Eden. My interest in these passages derives in large part from conversations with my mentor, Herb Morris, who taught me to appreciate the beauties and mysteries of this rich tale. For both us, the problem is explicating the deeper meaning of the story.

---

name aloud, and therefore use a euphemism that means "Lord." Thus the translation in English text of this name is typically "Lord God." "Jehovah" represents an attempt to render the Tetragrammaton Y-H-V-H in English.

8 Robert B. Coote, *In The Beginning: Creation And The Priestly History* (1991); S. R. Driver, An Introduction To The Literature Of The Old Testament (1891).

9 Genesis I-XXXIV: 2-5, 15-19 (H.C.O. Lanchester trans., 1923); Stephen Mitchell, Genesis: A New Translation Of The Classic Biblical Stories xxviii (1996).

Perhaps I put more emphasis on the original text than Morris does, but we share a common objective of understanding what the story can teach us about the human condition.

Thus, our first task is to review the words of Genesis 2, bearing on the story of Eden. The following is my own translation, with footnotes explaining the points of difficulty and providing cross-references to the leading scholarly literature on the subject.

Genesis 2:8 to 3:20

2:8) And the Lord God[10] planted a garden eastward in Eden, and there he put the Adam[11] whom he had formed.[12]

2:9) And out of the ground the Lord God made every tree to grow from the ground that is pleasant to the sight and good[13] for

---

10 I rely on the conventional phrase "Lord God," which is the marker of the "J" text.

11 In this and the following notes, I will note some of the complexities of translation from the Hebrew. These points are very important in resolving the basic moral and theological issues raised by the text. The Hebrew text refers both to *HaAdam* (the Adam) and simply to Adam without the definite article. The latter is clearly a proper name but the former could be translated as "the human being" or "the person." I have tried to retain this difference in the translation.

12 Another indicator of the "J" text is the way in which the process of creation is described. The first story, or "P" text, relies on the verb B-R-A to describe the way in which God calls Adam into being. This has come to be called *creation ex nihilo* because there is no apparent material from which, in the first story, God creates Adam. The second story relies, as in this passage and in the preceding Genesis 2:7, on the verb Y-TS-R, which means "to form."

13 The notion of *tov*, or "good," runs through the first three chapters of Genesis and has particular poignancy for the story of Adam and Eve in the Garden because it appears in the designation in the next clause in Genesis 2:9, for "the tree of the knowledge of good and evil." Tov is also the word that captures God's judgment that the creation is worthwhile. Genesis 1:4. "And God saw the light that it was good." Genesis implicitly endorses the distinction between instrumental and intrinsic good. The notion of "good for food" in this verse differs from God's seeing that the creation was good without specifying what it was good for.

food; the tree of life also in the midst of the garden and the tree of knowledge of good and evil.[14]

    2:10-14) (the location of the garden among the four rivers)

    2:15) And the Lord God took the Adam and put him in the garden of Eden to cultivate it and to keep it.[15]

    2:16) And the Lord God commanded the Adam, saying, Of every tree in the garden you (singular)[16] may eat freely,

    2:17) but of the tree of knowledge of good and evil you (singular) shall not eat, for on the day[17] that you eat of it you (singular) shall surely die.[18]

    2:18) And the Lord God said, it is not good for the Adam

---

14 The phrase in Hebrew is *tov v-ra*. There is little dispute about whether *tov* is properly translated as "good." The second word in the pair, *ra*, however, is problematic – it is not clear whether we should prefer "bad" or "evil" in English. Hebrew does not make the distinction. Nor does French, where the word *mal* suffices for both. German and English, however, do make the distinction between "bad" and "evil" (*schlecht und böse*). The way the translation "good and evil" has become ingrained in our thinking (in English) reveals a preference for reading the story as one about moral knowledge.

15 Note that in the first story of creation the Adam has no function in life. He/she is simply created in the image of God. Genesis 1:27. The plants grow without his/her assistance. Id. at 1:11. The first duty imposed on Adam is to be "fruitful and multiply." Id. at 1:28. In the second story, Adam has a purpose – his/her job is to cultivate the garden. Without his/her presence, the plants would not have grown. Id. at 2:5.

16 Readers in English cannot discern whether "you" is meant to refer to one or to many. This is important in considering whether, in addressing Adam, God is speaking to both the female and male halves that are later separated.

17 The meaning of the word "day" (*yom*) is one of the most mysterious in the book of Genesis. Genesis 1:5 – 2:2. According to the first story of creation, the world was created in seven "days." According the second version the "heavens and earth" were created in one day. Id. at 2:4.

18 The phrase "surely die" is a translation of the Hebrew manner of expressing emphasis by repeating the verb *mot tamut*, or literally, "die you will die."

to be alone. I will make (the Adam) a helpmate to offset him ....[19]

2:19) And out of the ground the Lord God formed every beast of the field and every bird of the air and brought them to the Adam to see what the Adam would call them. And whatever the Adam called the living creature that became its name.

2:20) And the Adam gave names to all the beasts and to the birds of the air and to every animal of the field but did not find a matching helpmate for Adam.

2:21) And the Lord God made the Adam fall asleep and the Adam slept and the Lord God took one of the Adam's sides[20] and closed up the flesh.

2:22) And the Lord God took the side from the Adam made into woman and brought her to the Adam.

2:23) And the Adam said, This is now bone of my bone, flesh of my flesh; she shall be called woman (isha) because she was taken from a man (ish).[21]

2:24) Therefore shall a man leave his father and his mother, and shall cleave to his wife and they shall be one flesh.

2:25) And they were naked, the Adam and his wife, and they were not ashamed.[22]

---

19 The wonderful phrase in Hebrew is ezer k-negedo – a "helpmate against himself."

20 There is some dispute as to whether the word tsela should be translated as "rib" or "side." The reading in favor of male supremacy obviously prefers the former, and that translation has entered into the conventional understanding of the text. My view is that "side" is a more accurate translation. This same term tsela is used again in Exodus 36:31-32 to refer to the sides of the ark of the covenant.

21 This is the first use of a word clearly indicating the genders of Adam and Eve. "The Adam," prior to the separation into isha (woman) and ish (man), should be understood as an androgynous being created both male and female in Genesis 1:27.

22 This sentence contains the first use of two critical words, "nakedness" (arum) and "shame" (busha, lhitbashesh). The premise of the statement is that people ordinarily feel shame when they are naked in front of other people. There is some reason Adam and Eve do not feel shame, and we have yet to discover what it is.

3:1) And the serpent was more naked (cunning)[23] than all the animals of the field that the Lord God had made, and he said to the woman, has God[24] said, you (plural) shall not eat of every tree of the garden.

3:2) And the woman said to the serpent, We may eat of the fruit of the garden

3:3) But of the fruit of the tree in the midst of the garden, God said you shall (plural) not eat, nor shall you (plural) touch it, lest you (plural) die.

3:4) And the serpent said to the woman, you (plural) shall not surely die.

3:5) For God knows that on the day[25] you eat of it, then

---

23 The word for "cunning" (*arom*) comes from the same root as "naked" (*arum*). The two forms are distinguishable by a single vowel sound. A proper account of this passage will have to explain the relationship between being naked and being cunning.

24 This is a very puzzling lapse in the way God is named in the second story. The text in Genesis 2:15 refers to *Jahwe Elohim* as commanding Adam (in the singular) not to eat of the tree of knowledge. The serpent refers to this warning, but changes the name of God to the form used in the first story, namely just *Elohim*. Significantly, Eve seems to understand the reference to God even though the name is different and the command was given before she was separated from Adam. At least this passage confirms that in some sense Eve was present in the single being that received the command not to eat of the tree in 2:15. Significantly, the serpent describes this command as having been issued in the plural-to both the man and the woman.

25 Again, the concept of "day" is ambiguous and elastic. It is best to think of the term as a vague reference to time span. *See* note 17.

your eyes shall be opened[26] and you shall be as gods[27] knowing good and evil.[28]

3:6) And when the woman saw that the tree was good[29] for food, and that it was pleasant to the eyes, a tree desirable to make one wise, she took of its fruit and ate, and she gave some to her man, who also ate.

3:7) And the eyes of both of them were opened and they knew they were naked,[30] and they sewed fig leaves together and

---

26 Implicitly, their eyes are not open, and this explains why they are naked but do not feel shame. According to the conventional understanding of shame, we experience shame in the eyes, in the gaze, of the other. When we are seen in situations that are ordinarily private-defecating on the street, experiencing a sexual reaction in public, falling asleep at a faculty meeting, we often feel shame at others seeing us exposed. *See* Gabriele Taylor, Pride, Shame, And Guilt: Emotions Of Self Assessment (1985). For a critical view of this thesis, see Michael Stocker, Valuing Emotions (1996). *See also* J. David Velleman, *The* Genesis *of Shame*, 30 Phil. & Pub. Affairs 27 (2001).

27 The word "gods" could with equal plausibility be translated as "God." This requires an explanation of the term *Elohim* that is used in the first story as the name of God. *Elohim* is, in fact, the plural form from *El* – therefore, the name of God is plural to begin with. The serpent uses the same word *Elohim* in this passage to describe both God and what Adam and Eve will become like if they eat of the fruit. This critical passage could be rendered, therefore, as "God knows that on the day that you eat of it ... you shall become like God knowing good and evil." The possibility of drawing this analogy between God and the consequences of eating the fruit may explain why the text has the serpent referring to God simply as *Elohim*, and not as *Yahve Elohim*.

28 There is, of course, a great mystery about what this knowledge of good and evil consists of. Apparently, it is not a matter of "good and evil" to know that one should follow God's commands, for that is already expected of Adam and Eve prior to their having knowledge of good and evil. Second, it cannot be simply a matter of knowing what is good, for in the next passage Eve will see that the tree is "good" (*tov*) for food.

29 The consistent translation of *tov* is "good." The word pervades the first account of creation, e.g., "(A)nd God saw the light that (or perhaps "because") it was good." Genesis 1:4.

30 This is the second reference to "nakedness," but note in this context

made themselves waistbands.

3:8) And they heard the voice of the Lord God walking in the garden in the wind of the day,[31] and the Adam and his wife hid among the trees of the garden

3:9) And the Lord God called to the Adam and said to him (it), Where are you (singular)[32] ?

3:10) And he (it) said, I heard your voice in the garden and I experienced awe[33] because I was naked[34] and I hid myself.

3:11) And the Lord God said, Who told you that you were naked?[35] Have you eaten of the tree which I commanded you that you should not eat?[36]

3:12) And the man said, the woman whom you gave to be

---

there is no reference to shame. The shame seems to be assumed in the reaction of their covering themselves up.

31 This is a poetic phrase – B'ruach hayom (spirit of the day) – that, so far as I can tell, has no bearing on the story as a whole.

32 This shift back to the singular is peculiar and hard to explain. It is almost as though God seeks to return to the kind of relationship He enjoyed with the Adam before the separation of man and woman, a time when God and the Adam were in a unique relationship of dependency – God dependent on the Adam to keep the garden, and the Adam dependent on God for knowledge of what he/she should do.

33 The critical word in Hebrew is yirah. The usual translation is "fear," but "awe" strikes me as more meaningful in this context. The phrase yirat hashamayim is typically translated as "awe" or "reverence" for God. The challenge in interpreting this passage is understanding the relationship between "nakedness" and the experience of yirah. There is no apparent logic in associating nakedness with fear.

34 This is the third reference to nakedness but in this context there is no apparent relationship to shame. A full account of the concept of nakedness (arum) would have to consider these three uses, plus the reference to the serpent as "clever" (arom).

35 This is mysterious when we realize that the more natural question would be: How did you realize that you are naked? God is still addressing Adam, still in singular, as a creature who can only know things when told them.

36 This story makes little sense if we attribute to God the characteristically divine attribute of omniscience.

with me, she gave me of the tree, and I ate.

3:13) And the Lord God said, What is this you have done, and the woman said, The serpent beguiled me and I ate.

3:14) And the Lord God said to the serpent, Because you have done this you are cursed above all the beasts and animals of the field, upon your belly you shall go and you shall eat dust all the days of your life.[37]

3:15) And I will put enmity between you and the woman and between your seed and her seed, he shall bruise your head and you shall bruise his heel.[38]

3:16) To the woman he said, I will greatly multiply the pain of your child bearing; in sorrow you shall bring forth children and your desire will be for your husband and he will rule over you.

3:17) And to Adam (God) said, Because you have listened to the voice of your wife and have eaten of the tree, of which I commanded you (singular) Cursed is the ground on account of you (singular).[39] In sorrow you shall eat of it all the days of your life.

3:18) Thorns and thistles shall it bring forth to you (singular) and (you) shall eat of the herbs of the field.

3:19) By the sweat of your brow shall you eat bread, till you return to the ground for out of it you (singular) were taken. For dust you are (singular) and to dust you shall return (singular).

3:20 And the Adam called his woman *Chava*, for she was the mother of all the living (*Chai*).

Androgynous God: Androgynous Adam

Seeking to uncover the meaning of the Hebrew text of Eden brings into the focus the way in which social forces have functioned to generate misconceptions of the meaning, and significance, of the biblical story of creation. It is generally assumed, for example, that both God and Adam are male, yet there is almost no evidence

---

37 The pattern of action and the curses follow the pattern ABCCBA.

38 The confusion in gender appears in the original. It is not clear why.

39 The description of the future of Eve and all womenkind is not presented as a curse, and there is no explanation offered for this future. By contrast, God refers to the prior command given to the Adam and then explains that the ground will cursed because of what Adam did.

for this view in the original text. The concept of masculinity exists and indeed the distinction between male and female is the central thread of the story, but there is no clear textual basis for assuming that God is male. True, the third person non-feminine verbal form is used to describe God's actions. But I hesitate to go on about this grammatical point without clarifying some basic points about the recognition of gender in various languages of the world.

Western languages recognize one, two, or three genders of nouns and pronouns. The most extreme mono-gendered languages are found in the Ural-Altaic family, typified by Turkish and Hungarian, which distinguish between male and female neither in nouns nor in pronouns. This would be a boon to English speakers constantly beset with the discomfort of choosing between masculine and feminine third-person pronouns and the familiar problem of saying and writing "he" or "she" or both. Romance languages – French, Italian, Spanish, Portuguese – go further and recognize male and female nouns and in many cases have both a male and female version of "they" – the third-person plural pronoun. This generates some problems in deciding which to use in mixed groups. Feminists are annoyed by the rule that in a room full of students, one male among a hundred females would be enough to require use of the male form of "they." The female plural – *elles* instead of *ils* in French – is therefore stronger than the male form, for it conveys the idea exclusively of women acting as the subject of the verb. The male form is better described as the non-feminine form because it applies to all subjects that are not exclusively female.

It is worth noting that this rule does not convey the idea of male superiority – at least by comparison with rules on defining minority races. The "one drop" rule – one drop of black blood or being 1/16th Jewish – took a small quotient to be sufficient for minority status. The assumption was that if a status is disfavored and scorned, it should be acquired by the slightest presence of the negative marking. The rule on choosing the non-feminine grammatical form is just the opposite; one man in the group is enough to require the use of the non-feminine form, a rule that implies either the supremacy of the female (which we might doubt for historical and sociological reasons) or simply that the non-feminine form conveys less information.

The Hebrew language – presumably like other Semitic languages – is supersensitive to gender distinctions. Not only is there a difference in the third person singular and plural, as in French, but there is a difference in the second person singular and plural as well. This means that in speaking Hebrew the speaker must make an instantaneous decision about whether he or she is speaking to a male or female and then choose the right pronouns and the right conjugations. In fact in the present forms of the verb, you have these distinctions in the first person as well. It is not hard for the speaker to remember the right forms, but those who have not learned these Semitic languages would be surprised at how difficult it is to translate consistently the visual impression of the gender of the person being addressed into a whole set of grammatical forms. Slips of the tongue in Hebrew are as common as the mistakes I have observed among native speakers of Hungarian in the consistent and correct use of "he" and "she" in English.

To complete this quick survey, we should note that Germanic languages recognize and use a neuter gender for people as well as for things. English recognizes the neuter pronoun "it" but it is offensive to apply this pronoun to people – at least to individual persons.[40] German has no difficulty whatsoever in treating *das Mädchen, das Fräulein, das Männchen* and other diminutives as neuter nouns. This is important because if God is in fact androgynous or hermaphroditic, then the appropriate gender for God would be neuter – in a language that recognized the neuter form.

The most that one can say about the description of God in Genesis chapters 1-11 is that the verbs used to refer to God are not the feminine form. But, because the non-feminine form in two-gender grammars is typically ambiguous, this grammatical choice in Hebrew, a two-gendered language, does not necessarily convey the idea that God is male. It would be fair to ask: Well, if the use of the non-feminine form of the verb is not enough to convey masculinity, what would be enough? In my view, it would be enough to find references to God with the masculine pronoun *Hoo*. But on this point, translations of the Hebrew text are typically

---

40 It occurs to me that it is fine to refer to humanity, or collective human subjects, as "it," though I am not sure why.

deceptive. In the English translation God is referred to repeatedly as "He," but there is no corresponding pronoun in the Hebrew text. The non-feminine form of the verb is used without a subject.[41] Some might argue that the use of this pronoun would convey no more information than the use of the non-feminine form of the verb. There is no way to resolve this debate except to recognize a warranted skepticism as to whether God is properly described as male.

Whether God is properly thought of as androgynous or hermaphroditic is another issue. "Androgynous" means that God has no sex at all. "Hermaphroditic" means that the nature of God includes both male and female. To reach the right interpretation on this point, we need to reflect on the nature of Adam as well. After all, Adam was created in God's image; what is true about Adam, therefore, should be true about God.[42]

The male bias in biblical translation is at least consistent. As it is commonly assumed that God is male, so it is taken for granted that Adam is male. In fact, there is as little evidence for one as for the other. Because the first human was created *ex nihilo* – from nothing – there is ample reason to think that "the Adam" encompasses both male and female dimensions. And yet the translations typically describe Adam as "him" and assume that God should be referred to as "He."[43]

Here we can bring to bear our reflections about grammars that contain three genders and permit the description of human beings in the neuter. Hebrew does not allow this option and therefore there is a problem translating Genesis 1:27, which reads

---

41 For example, in the all-important passage in Genesis 1:27, the Hebrew text reads: "*Btselern Elohim barah oto, zachar u-nkevah barah otam.*" Literally, this reads: "In the image of God created (him/her) male and female created them." The English translation is typically: "In the image of God He created him; male and female He created them." The two references to "he" are simply added in the English text even though there is no corresponding masculine pronoun in the original.

42 Genesis 1:27.

43 See supra note 41 for an explanation of the way the masculine pronoun is read into the text. The only translation that resists this bias, so far as I know, is Everett Fox, The Five Books Of Moses 15 & n.27 (1995).

that God created *oto* – the original being. In the same sentence, the text tells us that God created *oto* masculine and feminine. We should insist on good reasons for translating the pronoun *oto* as "him." For example, if Hebrew had the option of identifying Adam as neuter and rejected it, then we would have a sound basis for treating Adam as masculine.

If Adam is not just feminine and not just masculine, the problem remains whether we should describe *oto* as androgynous or hermaphrodite. The more accurate description is probably that Adam is hermaphrodite – containing both male and female sides. The separation of the male and female occurs in 2:21 when God takes one side (not "rib") of Adam and fashions it into a woman. This is the first time we find a reference to Adam as a man.[44] That is, the process of separation creates both man and woman.

We can reason backwards from Adam to that of which she/he is an image – namely, to God. If Adam (as the image) contains both sexes, then God should also contain both sexes. Here, we run into a theological problem, however, for recognizing the male and female sides of God raises an issue about the unity of a monotheistic supreme being. These problems are familiar in the Christian efforts to reconcile the Trinity with a single divine source. Jewish mystical thinking coped with the feminine side of God by positing the notion of a *Shikhinah* – or "female presence" surrounding God.[45] The theological niceties of a hermaphrodite God seems to make it more appealing simply to think of God as androgynous, as beyond sexual identity.

It should be obvious why the biblical text has been so persistently misread. People can find in any written material passages to support their preconceptions, and during historical periods in which men were assumed to be the only relevant actors on the stage of history, it was natural to think of male figures as the original agents of creation.

---

44 Genesis 2:23.

45 *See* Rav P. S. Berg, The Essential Zohar: The Source Of Kabbalistic Wisdom (2002); Sanford L. Drob, Symbols Of The Kabbalah: Philosophical And Psychological Perspectives (2000); Gershom G. Scholem, On The Kabbalah And Its Symbolism (Ralph Manheim trans., 1965).

Nakedness, Shame, And The Fall

The writers of the Gospels never refer to the story of Adam and Eve. Beginning with Paul in Romans 5:12, we find references to a doctrine that has altered the Western understanding of the human condition. As Paul wrote: *"(B)y one man sin entered into the world, and death by sin."*[46] Augustine elaborated the claim: "The deliberate sin of the First man is the cause of original sin."[47] Thus was born the dogma of original sin. Even though many Protestants have since rejected the idea of sin passed on from parents to children, I am not sure that Christianity remains a coherent religion without it. Let me explain.

Paul and Augustine respond to one critical problem in the text. If God says, "on the day that you eat of it you (singular) shall surely die" (2:17), this must mean exactly what it says. Admittedly, there is some problem about how long a day is, but the natural reading of the words implies that Adam (and implicitly Eve) were immortal before they ate of the fruit, and that by eating they became mortal. Thus, God banishes them from the Garden, lest they also eat from the tree of life.[48] The Fall signals, therefore, not only sin but mortality. This combination explains the tension in Christian theology between an emphasis on the crucifixion (conquering sin) and the resurrection (conquering mortality).[49] And yet both are intimately linked to the idea that Adam's disobedience was "the deliberate sin" that brought "death by sin" into the world.

Despite the centrality of the idea of original sin to Christian theology, the history of religious thought has clearly been opposed to the Catholic reading of the Garden of Eden. First Islam rejected

---

46 *Romans* 5:12 (emphasis added).

47 Augustine, *De nuptiis et concupiscentia* (On Marriage and Concupiscence), II, xxvi, ch. 43 (420), *in 5* A Select Library Of The Nicene And Post-Nicene Fathers Of The Christian Church: Saint Augustine: Anti-Pelagian Writings 257, 300 (Philip Schaff & Peter Holmes eds. & trans., 1971).

48 Genesis 3:22.

49 I am indebted to James Carroll for explaining these ideas to me over breakfast in Jerusalem in October 2001. *See* James Carroll, *Constantine's Sword: The Church And The Jews: A History* (2001).

the idea, thus returning to the teachings of the Jews about this and other issues.[50] Then, with the Reformation and the Enlightenment's emphasis on the Kantian idea of individual ultimate worth, the idea of original sin became an idea whose time had come and gone. For Nietzsche, the doctrine of original sin *"lay like a cancer in the bowels of an entire civilization."*[51] The creed of Joseph Smith, the founder of Mormonism, explicitly rejects the idea as incompatible with individual responsibility: "We believe that men will be punished for their own sins, and not for Adam's transgression."[52] Contemporary theologian Douglas Farrow apparently subscribes to the view, attributed to Enlightenment thinking, that the doctrine is a perversion.[53]

If the Fall is so important to Christian thinking, then it is remarkable that so many Christian denominations have turned against it. Joseph Smith provided a good reason – liberal to its core. The descendants of Adam should be judged by what they do, not tainted by some deed committed in the genesis of the species. The very idea that some taint is carried forward from generation to generation – some scar or defect that renders humanity imperfect – would be enough to offend anyone who believed in the grandeur and the perfectibility of the human species.

A sound humanistic interpretation of the Garden story, then, would rescue Adam and Eve from the defect that the legend of the Fall has introduced into our culture. There would have to be alternative account of the text that stresses the act of eating the forbidden fruit not as an occasion for corruption of the species, but as a moment of growth.

The Fall is no more an inevitable part of the story than is the masculinity of God and Adam. Both were read into the text with

---

50 The Islamic commitment to law (*Shaariyah*) is very similar to the Jewish view of law (*Halachah*), and both are clearly opposed to the anti-legalistic message of the Sermon on the Mount. *Matthew* 5:27.

51 Douglas Farrow, *Fall, in* The Oxford Companion To Christian Thought 233, 233 (Adrian Hastings et al. eds., 2000) (emphasis added).

52 The Mormon Articles of Faith, art. 2, *available* at http://www. sacredtexts.com/mor/morartf.txt (last visited March 31, 2003) (on file with the Quinnipiac Law Review).

53 See supra note 39.

purposes in mind other than simply providing the best possible account for the words on the page. Yet it is apparently easier for some believers, like Muslims and Mormons, simply to reject the doctrine than it is for secular thinkers to abandon a myth of corruption, a story that has taken on so much importance in the arts of the West. (This, I believe, is Morris's position. He seeks an interpretation of the Fall that could make sense to a reader of modem sensibilities. Presumably he does not want to endorse an idea of sin that renders all of humanity defective because *"by one man sin entered into the world, and death by sin."*)[54]

Could one really believe that all of humanity was condemned and punished simply because two people took a bite of fruit? Surely there is a problem of proportionality here, which could not but fail to turn someone committed to retributive punishment away from this primitive and anti-humanistic mythology by which the sin of one generation forever changes history.[55]

The doctrine of original sin should be understood historically in the same way that we understand the bias toward male figures as the dominant actors in the creation story. Theologians read the Fall into the text, as generations of readers simply assumed that both God and Adam were masculine. Returning to the text might liberate us from both of these mistakes.

An adequate account of the entire story must address the central difficulty of what happens when Eve and then Adam eat of the forbidden fruit. The text is silent about their inner experience, so we have to try to imagine what happens to them. According to God's statements and the descriptions of the text, at least five

---

54 See supra note 46 (emphasis added).

55 In my view, the invention of original sin correlates with the emergence of anti-Semitism in Christian thinking. Both doctrines have a similar structure. The Jews are condemned forever as the "sons of the devil" (*John* 8:44: "Ye are of your father the devil .... ") for the role of the crowd in approving of the crucifixion (*Matthew* 27:25). They – like the descendants of Adam – are in need of redemption, a redemption that until recently the Church believed only it could provide. Thus, the sins of some of the fathers are visited on all the sons. Both doctrines aggrandize the Catholic Church. Under the influence of Pope John XXIII, the Church gave up its anti-Semitic teachings and adopted a more respectful attitude toward Judaism. They have yet to alter the teaching on original sin.

events occur:

1. They should die "on that day,"
2. They become like God or gods,
3. They realize the difference between good and evil,
4. Their eyes are opened, and
5. They become aware of their nakedness.

The fifth factor is the only experience that we can reliably establish on the basis of the text.[56]

Of the all the events that *do not* happen after the eating of the forbidden fruit, there is no sign that Adam and Eve feel guilt for their disobedience. One would think that if this were a serious sin, a great act of disobedience that brought death into the world – and they also had knowledge of good and evil – Adam and Eve would feel *something* about having committed this great wrong. But they reveal no sign of guilt.

Given the dimension of their sin in Christian theology – they have condemned humanity to the taint of the Fall – we can only be puzzled by their appearing to feel nothing except possibly a sense of shame about their nakedness. It is true that in the next verse when God enters the Garden they hide because they realize that they are naked. This I believe is a key passage, and again the key word is "nakedness." There is no mention either of shame or guilt.

The proponents of the Fall begin their reasoning, it seems, from the supposedly implicit fact that the couple experiences shame upon discovering that they are naked. The factor of shame is assumed because in the preceding reference to nakedness, "(T)hey were naked... and they were not ashamed."[57] Thus, when their eyes are opened and they realize they are naked, they are assumed to experience shame. They respond to their shame by covering themselves up.

The reasoning is fallacious: it assumes that eyes closed equals no shame whereas eyes opened is equivalent to shame. But the conclusion hardly follows from the premise. Their eyes might

---

56 Genesis 3:27.

57 Genesis 2:25.

be open and they would experience no shame. Yet, to be sure, several reasons lead one to make the association in this context of awareness of nakedness and shame. First, we associate shame with the genitals. (It is not clear why and I address this issue in detail below.) Further, there is a conceptual connection between shame and being exposed to the opened eyes and the gaze of the other. We experience shame in the sight of others, or at least in the eyes of some imaginary observer. Third, the natural response to shame is to cover the source of the shame, and this is precisely what Adam and Eve do when they cover themselves with fig leaves. All of these factors come together to support a view of the text that I shall call the "shame thesis."

After struggling with the shame thesis, I am becoming more skeptical whether the concept provides the right anchor for navigating the nuances of these passages. First, what does it mean to say that people feel shame about their genitals and how does covering themselves respond to the shame? One common argument is that our genitals remind us of our animal nature and in the moment that Adam and Eve should become like gods they are reminded of their baser side. The dissonance leads them to deny their similarity to animals by covering themselves with fig leaves. But how do they (or we) resemble animals? In fact, human beings have at least four highly distinctive traits in common with cats and dogs – sex, eating, sleeping, and eliminating waste by urination and defecation.[58] We feel no shame about eating and sleeping, even though these acts might remind us of our natural nature.

Why, then, should we assume that Adam and Eve experience shame because their genitals are exposed? If they were in a nudist colony, they would not feel ashamed. And even more troublesome is the problem of linking the shame thesis with the first three factors in the text: (1) death, (2) becoming like gods, and (3) knowledge of good and evil. Perhaps there is more to be said on behalf of the shame thesis, but an alternative account warrants our attention as well.

The alternative thesis takes the central word in the passage

---

58 I do not mention the infinite number of other physical acts that animals and humans have in common – e.g., walking, touching, smelling, hearing, seeing, emitting noises from the mouth, etc.

to be not "shame," but "nakedness." In fact, the concept of "naked" recurs four times:

1. They were naked and not ashamed;[59]
2. The serpent is described as "naked" or something like "naked' in being more *arom* than all "the animals of the field;"[60]
3. They eat of the fruit and realize that they are naked;[61]
4. Adam explains his hiding from God because he experience awe (or fear) because he was naked.[62]

An adequate account of the story must provide an explanation of this recurrent theme of nakedness and the way in which these four passages interweave to create a tale of moral and theological significance. The key to understanding both the use of the word "nakedness" and the story as a whole is the concept of separation-the separation of Adam from Eve, and the separation of human beings from their Creator.

In the first passage, when their eyes are still closed and they have not yet "disobeyed" God, they are not aware of being distinct beings – neither distinct from each other or from God. After eating of the fruit, they realize that they are separate beings. They can see with their own eyes that they are separate and different. As a result of becoming consciously as well as physically distinct persons, they also realize that they are separate from God. The sentiment they experience, *yirah*, is the first recorded religious sentiment in the creation story, and it is best translated as "awe" – an experience of reverence for the power of God as a being apart from themselves.

With this context in mind, however, it becomes clear that nakedness is a metaphor for something deeper – for an inability of human beings to function on their own without being tied to their Creator. This deeper association becomes evident in contemplating

59 Genesis 2:25.

60 Id. at 3:1.

61 Id. at 3:7.

62 Id. at 3:10.

the similarity between the nakedness of Adam and Eve and the cunning nature of the serpent. There is no doubt that the serpent represents some kind of force that comes from outside the intimate relationship between God and the Adam. First we are told of the physical separation of the two halves of the first created being, that there was man and there was woman but they were no yet aware that they were distinct being[63] and suddenly there enters a foreign force – also naked (*arom*) in its cunningness.[64] The foreign force becomes the necessary instrument in the final separation in consciousness between man and woman.

The linguistic proximity of *arum* and *arom* – nakedness and cunningness – is too close to go unnoticed and yet lies camouflaged in all the translations of which I am aware. The serpent has something in common with Adam and Eve before and after they eat of the fruit. But what is it?

One account in the Jewish sources derives from the special place of the law in Jewish thinking about the way in which human beings must function in the world. The serpent is cunning in the sense that it exists outside the law – it knows no rules of proper conduct. It can lie and deceive and tempt. It can foster rebellion and awaken desire. According to a *Midrash*, the serpent even seduces Eve. This homiletic account has an appeal. It permits an easy transition to the place of nakedness in Adam's experience of awe in the presence of God. The law has yet to unfold in the narrative. Unclothed in the sense of having no covenant with God, no law by which to live, he experiences fear, trembling, and awe. He hides. He is separate from God, and does not know how to respond in worship.

The separation thesis has the appeal of presenting the eating of the fruit not as the Fall or as a sin but as a necessary step in the evolution of God's children. In our contemporary way of putting it, they must grow up and leave the parental Garden.

Admittedly, some puzzles remain. For one, it is not clear why Adam and Eve feel no shame when their eyes are still closed. There seems to be little explanation except that nakedness is a cause of shame; but if the nakedness is not seen they feel no

---

63 Genesis 2:22-24.

64 Id. at 3:1.

shame. This factor leads one back to the shame thesis, that it is not nakedness per se that matters in the story, but only nakedness so far as it leads to shame. I am unable to account for the seeming anomaly of the passage: "And they were naked ... (and) were not ashamed.[65]

Another puzzle is the status of God's prophecy (or threat) made to Adam prior to the separation of Eve that the eating of the fruit will have fatal consequences. Someone is expected to die, and yet this does not happen. There are various ways of coping with this mystery in the text. Perhaps because of their eating of the fruit, human beings become mortal, but then one might have expected God to say something about their mortality in the curse given afterwards.[66] Perhaps they simply become conscious of their mortality as a result of knowledge of good and evil. Or perhaps the death that occurs is not to them as individuals but to their capacity as aspects of a single harmonious existence, two beings still united in one and tied to their Creator.

The biggest puzzle of all, however, is the interpretation of "knowledge of good and evil." This is the core of the story and it is difficult to comprehend exactly what Adam and Eve learn that could be called knowledge of good and evil. Morris claims that they acquire moral knowledge, but we can search the sources in vain for a clue about the content of their knowledge. My sense is that the Western tradition has exaggerated this aspect of the story by consistently translating the acquired knowledge as being about "good and evil" instead of "good and bad." Perhaps a less ambitious reading would further the point of the story.

My suggestion is that the knowledge they acquire – the knowledge that makes them like God – is the capacity to make distinctions and to see the difference between opposites. The entire story of creation focuses on the carving out of distinctions from the background of chaos – of *tohu v-vohu*.[67] First, there is the

---

65 Id. at 2:25.

66 God is afraid that they will eat of the tree of life, but the existence of this second tree in the center of the Garden also raises problems. Genesis 2:9. If Adam and Eve were immortal prior to the eating the fruit, it is hard to understand the point of a tree of life. For whom?

67 Id. at 1:2.

distinction between darkness and light; then, in rapid succession, between night and day; sky and earth; sea and land; creatures of the sea and birds of the sky; animals of the field and human beings. All of these distinctions are described as "good" or "very good." We don't really know what the opposite category of bad represents, but we are told that it is "not good" for Adam to be alone.[68] Goodness requires opposition. If Adam remains alone, there is no opposition, no counterpart, no foil for conversation and argument. Eve is brought into the world as his "helpmate to offset him."[69]

The human being, the Adam, is finally refined as man and woman. It is not until the eating of the fruit, however, that Eve and Adam become aware of their difference. They see their difference in the part of the body where it is most marked, in their naked genitals. Thus, their eyes are opened and they become aware of the organizing distinctions of human existence. This is the sense in which they become like gods or God.

The final realization of separation and difference comes when God enters the Garden and Adam and Evil hide because they do not know how to respond to God as a totally separate being. Again the word "nakedness" functions as the critical marker of difference.

Let us review, then, the five desiderata mentioned at the outset and consider whether the separation thesis satisfies them:

(1) *They should die on that day.* When they eat of the fruit, their separation becomes complete. The single being created "male and female" in the image of God is dead.

(2) *They become like God or gods.* They organize the world they perceive on the basis of distinctions and oppositions.

(3) *They know the difference between good and evil.* The knowledge is better described as the distinction between good and bad, and it stands for the value of all knowledge based on the perception of distinctions.

(4) *Their eyes are opened, and*

(5) *They become aware of their nakedness.* Thus, they are able to understand the difference between male and female.

Therefore, the separation thesis accounts for all of these

---

68 Genesis 2:18.

69 See supra note 19.

factors and does so without engaging in the anti-humanistic errors of original sin, misogyny,[70] or sexual repression. If this is a better account of Eden than the one that runs through Western culture, then we should realize the conventional understanding of the Fall tells us more about innate biases than about the inspiration we can derive from these words repeated so often, and understood so little.

---

70 I have hesitated to explore the theme of misogyny in this paper, but here is the outline of the argument: If we read the text to imply shame for sexual urges, then Eve, as the bearer of desire for her husband, becomes tainted as the symbol of desire. Genesis 3:16. Not only does she desire the apple, she becomes responsible for leading Adam astray, both in Eden and in bed. This attitude toward women has found expression in Orthodox Jewish and Islamic images of the woman as seductress. To avoid distracting men and awakening their unholy desires, she must cover her hair and even, in the extreme version of the Taliban, her entire body.

CHAPTER THREE

The Absent And Present Serpent In Nicolas Poussin's "Spring"

Herbert Morris

The Serpent is as central, and as apparently indispensable to the drama depicted in Genesis 3 as Iago, with his deviousness, is to Othello's tragic story. Accordingly, painters from the earliest period of Western art through Dürer, Raphael, Michelangelo, Cranach the Elder, Cranach the Younger, Tintoretto, Titian, Rubens and Domenichino, all not too distant in time from Poussin and several having a clear influence upon him, insert a snake in their pictorial representation of the tale of Adam and Eve. Poussin, who takes the tale as the subject for Spring or The Earthly Paradise (Fig. 1), the first painting in his series of paintings, Four Seasons,[1] alone among painters, and

---

1 Poussin and Nature: Arcadian Visions, ed. P. Rosenberg/ K. Christiansen (New Haven and London: Yale University Press, 2008). Professor Rosenberg writes, "The paintings of the Four Seasons are incontestably the most famous works by Poussin and the most often illustrated as has been frequently repeated, they constitute his 'artistic and spiritual testament.'" 292. See general discussion 292-296. See also N. Milovanovic, Nicolas Poussin Les Quatre Saisons (Musée de Louvre: Paris 2014). The du de Richelieu, grand-nephew of Cardinal Richelieu, commissioned the

Fig. 1: Spring or Earthly Paradise, 1660-64.

indeed sculptors, who have treated the subject prior to him, to my knowledge, does not include a snake, the form taken by the character in the tale referred to as "the Serpent."

The painting does depict, as expected, the obligatory nude figures of Adam and Eve.[2] Both catch the early morning sunlight and are diminutive in size compared to the immensity of the luxuriant natural setting in which they are situated. We see Eve kneeling beside a reclining Adam with his left knee raised, her right hand gripping his left upper arm, and her left arm raised, her

---

paintings, and then, either paying off a debt to King Louis XIV occasioned by losing a tennis match or selling the paintings to the King, delivered them in 1665 to the King who, in turn, arranged for them to be hung in the Louvre. Poussin is known to have worked on the paintings during the period 1660-64, a period in which he suffered from the effects of both age (1594-1665) and illness. It is not known in what sequence the paintings, each of which is on a Biblical story – Adam and Eve, Boaz and Ruth, The Gathering of the Grapes, The Flood – was painted.

2 I refer to the woman as "Eve" even though she is only so named in Genesis 3:20 after the events discussed in this essay.

Fig. 2:
Masaccio, Expulsion
from the Garden of
Eden, c. 1425.

hand pointing toward what we are clearly to understand as a representation of the Tree of Knowledge with its hanging fruit interspersed with flowers. A short distance from this tree, to its left, in deep shadows, is another tree laden with fruit, absent any flowers, which it is reasonable to assume is meant to symbolize the Tree of Life that God informs Adam he has placed in the midst of the garden.[3] The Creator floats in billowy dark clouds above, facing forward, his left hand extended and directed ahead. Our eyes, guided by our knowledge of the biblical tale and its many pictorial depictions, and influenced by an ingrained mental habit that has resulted, survey the scene. We search for the tale's Serpent in the vicinity of the Tree of Knowledge, but he is nowhere to be seen. He is neither wrapped around the trunk of the Tree nor slithering along it nor hanging from a branch nor poking his head out from some thick foliage nearby nor simply on the ground in plain sight.[4] We do not expect a representation of the Serpent in a scene of the Expulsion, such as that of Masaccio (Fig. 2), but when the action described takes place in the Garden, the scene of the temptation, we do.

The absence of the Serpent alone arouses puzzlement that deepens for those of us aware of the particular appeal that the snake had for Poussin as a vehicle of symbolic significance.

A snake appears in a number of his most famous landscapes. One is to be found in his Landscape with Orpheus and Eurydice (Fig. 3), in Landscape with a Man Killed by a Snake (Fig. 4), Landscape with a Man Pursued by a Snake (Fig. 5), and in Two Nymphs and a Snake in a Landscape (Fig. 6). A snake, the python, wrapped around the base of a tree, also appears in the painting Apollo and Daphne

---

3 Gen. 2:8.

4 A common pictorial representation of the serpent, of course, has its upper body as that of a young woman despite Genesis 3:1 in which the Serpent is identified as male.

Fig. 3: Landscape with Orpheus and Eurydice, c. 1650.

Fig. 4: Landscape with a Man Killed by a Snake, c. 1648.

Fig. 5: Landscape with a Man Pursued by a Snake, 1648.

Fig. 6: Two Nymphs and a Snake in a Landscape, 1659.

Fig. 7: *Apollo and Daphne, 1664.*

Fig. 8: *Winter or The Flood 1660-64.*

(Fig. 7), dated the year before his death.[5]

Whatever the level of perplexity occasioned by these facts, it is heightened by what we observe in Winter or The Flood (Fig. 8), the last in the series of four paintings. In that painting we see a snake, the longest and thickest of any before painted by Poussin, splayed out upon a large dark rock in the left foreground of the painting and still another, much smaller, attached to the trunk of a tree just off the center of the scene on the right. Where we expect a snake, we see none. Where we do not expect a snake, we see two. It is as if the sly Serpent, split into two in some manner, and then slithered away from Eden in the spring where he belonged, to a stormy wintry scene of horror, accompanied by a smaller companion, where he does not.

Poussin, then, has presented us in Spring and Winter with a conundrum of absence and presence. The fact that the paintings come from the same series compounds our puzzlement. I consider in this paper Spring alone. I claim, firstly, that the Serpent's absence from where we expect to see him serves Poussin's purposes better than would the Serpent's presence there. Poussin gains something from non-representation of the Serpent as represented in Genesis. He also means to convey something to us by non-representation.[6] Secondly, I claim that the Serpent is in plain sight but not at all where we expect to see him or in his familiar embodiment. He appears in the Tree of Life, offering a deceptively appealing illusion

---

5 A. Blunt, Nicolas Poussin (New York: Pallas Athene, 1967), I, 315, Fn 3: "The snake, which is the central theme of the Landscape with Two Nymphs, appears to have become something of an obsession with Poussin in his later years." See also T.J. Clark, The Sight of Death (New Haven and London: Yale University Press, 2006) " Snakes, it is clear, were the members of the animal kingdom Poussin was most drawn to: they appear in paintings and drawings all through his life, time and again charged with a specially repellent beauty," 178. Professor Clark's discussion of snakes is the most thorough in the Poussin literature, but however illuminating his remarks about a snake when it appears, he neglects to shed any light on the issue that is dealt with in this paper, not saying anything about the absence of a snake in Spring.

6 See on the difference between "causing" and "meaning" H.P. Grice, "Meaning," Studies in the Way of Words (Cambridge: Harvard University Press, 1989), 213-23.

of overcoming death while Eve is about to grasp knowledge and the reality of human mortality. My view is that Poussin in Spring provides a radical and illuminating revision of the biblical tale of Adam and Eve from a Stoic perspective on life.[7]

In Part I, I consider several possible explanations for the biblical Serpent's absence. While the Serpent's absence has been noted by a number of art historians, to my knowledge there is no published work in which there is no systematic attempt to resolve the mystery. I reject a number of possible explanations that may come to mind and then offer one of my own. In Part II I offer supporting argument for my second claim.

Part I

One suggested explanation for the Serpent's absence in Spring is that Poussin depicts a moment in time before the temptation and Fall. The Serpent has yet a role to perform. All is, as yet, complete innocence. Eve is simply drawing Adam's attention to the attractiveness of the fruit on the Tree, but without either of them having thought of eating from it in mind. But, problematically, the Tree, on this view, is without any symbolic significance, and it is a mere accident that, at the moment, Eve finds this tree, rather than any other attractive tree in the Garden, visually appealing. Yet another problem with this view is the fact that in the biblical telling of the tale, Eve's focus on the Tree of Knowledge occurs only after the Serpent's question to her about eating the fruit of the trees in the garden.[8] The painting, in light of our knowledge of the tale would seem strongly to suggest that Eve, with her left hand pointing to the Tree and her right on the upper left arm of Adam, is beckoning him to eat.

Another possible interpretation for the Serpent's absence is significantly different from the first. We can label it "the Miltonian interpretation" because its basic features accord with the depiction of the Fall in Paradise Lost.[9] On this view, once the Serpent's guile

---

7 On the topic of Stoicism and Poussin, see Blunt, 157-76.

8 Gen. 3:1

9 K. Clark, Landscape into Art (London: Penguin, 1956) 81: "...the Spring, that perfect illustration to Paradise Lost, which by the art of design our

proves successful and Eve gives way to temptation, the Serpent's work is complete and he vanishes. He has no further role to play. Eve then tempts Adam and he, too, eats of the Tree of Knowledge, but the Serpent is not there to witness this final act of the Fall. The claim, then, is that the painting captures that moment in time after Eve has eaten and now approaches Adam, inviting or beckoning him so that he might join her. It is a tale of two temptations each one of which attains its goal.[10]

Several obstacles stand in the way of accepting this interpretation. Firstly, the painting itself does not warrant the story imposed upon it of Eve's already having been tempted by the Serpent and eaten the fruit. We see no signs of her having bitten into fruit or possessing fruit, and the biblical tale has her only offering Adam fruit after she has tasted it. Spring does not portray such a scenario. For all that we can tell from the painting, she may have come upon the idea of eating without anyone's tempting her to do so. Secondly, the position and gaze of God in the clouds above seems perplexing in light of the tragedy unfolding below. We would expect a focus, not on what is in the distance ahead of him, but rather on what is below him and, given the biblical tale, what he will soon with great displeasure address.

A final suggestion can be constructed from the views of Willibald Sauerländer.[11] He argues that the four paintings in the series Four Seasons must be viewed as a whole and that a symbolic Christian conception of historical development is the key to understanding the movement from spring to winter. True there are

---

first parents are given their true place in nature."

10 J. Milton, Paradise Lost, ed. M. Y. Hughes (New Jersey: Prentice Hall, 1957), Book IX.

11 See W. Sauerländer,"Die Jahreszeiten: Ein Beitrag zur allegorischen Landschaft beimspäten Poussin," Munchner Jahrbuch der bildenden Kunst 7 (1956), 169-84. W. Sauerländer, "Nature Through the Glass of Time: A Reflection on the Meaning of Poussin's Landscapes," 110-17. I am unconvinced by Professor Sauerländer's claim that an understanding of each painting in the series depends upon an understanding of the series as a whole. See R. Wollheim, Painting as an Art (Princeton: Princeton University Press, 1987) 367-368 for a critique of Professor Sauerländer's views on this issue.

intimations of the Fall and mortality in "Spring". Yet what Poussin intends to depict is the world before the Fall, a world in which Eve is pointing at the Tree but has yet to reach for its fruit. Sauerländer, writing some fifty years after first proposing his interpretation, summarizes it this way:

> The Creation of the world is finished, and God is seen high in the sky blessing his work. As in Poussin's other landscapes, however, felicity is overshadowed by immanent (sic) misfortune and death. Eve, who is seen in the center of the garden, points to the fruits of the Tree of Knowledge and invites Adam to taste from them...It is the moment just before the Fall, the moment of expectation...The Golden Age is coming to an end. The scorn of God and the Expulsion from Paradise are imminent.[12]

Sauerländer does not directly address the issue of the Serpent's absence, but it is plausible to attribute to him a view similar to the one taken by Milton. Sauerländer views Spring as depicting the world before the Fall, but because he views Eve as "inviting" Adam to eat, we must imagine that Eve has already succumbed to the Serpent's temptation. And, as with Milton, the Serpent is a character in the tale whose role has already been performed, and he need not be depicted.[13]

This view, while not open to the criticism that there is no evidence of Eve having eaten, is vulnerable to the criticism that there is an incongruity between the events taking place in the Garden and the depiction of God. More importantly, even if we

_____

12 Poussin and Nature, 113.

13 Milovanovic in his recent Les Saisons Quatre generally follows Sauerländer's Christian interpretation of the series of paintings. He observes, "Dans le tableau de Poussin, ce n'est donc pas le demon qui est en cause, mais le coeur humain." p. 12. We can, perhaps, conclude from this that Milovanovic believes the Serpent is not present because he is unnecessary. This would differ from the view that I attribute to Sauerländer. Milovanovic sees the painting in exclusively Christian terms and does not discuss the Tree of Life or the significance of God's position and gesture.

were to grant the truth of either the Miltonian or Sauerländer view, we would not have been provided with an answer to the question, "Why would Poussin have selected such a narrative out of all the possible ones?" What of any significance turns on whether the time depicted is just after Eve's temptation or just before it? The fact alone of the Serpent's absence seems of so much more significance than either of these proposed scenarios that we have considered that seek to account for the fact. I want now to offer another explanation not open to the objections so far put forward.

It cannot, I believe, reasonably be doubted that one of Poussin's purposes in the painting of Spring was to raise for viewers of the painting the very question addressed in this essay. He would be aware of the uniqueness of his painting in not depicting a snake on or in close proximity to the Tree of Knowledge in a tale that has the Serpent as one of the central characters. Having planted the seed, "Why no Serpent?" I believe that his hope was that this seed would germinate into a heightened attentiveness to every detail of the painting and to reflection associated with the topics the tale raises, topics such as human responsibility, good and evil, and death. Were Poussin to follow the path of all his distinguished predecessors and paint a snake, one wrapped around the trunk of the Tree of Knowledge, habits of mind would be triggered and the Serpent would be given but a glance, confirming viewers' expectations. Poussin is then, I believe, exploiting a familiar phenomenon. Disappointment of an expectation is likely to draw more attention than its satisfaction.

We can now turn from the causal effects on viewers of noticing the absence of a snake to what Poussin meant to convey by the biblical Serpent's non-appearance. My claim is that Poussin intended to gain special attention as a result of his non-representation; but he also intended this non-representation to convey meaning in addition to the meaning conveyed by the Serpent that is depicted in the Tree of Life.

We have seen that on both the Miltonian or Sauerländer views the Serpent has a role, one already or imminently to be performed. I suggest that the Serpent, as usually understood, has no role to play in tempting Eve to eat of the Tree of Knowledge whatsoever. Poussin likely believed that a fantasy of a serpent with feet, mouthing words, in what language we can have no idea, a being apart from humans, one capable of subtle thought, distracts from what is the morally serious point. Two individuals, capable of free choice, have chosen to acquire knowledge and are prepared to disobey their creator, even facing death as a consequence, in order to do so. It all lies within us; it is our nature, both the susceptibility and the occasional surrender. We know that, as we develop, we shall acquire knowledge of good and evil. We know, too, that at a certain point in time that we shall die. The tale, if taken literally, presents a history of how these facts about human life have come about. Poussin keeps what he believes to be essential truth and discards what he cannot take seriously. He exploits for his purposes the tale, but through his form of telling a story, through pictorial images, he leaves out an expected pictorial representation of the Serpent, modifies in this manner the accepted story, and conveys an important moral truth.

The biblical Serpent is, then, a fantasy that should be cast aside, but what remains of it is the idea of a powerful, irrepressible force, a fundamental part of human nature, something within that seeks knowledge, a force so powerful that it may lead us into painful conflict with other strong attachments. The biblical Serpent is not only a phantom but also, importantly, one too seductively available as an object upon which to place responsibility. Poussin, by not representing the biblical Serpent, is portraying Adam and Eve in such a way as to place all responsibility, whether it be for good or for evil, upon them. Eve, as he depicts her, does not have available the excuse, "the serpent beguiled me." Nor does Eve have the reassurance provided by the Serpent that she will not die if she eats. Nor does one come away from the depicted scene imagining Adam shifting his guilt onto Eve. Each is fully responsible, and, given that Eve has not yet eaten, the powerful motives of love and compassion Adam might possess, as on the "Miltonian" view, to join her in eating, are not in play. There is no room for Eve to blame the Serpent or for Adam to blame Eve. Poussin disposes of what we all now take for granted as the lamest of excuses, however we might in subtle ways continue to employ it, "the devil made me do it."

This concludes my explanation for the biblical Serpent's non-appearance. If true, Poussin has already modified the biblical tale in an obviously important respect. He is telling a different story but keeping two of its main characters. I shall now argue that his version of the tale of Adam and Eve is even more radical. They are to be regarded, not as fallen creatures, not as the earliest human malefactors, the cause of so much human suffering. Rather, they are creatures about to experience a rebirth, appropriately occurring during spring, transformed into creatures capable of a more elevated form of life.

Part II

There is, I believe, a temptation many viewers will feel when looking at Spring. What will immediately come to mind is a biblical tale with which they are bound to have some familiarity. They expect to see the Serpent, and this expectation would be reinforced if they have familiarity with other pictorial representations of the tale. All have a snake and all have that snake on or close by the Tree of Knowledge. Aware of what awaits us in Winter, we may also think that Poussin's intent was to have the Serpent associated with tempting Eve to eat of the Tree of Knowledge, present for some reason in a scene depicting God's punishment for human disobedience. The Sauerländer and Miltonian views presuppose such a fixation of attention, influenced by ingrained expectations. Should our view be constrained by these expectations, we run the risk of failing carefully to attend to an all-important detail of the painting, Spring – The Tree of Life.

Let us, then, shift our focus of attention to this tree. In Genesis 2 we learn that God has placed within the garden numerous trees, two of which are named, one the Tree of Knowledge, the other the Tree of Life. God informs Adam that he might eat of the fruit of any tree in the garden except for the Tree of Knowledge. It is reasonable to assume that the Tree of Knowledge is the tree toward which Eve is pointing and from which she and Adam shall soon eat. They do, after all, gain knowledge of good and evil, and nothing is presented that suggests that they have eaten of the Tree of Life, which, arguably, if they had, would have made them invulnerable to death. So the Tree of Life is the tree, for the most part painted in dark colors, shaded from the sun, atop of which is a dark rock formation, the tree with hanging fruit that appears in the left foreground of the painting. At the very end of Genesis 3 the Tree of Life is again referred to, following the expulsion of Adam and Eve from the garden:

> ...and he placed at the east of the garden of Eden Cherubims, and a flaming sword which turned every way, to keep the way of the tree of life.[14]

---

14 See Blunt, Poussin, Chapter IV, "Poussin and Stoicism" for the most thorough discussion of Poussin's paintings dealing with Stoic heroes such as Phocion, Camillius, and Diogenes, and his general attachment to Stoic thought. "His basic principle for the conduct of life is to live according to nature and reason. For him, as for the Stoics, these are more or less indistinguishable, and to live according to one is to follow the other." 167 Poussin would have also been acquainted with the works of a number of Neo-stoics, among them Justus Lipsius, Guillaume du Vair, and Pierre Charron, each of whom, while attached to the thinking of the ancient Stoics, sought to harmonize Stoicism and Christianity. On the issue of personal responsibility most relevant is Justus Lipsius rejection of philosophic determinism, a view espoused by leading classical Stoics, see J. Lipsius, Two Books of Constancie, trans. by Sir J. Stradling; ed. by R. Kirk (New Brunswick, N.J.: Rutgers University Press, 1939) "Four Modifications of Ancient Stoicism," 1.20. My argument presupposes that Poussin believed, as Lipsius did, in personal responsibility and his admiration for the ancient Stoics did not go so far as his relinquishing the idea of personal responsibility whether or not the ancient Stoics in fact did so. Attesting to the popularity of Neo-stoic ideas in France of the 17th century is the fact that P. Charron's De la Sagesse livres trois (Bordeaux: Simon Millanges, 1601) appeared in 36 editions by 1672. See "Neostoicism" in International Journal of Philosophy. See also Chapter V, "Poussin's Religious Ideas," in Blunt and the little that is known about them. It should, perhaps, be mentioned that there is a distinction between attachment to everlasting life and a belief in the immortality of the soul. There is no Christian doctrine of which I am aware that supports the idea of an everlasting human life of the kind associated with the Tree of Life. In addition to the influence of Stoicism upon Poussin and, in particular with regard to his attitudes toward death, there would very likely be the influence of Lucretius and Montaigne both of whom he greatly admired. See E. Cropper and C. Dempsey, Nicolas Poussin: Friendship and the Love of Painting (Princeton: Princeton University Press, 1996), 177-215. See also Michel de Montaigne, The Complete Essays (London: Penguin Books, 1987), trans. by M.A. Screech. Essay 20, 89-108, "To philosophize is to

Were Adam and Eve to eat of the Tree of Life, God's assurance, expressed to Adam, that he would surely die if he ate of the Tree of Knowledge, would presumably turn out to be false, for Adam and Eve would, by eating, gain everlasting life.

Poussin, with perhaps the sole exception of Lucas Cranach the Elder (Fig. 9), among his distinguished predecessors, inserts the Tree of Life into his depiction of the Garden of Eden. He is not a painter inclined casually, indifferent to its symbolic significance, to include such an element in his painting. What meaning might it carry? If we focus our attention

Fig. 9: Lucas Cranach, the Elder, The Fall of Man, 1530.

upon this tree, we are confronted with a stunning sight, the sole aspect of the painting that conveys a sense of dread that, if we stay with it, can make our skin crawl, not dissimilar to our response to the large snake in the left foreground of Winter. The Serpent, whom we have vainly sought, where our expectations led us to believe he would be present, is now before us, disguised to be sure, in the multi-trunked Tree of Life where we never expected to see him. We spot him in the dark, narrow, contorted and twisted trunks and limbs forming all that we can see of the lower portion of the tree. The word "serpentine" leaps to the mind (Fig. 10). It seems as fitting a description as any to apply to those shapes. No other trees in the large corpus of Poussin's paintings, apart from the shapes of several battered branches in Winter, have trunks of a shape remotely similar to the Tree of Life. It provides a marked contrast to the erect trunks of the bedazzling Tree of Knowledge with its flowers scattered amidst its hanging fruit. If we were indeed meant to view the Serpent as situated there, Poussin

---

learn how to die," is particularly relevant.

Fig. 10: Detail of the Tree of Life in Fig. 1.

would be alone among a long list of distinguished painters to have chosen him to be so situated. That we should find the Serpent in this tree seems, however, peculiarly fitting, even while we must acknowledge its dramatic divergence from the biblical tale. The Serpent is proverbially thought to be adept at hiding, and he appears to have beguiled us to look elsewhere for him when all the time he was residing in this unexpected locale, blending into the rich foliage, until that is, our attentive eyes fix upon him and bring him to light. He is also known to be immortal because of the repeated sloughing off of his skin, his powers of renewal, and here he is fittingly ensconced in the tree that promises everlasting life.[15]

What is to be made of all this? What is to be made of the Tree of Life, holding out its promise of everlasting life, depicted in a dark setting, with shapes giving rise to a feeling of unease, while the Tree of Knowledge, the eating from which brings death, is

---

15 Gen. 3:24.

sprinkled with bright flowers? What accounts for Eve, a temptress, not unlike the Serpent, being struck by the sun's rays, a luminous figure in marked contrast to those trunks supporting the fruit hanging from the Tree of Life?

I believe some answers to these questions may lie in supplementing the Sauerländer and Blunt Christian and Pagan interpretations of the "Four Seasons"[16], by regarding "Spring" with Poussin's well-known attachment to a Stoic mode of thinking in mind – its veneration of knowledge, reason, and nature.[17] He has, I believe, uprooted Adam and Eve from the tale historically associated with them and fashioned a tale of a significantly different kind, one in which Eve is fairly described as a Stoic hero.

I reach this conclusion by imagining Poussin's thought process, quite consistent with fundamental themes at the heart of Stoicism, moving forward with a focus on nature and reason. There are several simple observations. Everything living dies. Among all living things, animals flee the prospect of imminent death. Among the animals, humans alone possess the concept of death and are capable of contemplating it when it is not proximate. This thought arouses in many a fear of death, and this fear gives rise, in turn, to thoughts of how it might be avoided. And a tempting fantasy, then, not infrequently enters the human mind that one might live forever, and one witnesses this fantasy at work in the familiar emotional inability to imagine one's own death. We often fail to live in a manner that reveals a genuine conviction that life at some point ends and this fact is an important aspect of why it is something to be treasured. In these circumstances we fail to face a fundamental truth of nature that we all die and opt instead, as is evident from much of our conduct during life, the illusion of everlasting life. This behavior is contrary to reason.

It is also contrary to reason to believe, and behave as if it were true, that such a life without end was clearly an indisputable good to be chosen if offered to one. Reason rejects a choice of some

---

16 J. H. Charlesworth, *The Good and Evil Serpent* (New Haven and London: Yale University Press, 2010), 32-57, 269-351.

17 See Blunt, Poussin, 334-335 where he suggests that each of the paintings in the Four Seasons can be seen as representing a different pagan god, in the case of Spring the god, Apollo.

purported good when the prospect of attaining it brings before our minds an idea that we cannot get our minds around, an idea whose intelligibility we cannot grasp. Our imagination, if active on the issue, as it is bound to be, presents us with possibilities, none of which we can test in advance, of eternal suffering or unbearable tedium or a loss of deep involvement in life with never any escape. Reason instructs us that death appears an evil to be avoided at any cost, but it is in fact a blessing provided by nature. No reasonable person would choose this false, tempting, good. A lengthier life, provided certain conditions, such as good health, obtain, yes. Seeking an everlasting life, with all its unknowns, no. The Tree of Life offers, then, what might appear as an inestimable good, but on reflection, nature is preferable to illusion.

Eve's back is to the Tree of Life, suggesting a rejection of what the Serpent may have tempted her to eat. The bright light of a morning sun, evoking the light that knowledge, shines upon her. We can imagine her possessing instinctive good sense, on Poussin's view of the matter, and that she prefers the genuine good of knowledge to the false promise of everlasting life. There is no Serpent, as we know in this version of the tale, to either tempt her to eat of the Tree of Knowledge or to assure her that she shall not die if she does. We see her before the moment that she and Adam move forward toward the tree and eat its fruit, believing that when they do, they shall die. We must assume, for God's words to have significance at all, that they are instinctively aware of death as an evil to be avoided. They move forward, despite the warning, and eat. This is a portrait, not of creatures that, as a consequence of disobedience, will fall, but, rather, of individuals capable of acting courageously, prepared to suffer death to obtain knowledge.

Spring is the appropriate season for this event to take place, given that when Adam and Eve eat, there is a rebirth, and a new life comes into being. The two become recognizable human beings with the capacity to reflect on their conduct and adjust their conduct to norms of their choosing. Virtuous action becomes a possibility. They acted nobly in eating; and now after eating, the idea of a noble action, not before available to them, can guide their future conduct. They can now reflect upon death and consider whether or not it is in all circumstances evil, and they can think about knowledge and reflect whether in all circumstances it is productive of good. With such thoughts they would move from knowledge to wisdom. They were before as children to be admired and to be loved; now they are creatures capable of dignity and worthy of respect. Poussin has depicted two individuals whose conduct is not distinguishable from that of noble Stoic heroes whom he has on a number of occasions depicted.[18]

What is it, should we accept this pictorial re-invention of the Adam and Eve tale, that we are to imagine God, floating in the clouds above, thinking about it all?

His ways are notoriously inscrutable, and prohibiting his creatures from acquiring knowledge of good and evil, central to the biblical tale, is significant evidence that this is so. Can a loving God intend for the human beings that he has created to remain forever as children, that there be no place in human life for moral beauty, for moral virtue, for a realization of all of the human's natural capabilities? What could be made of the idea of a human being made in the image of God if they remain as little children? Still, the biblical tale is one in which God informs Adam that on the day he eats of the fruit of the Tree of Knowledge of Good and Evil he shall surely die. Such language does suggest death as a punitive response and God's desire for obedience. God turns his back on Adam and Eve and this suggests disappointment, turning away from them, because God foresees their disobedience, in their imminent turning away from him.

My conjecture on this issue is as follows. First, there is another example in Genesis of God commanding what one may find perplexing. He commands Abraham to sacrifice what is most dear to him, his son Isaac. He does so to test the strength of Abraham's faith. God is ultimately pleased with the evidence Abraham provides of his willingness to kill Isaac and the strength of attachment to his Lord.[19] Likewise, we may suppose that Poussin's God, in his Stoic re-telling of the tale, means to test the strength of Adam and Eve's attachment to knowledge by indicating death as the outcome of

---

18 Blunt, Poussin, 160-68. See also Elaine Pagels, *The Gnostic Gospels* (New York: Random House, 1989), Chap. 3 for discussion of gnostic perspectives similar to those that would inform a Stoic approach to Adam and Eve.

19 Gen. 22.

Fig. 11: Detail of God in the clouds above from Fig. 1.

Fig. 12: Landscape with Hagar and the Angel, 1660.

obtaining it. They pass the test.

Second, God is looking forward and his left arm is raised, his hand facing forward (Fig. 11). Some scholars view God's hand as raised in a blessing.[20] This interpretation is highly improbable, not simply because the hand does not appear raised, but, more significantly, because neither God nor priests bless with other than their right hand and, of course, it is God's left hand that is stretched out in a forward direction.

What meaning, then, is to be attributed to this hand gesture? There is another similar gesture in Spring itself and another in a Poussin painting, dated 1660 (Fig. 12), and the gestures serve to direct attention, either to a subject within the painting or to the viewer of the painting. Eve's left hand is raised and points to the Tree of Knowledge. God's left hand is directed toward the light of the morning sun, a light that illuminates the world, the most fitting of symbols for knowledge. God, by this gesture, appears to be validating, rather than condemning, Adam and Eve's conduct. The radical reconstruction of the tale from a Stoic perspective is completed with a significantly radical depiction of God.

Spring was painted between 1660-1664. Poussin was ill and his hands were trembling. He died in 1665. It is reasonable to believe that his attention focused, at least occasionally, on his own death and how he would confront it. No more light; no more color; no more shapes; no more giving and receiving love; no more thought and knowledge. There is reason, I believe, to think that with Spring Poussin was preparing himself to die in the manner of the wise man so revered by the Stoics, surveying in his mind's eye much of what he so cherished in life, and at the end – a sense of gratitude and a calm acceptance of what nature brings to all that is living.

---

20 Sauerländer, see note 11 above; Poussin and Nature, 293.

CHAPTER FOUR

A Rudimentary Attempt At A Case Brief Of The First Three Chapters Of The Book Of Genesis

Richard V. Meyer

In the shared introduction to his two poignant pieces, "The Jurisprudence of Genesis," and "Thinking about Eden, A Tribute to Herbert Morris," my teacher, mentor, and friend George Fletcher compares Biblical interpretation by the Holy See to a Supreme Court decision explaining the Constitution. Fletcher makes this point to decry that lack of support within Genesis for the foundational Catholic doctrine of original sin. As always, Fletcher was looking deeper than those around him and many of his conclusions were based upon a more accurate translation of the Hebrew text. This caused me to reread and reflect on passages that I had known since childhood and to try to evaluate them through a legal rather than theological lens.

Specifically, I decided to use the case brief method and rules of legal interpretation to clarify the "law" contained within the first three chapter so Genesis. This piece is the product of that analysis.

Introduction To The Case Brief Method

Any first year law student will tell you that reading cases

is hard. Case opinions do not follow easily discernible patterns. Sometimes a mesh between poetry and prose, their statement of law can be hidden behind poor wording, covert assumptions, and literary device. Obtuse statements cannot be disregarded and apparently clear statements cannot be accepted at face value. Law students begin their search for order in a world of chaos.[1]

The case brief is a step by step process that converts and translates the opinion into a summarized and functional format. If Genesis is a poetic source of law, than the case brief might be a useful method to glean the specific statements of law contained therein.

What follows is my meager attempts to apply this method to the "case" against Adam, Eve, and the serpent in first three chapters of Genesis. I deviate from pure case analysis in that I also apply statutory rules of interpretation. For example, I will assume that every word or phrase is relevant to determining the rule or rules. This is not part of case analysis, where a jurist might include "dicta" or irrelevant statements. I am not attempting to identify any theological truths in this section, but only to see what this method of legal interpretation adds to the discussion of this Book.

My case brief sections with be: 1) The Case Name, Citation and Parties; 2) The Facts; 3) The Issues and Holdings, 4) The Reasoning, and 5) Comment.

Case Name, Citation, And Parties

Any case brief will normally start with a case name and citation. In addition to helping identify and locate the record of the case, the citation also identifies the jurisdiction. The jurisdiction portion is important because it tells us which Court made the decision and where the law of the case will apply. Genesis obviously does not contain a case citation. However, in nearly all sources of law, jurisdiction is mentioned at the start (e.g. the Constitution

---

1 Although neither the father of the case briefing method, Christopher Columbus Langdell, nor Karl Lelewellyn in the landmark The Bramble Bush: On our Law and Its Study (Ocean publications, 1930) proposed that case briefing would bring order from chaos. However, the step by step process they espoused has produced this effect for the amateur case reader.

of the United States). Even mere allegations/complaints assert jurisdiction at the very beginning. Applying this to Genesis, the first verse of the first chapter: "In the beginning Élöhîm created the heaven and the earth" would identify the Court and the area of application. Thus God is the court, and all of existence is the area of legal application.

The next step is to identify the parties to the case. There are four named individuals in Genesis. They are, in the order they are introduced: 1) Élöhîm/Yähwè Élöhîm; 2) Adam; 3) the Woman; & 4) the serpent. (For reasons explained later, it is important that the third potential party be referred to as "the woman" rather than her subsequent name of "Eve.") For this essay, I have decided to focus on the cases against Adam and the Woman.[2]

Since Adam and the Woman are being charged for actions arising from the same series of transactions and course of conduct, their cases can be joined into a single case. However, they are not the only defendants. The judgments also apply to some unnamed individuals. Specifically, the offspring of the Woman. Since a court can only issue a judgment concerning parties, they must be added to the case names.

Therefore my case name is:

Yähwè Élöhîm *vs. Adam, The Woman et al.*

The Facts[3]

The facts are those events that give rise to the application of the law. These appear to be contained in sections 3:1 to 3:13 of Genesis.

> *1 Now the serpent was more subtle than any*
> *beast of the field which the Lord God had made. And*
> *he said unto the woman: "Yea, hath God said: Ye shall*

---

2 The case against the serpent is certainly interesting, but it appears to reference a criminal prohibition not included in the text.

3 Since Genesis describes a trial rather than an appellate case, I am skipping the procedural history section and moving directly on to the facts.

not eat of any tree of the garden?"

*2 And the woman said unto the serpent: "Of
the fruit of the trees of the garden we may eat;*

*3 but of the fruit of the tree which is in the
midst of the garden, God hath said: Ye shall not eat
of it, neither shall ye touch it, lest ye die."*

*4 And the serpent said unto the woman: "Ye
shall not surely die;*

*5 for God doth know that in the day ye eat
thereof, then your eyes shall be opened, and ye shall
be as God, knowing good and evil."*

*6 And when the woman saw that the tree was
good for food, and that it was a delight to the eyes,
and that the tree was to be desired to make one wise,
she took of the fruit thereof, and did eat; and she
gave also unto her husband with her, and he did eat.*

*7 And the eyes of them both were opened,
and they knew that they were naked; and they sewed
fig-leaves together, and made themselves girdles.*

*8 And they heard the voice of the Lord God
walking in the garden toward the cool of the day;
and the man and his wife hid themselves from the
presence of the Lord God amongst the trees of the
garden.*

*9 And the Lord God called unto the man, and
said unto him: "Where art thou?"*

*10 And he said: "I heard Thy voice in the
garden, and I was afraid, because I was naked; and
I hid myself."*

*11 And He said: "Who told thee that thou
wast naked? Hast thou eaten of the tree, whereof I
commanded thee that thou shouldest not eat?"*

*12 And the man said: "The woman whom
Thou gavest to be with me, she gave me of the tree,
and I did eat."*

*13 And the Lord God said unto the woman:
"What is this thou hast done?" And the woman said:
"The serpent beguiled me, and I did eat."*

I will treat everything prior to 3:1 as a recitation of the relevant law. The sections after 3:13 appear to contain the holdings, judgments, as well as some of the reasoning.

The Issues And Holdings

Crafting the proper issue is possibly the hardest part of the case brief. Here are my feeble attempts to encapsulate the legal issues raised by the "case."

Issue #1: Does 2:17 create a criminal prohibition against eating the fruit, or merely a warning of scientific consequence?
Holding: 2:17 is a criminal prohibition.

Issue #2: Can the Woman be punished for violating the criminal prohibition of 2:17?
Holding: No. Although she had the legal status of a person under the law, she did not subjectively or objectively know of the moral prohibition contained within 2:17.

Issue #3: Is there justification for the negative consequences assigned to the Woman?
Holding: Yes. The woman breached her contractual duties to Adam inferred by 2:18, and was found liable.

Issue #4: Do the punishments and penalties assigned to Adam and the Woman apply to their offspring.
Holding: The denial of the Garden, changes to the land, and the enmity with the serpent apply to offspring, but all others do not.

The Reasoning

A.   Reasoning Issue #1: Does 2:17 create a crime?

In order for there to be a criminal prohibition, we must have two things: A) A prohibition against conduct; B) Issued by a sovereign.

1. Is 2:17 a prohibition of conduct or merely a warning of scientific consequence?

If a government sends out a health warning to its citizens like "Do not eat lemons because they cause cancer" it does not create a crime that can be violated. If a citizen, in response to the warning, eats a lemon, the State will not punish the citizen. The purpose of the message was to provide information rather than to control conduct. If that is the case with 2:17, Adam could not have committed a crime.

Applying the of plain meaning rule of legal interpretation (absent evidence to the contrary, lawmakers are presumed to intend the "ordinary meaning" of the language) to the wording of 2:17 ("but of the tree of the knowledge of good and evil, thou shalt not eat of it; for in the day that thou eatest thereof thou shalt surely die") it appears to be a warning of a worldly consequence rather than a criminal prohibition. "Don't eat this fruit because it is poisonous." However, this interpretation is in direct conflict with the rule of 2:9 that the fruit to be "good for food,"[4] the factual finding that the Woman found it "good for food" in 3:6, and finally the fact that it did not act as a physical poison against Adam or the Woman. Since the plain meaning causes textual conflict, we need to look elsewhere to resolve it.

The next potentially relevant rule of legal interpretation is *Noscitur a sociis*, which loosely translates to "a word is known by the company it keeps." This allows us to look elsewhere in the statute to determine the meaning of the section. Using the approach, I believe 2:17 does not warn of a scientific consequence, but instead identifies a crime (do not eat the fruit) and an associated punishment (or I will kill you.) I reached this conclusion by using legal interpretive rules to determine the meaning of the word "day."

Day first appears in the first chapter. In the first creation story of Genesis, we are introduced to a creator God (or Gods) called Elohim. In subsequent periods of time called "days," He creates Light, dry land, plants, animals, the sun, moon & stars, animals, and mankind. He also granted mankind "dominion" over the other

---

4 Genesis 2:9 tells us generally that the trees God made were pleasing to the eye and good for food prior to introducing the two specific trees.

products of his creation before having a seventh "Blessed" day of rest. His story covers the entire first chapter carries into the first few verses of the second. Then we meet Yahweh Elohim or the Lord God. However, he apparently completes creation in a single day, and he initially only creates a single human rather than the simultaneous creations of male and female humans of the prior creator. As a literary or historical narrative, the two stories seem hopelessly in conflict and have been reduced to the status of mere poetry by many. However, the two stories may not be in conflict at all, but instead tell the story of two different creations within the same physical world.

As a recitation of what science tells us about the creations of the world, the first creation story is not that far off. It starts with some new light (Big Bang) followed by the creation of a planet followed by dry land. Then come plants and a fixing of the solar system and galaxy. Next comes animals beginning in water and then moving to dry land with an instinctual desire to be fruitful and multiply, and then finally a world-dominating mankind. With the exception of plants arriving before the solar system was fixed, this appears to the order and manner of creation under modern evolution theory. The only problematic term appears to be the word "day."

If we apply a plain meaning interpretation to the word, we are left with a day being either one full rotation of the earth (24 hours) or a period when the sun is shining in the sky. In addition to requiring a creation process that is much faster than indicated by the archaeological record, it seems odd that the author would apply a term in the fifth verse (the First Day) that does not gain its relative meaning until the sun and moon are fixed in the sky in the sixteenth verse (the Fourth Day). Since the plain meaning rule of legal interpretation requires a single, unambiguous definition of a word it does not appear to be useful in this instance.

However, when the Supreme Court talked about the plain meaning rule in *Caminetti v. United States*, they made the statement that "... the meaning... in the first instance (is) sought in the language in which (it) was framed." In other words, if a law provides a definition of the word, we use that definition, even if that is in conflict with ordinary uses of the word. So how is "day" defined within the text? The term is introduced in the Hebrew "élohiym *Bëyn häôr ûvëyn hachoshekh*" *waYiq'rä* élohiym *läôr yôm w'lachoshekh' qärä läy'läh*" is normally translated to "Elohim divided the light from the darkness and Elohim called the light Day, and the Darkness he called Night."[5]

So we start with the definition that day is "the light." Since the sun was not created until later, this "light" cannot mean sunlight but must refer to something else. Using *Noscitur a sociis* again, we can look at the surrounding text to find the meaning of "the light."

Immediately after defining the term day to mean "the Light," the text provides seven applications of the term. Day refers to: when God separated the Light from the Darkness; when He separated the earth from the heavens; when He separated the earth and the waters and provided plant life; when He created the great lights in the sky and fixed them there; when He created animal life; when he created mankind; and when He blessed a day and chose not to act. These are separated by periods when the Light leaves (dusk) and when the Light returns (dawn).

Note that our seven examples appear to be events. Thus, if we segregate out any residual mental vestiges of a sun based "day," the text does not actually verify the common assumption that the term "day" denotes a unit of time. Instead, the text supports a definition of day as having two aspects: 1) A period of light; 2) a period when God acts.[6] If we look at these as separate elements, a day would be whenever "God acts in the light." However, if we look at these two as alternate descriptions of the same element, the presence of Light is synonymous with God acting. Thus, for the purposes of this law, a day would be defined as whenever God (The Light) acts.[7]

---

5 However the term "yôm" that is translated as "Day" is more accurately translated as a "period of warmth."

6 The seventh day seems problematic for this definition because it does not describe any physically creative acts. However, the law defines an act to include an omission (a voluntary decision not to act). Thus the seventh day is distinguishable from the period of darkness because God still "acted" by choosing not to act. Further, on the seventh day, God did act to create a normative value in that he declared the day to be "blessed."

7 This alternate definition of day does start to alleviate the conflict between the two creation stories. For example, consider the conflict that

Getting back to 2:17, if we substitute the definition of day, we get:

"but of the tree of the knowledge of good and evil, thou shalt not eat of it; for (when I act after you eat it) thou shalt surely die"

2:17 identifies the prohibited conduct (thou shalt not eat of it) as well as the applicable penalty from the sovereign (if you do, I will act and you will die). This interpretation is textually consistent with the Lord God's announcement of the findings and sentence against Adam. After finding him guilty:

And unto Adam He said: "Because thou hast hearkened unto the voice of thy wife, and hast eaten of the tree, of which I commanded thee, saying: Thou shalt not eat of it."

...the Lord God sent Adam out of Eden as his sentence. The effect of being banished from the paradise like garden is twofold. First, Adam will now have to work to grow food rather than have it easily available. Second and more importantly, Adam will be cut off from the tree of life and eventually die

"...till thou return unto the ground; for out of it wast thou taken; for dust thou art, and unto dust shalt thou return."

Thus, because Adam violated the law of 2:17, the Lord God acted to cause his death. 2:17 is a prohibition on conduct.

2. Is Yähwè Élöhîm/Lord God a sovereign and therefore capable of issuing criminal laws?

the first creation story took at least four days to create the heavens and the earth, whereas the second story, in Genesis 2:4, has them created in a single day. However, if you apply this alternate definition of day, then Genesis 2:4-7 would read "while God was acting to create the heavens and the earth but before plants had arrived, He created a man by breathing "... into his nostrils the breath of life, and man became a living soul."

Not all command are laws. As H.L.A. Hart discussed in his attack on Austin's definition of law, when a gunman threatens to shoot if you disobey, this does not create law. Normally, laws must be the product and will of some sovereign. For Adam to be found guilty of a crime, the Lord God must have sovereign status when he issued 2:17.

As mentioned earlier, the second story focuses in the actions of a Lord God rather than God (or Gods). The addition of the word "Lord" to the name appears to signify the Creator in the second story is either a different person or has a different role in the second story. Since Genesis 2:4 has the Lord God being the individual that created the heavens and the earth, the later (that God and Lord God are the same being but operating in different roles) seems most supported by the text. Assuming that to be correct, we have to determine the reason for the name change.[8]

The title Lord God carries with it some aspect of authority that was not present with the title of God. If the second story adds to, rather than merely repeats the first story, it seems to follow that its significance is somehow linked to this new mantle of authority. God gives a command to the primal forces of the universe ("Let there be light") whereas the Lord God gives a command to Adam ("Thou shalt not eat"). God has power over science & nature, and the Lord God has power over morality and man, or as Jefferson referred to them, the Laws of Nature and Nature's God.[9] The Lord God does appear to be a sovereign capable of issuing law.

The prohibition on conduct in 2:17 is a prohibition on conduct issued by a sovereign, so it does create a crime.[10]

---

8 The Wellhausen hypothesis proposes that the Torah is a product of multiple authors combined by a series of redactors. This might provide an historical reason for the name change, but for this analysis I am operating under the restriction that all words and wording are intentional and vital to divining the correct legal message.

9 (I find it interesting that these are plural and singular in the same way that Elohim is first plural and then becomes singular once Yähwè (Lord) is attached.)

10 While this could also be considered the creation of a tort, the specific consequence that does not appear to benefit any victim leads me to conclude it establishes a crime.

B.   Reasoning Issue #2 – Did the Woman violate the criminal prohibition of 2:17 and if so, what conduct constituted this violation?

In order to for the Woman to be punished for violating 2:17, she would need to have the legal status of a person under the law and have known or should have known of the criminal prohibition prior to her act.

1.   What was the legal status of the Woman?

The first creation story has male and female humanity created simultaneously on God's sixth day as the final creative event, and the second story has man created first and then a garden followed by animals and then finally a "woman" created from part of the man. While these could be two different descriptions of the same events, the rule of legal interpretation against "surplusage" requires us to avoid finding redundancy and instead prefers an interpretation that would give important meaning to both stories. The rule against surplusage would lead us to think of these two stories as separate events.

If we view these stories as in parallel rather than repetitive, than the creations of the Lord God role are different than those of the God role. The former creates the general and the later creates the specific. God created the waters of the earth, and the Lord God created four specific rivers; God created plants and trees and the Lord God created the Garden; and God created the beasts of the earth, whereas the Lord God created at least one example of each specific beast in the garden so that it could be presented to Adam for naming. If we follow this pattern, God created the species (homo sapiens) and the Lord God made Adam and the Woman in separate creative acts.[11]

---

11 This approach seems supported by the text not only within the two creation stories, but it solves the problem of Cain's wife as posed by Fletcher. If a species of humanity was created separate from the two created in the Garden, then Cain could have found a biological mate other than an unnamed sister. On objection is that this would support racist claims that some humans have souls but others do not. However, the later portion of the "law" contains the story of Noah. In that story, the soul-less,

This does not help us resolve the status of the Woman. If she has a status as less than human, she would not be subject to criminal law, but only negative consequence. We do not "punish" our pets when we smack them on the nose with a newspaper any more than we punish a tree by removing limbs that threaten our roof. Punishment is more than negative consequence because there is an aspect of morality associated with justification for the sentence. If the Woman is not a peer (or near peer)[12] of Adam, she is not subject to punishment.

There is at least some textual evidence that a woman might be less than Adam. She (the helper) is sought from among the beasts of the field. We know from the first story that man has a status of dominion over these beasts. If a "help meet" had been found among those beasts, than presumably she would have been subordinate to Adam. However, she was not found among the beasts but created from Adam as a peer.

Perhaps the most important part in Fletcher's work in evaluating the jurisprudential messages of Genesis is his exposition that the original text does not support sexual inequality. Noting that Eve was created by a "side" rather than a "rib" of Adam's rises women from the status from that of a spare part to a peer. I want to take this one step farther and argue that Eve's gender was, at most, tangential to the story.

This train of thought starts with the question "Why did the serpent talk to Eve instead of Adam?" The misogynist answer is that the woman was the "weaker" sex and more susceptible to temptation. Even when rebutting this justification for sexism, Fletcher still fails to comment on why Eve was the target of the serpent's "cunning." Assume for a second that Eve's gender was irrelevant. She is still significantly different than Adam.

First, she is younger and less experienced. Whereas Adam has been shown every beast of the field and fowl of the air, the narrative goes from Eve meeting Adam to the serpent talking to

---

wicked humanity was wiped out and all that are left are descendant of Noah, a direct descendant of Adam.

12 The use of the word peer in this context might be a bit misleading. Slaves were certainly not peers with citizens in the antebellum South, yet both were subject to the criminal laws.

her with no mention of what, if anything, occurred in between. We could surmise that God talked to Eve, since she was aware of the prohibition against eating certain fruit, but that begs a very important question: Why was the Eve's recounting of the prohibition different than what the Lord God said in Genesis 2:17?

Eve's account expanded the prohibition; in addition to eating of the fruit, even touching it was forbidden. Further, Eve adds a level of confusion as to which tree was prohibited. According to Genesis 2:9, the Tree of Life is in the "...midst of the garden." The text is not clear, but it seems to support that the Tree of Knowledge was also in the middle of the garden. God left no confusion in his instructions to Adam, identifying the prohibited tree by name. Eve, however, refers only to the tree "... in the midst of the garden." Why doesn't she refer to the Tree by name and why does she expand upon the prohibition? Again, if we apply the rule against surplusage, then the Eve's different rendering of the prohibition has significance.

The differences appear to be the product of translation/transference. The prohibition was originally spoken from God to Adam and Eve must have learned about it from Adam. It would be very "human" of Adam, in the interests of safety, to add to the prohibition just to avoid confusion. While he understood exactly which tree and which act was forbidden, the safer approach when explaining the rule to Eve would be to expand the prohibition to not even touch the fruit of either tree. Thus Adam got the rule out of God, and Eve got the rule "out of man."

My awkward wording of the last sentence was purposeful. I have been referring to one of the characters as Eve in this discussion, but she does not actually gain that name till the end of the chapter. At this point she is referred to only as woman, a word meaning "out of man." She lacks a name and any identifying experiences or physical characteristics. She is simply "out of man." Further, it is interesting that this label came from both God and Adam. In Genesis 2:23 Adam names her "out of man" just like he had previously given names to all other animals. However, the preceding text in 2:22 already labels her "out of man" (the term iSHäh is used on both verses). This cannot be just author's convenience or a generic term of a gender. 2:22 does not refer to her as female or ûn'qëväh as the term is introduced in the first creation story and it continues to refer to Adam as *häädäm* in both verses. Since that is her only identifying characteristic/label at this point in the text, it is the only textual answer to our question. The serpent targeted her not due to her gender, but because she was "out of man."

2.   Did the Woman know or should she have known of the criminal prohibition?

Based on her own "testimony" the Woman was aware of the prohibition in 2:17. However, the text does not support that she knew this a morality based command rather than a mere warning of worldly consequence.

At this point we need to step back to the roles of God and Lord God. Earlier I mentioned that God was the creator's role in the first story creating the general items of the universe, and Lord God was the role in the second story creating the specific items within the Garden. The former is the role that created the laws of science, the latter role created the laws of morality. With that as background, I find it interesting that the Woman quotes Elohim rather than Yähwè Elohim to the serpent. One could argue that this is the product of Jewish tradition not to use the term Yähwè but that tradition would replace it with Adon (Lord). If we accept that the God of the first story created the laws of science, than by quoting Elohim rather than Yähwè Elohim, the Woman is reducing the prohibition from the status of a (moral) command to merely a warning of (scientific) negative consequences. This difference is tectonic.

Compare the threatened consequence from the quote from the Woman ("Élöhîm hath said, Ye shall not eat of it, neither shall ye touch it, *lest ye die*") to the command from the Lord God "...for *in the day* that thou eatest thereof *thou shalt surely die.*" At first glance, both seem to be a warning that if you eat the fruit you will surely die. However, the Lord God's command included that interesting word "day." If we set aside the idea that "day" is a unit of time and is "when God acts," then the Lord God is telling Adam, "If you eat of that fruit, *I will act* to cause your death." The source of the danger is no longer the fruit, but *the reaction of God*.[13]

Adam received a command, whereas the Woman received only a warning of scientific consequence. A warning of (scientific) negative consequence is more open to challenge. If a child is told "Do not touch a strange dog or I will punish you," they will avoid touching even the friendliest of canines. However, if the child receives a warning rather than a command "Do not pet strange dogs lest they bite you," they are far more likely to reach out to the small dog with wagging tail. They trust their own perception and awareness of the scientific situation.

Like the child reaching for the apparently friendly small dog, the Woman does her own scientific analysis of the danger posed by the fruit. She sees that, contrary to the warning, it is "good to eat." She also hears the words of a witness (the serpent) that agree with her scientific analysis and promise hidden benefits. Enticed by the possibility of greater knowledge and the apparent absence of the forewarned scientific threat, she elects to touch and eat the fruit.

Even though she had the status of a person under the law, because the Woman did not know nor should she have known of the criminal prohibition against eating the fruit, she cannot be punished for violating 2:17.

C.   Reasoning Issue #3 – Is there justification for the negative consequences assigned to the Woman?

If the Woman was not subject to punishment for a violation of 2:17, it seems odd that the Court (Lord God) would announce the negative consequences against her (3:16) as well as her offspring (3:15). I believe these consequences were the result of civil liability for negligence rather than criminal punishment.

When the Lord God punished Adam, he started by linking the punishment directly to the offense:

---

13 Note that once again the story seems to support the idea that a day is better defined as "when God acts" as opposed to a unit of time. Adam did not die that "day" but lived for hundreds of years after eating the fruit. However, after he ate the fruit, God acted to deny Adam access to the Tree of Life and that did ultimately caused Adam's death.

> *"Because thou hast hearkened unto the voice of thy wife, and hast eaten of the tree, of which I commanded thee, saying: Thou shalt not eat of it..."*

... is followed by a list of negative consequences and a punishment (death). He does the same with the serpent:

> *"Because thou hast done this, cursed art thou from among all cattle, and from among all beasts of the field; upon thy belly shalt thou go, and dust shalt thou eat all the days of thy life."*

However, there is no such justification provided for the actions the Lord God takes against the Woman. He just jumps right to the consequence:

> *"Unto the woman He said: I will greatly multiply thy pain and thy travail; in pain thou shalt bring forth children; and thy desire shall be to thy husband, and he shall rule over thee."*

This appears to support the idea that the negative consequences to the Woman are not the result of her failure to obey the law from the Lord God. Than what is their justification?

I always found it interesting that Adam, when accused of violating God's command, assigns responsibility to the woman for his action:

> *"Hast thou eaten of the tree, whereof I commanded thee that thou shouldest not eat?"*

> *And the man said: "The woman whom Thou gavest to be with me, she gave me of the tree, and I did eat."*

Why would Adam think that the fact that the Woman provided him with the fruit is in any way relevant to his criminal conduct? Prior to this legal evaluation of the text, I had never considered that this was not a claim of defense at all, but rather a cross claim against the Woman. Consider the text where the

Woman was made:

> *And the Lord God said: "It is not good that the man should be alone; I will make him a help meet for him."*

> *And the man gave names to all cattle, and to the fowl of the air, and to every beast of the field; but for Adam there was not found a help meet for him.*

> *And the Lord God caused a deep sleep to fall upon the man, and he slept; and He took one of his sides, and closed up the place with flesh instead thereof.*

> *And the side, which the Lord God had taken from the man, made He a woman, and brought her unto the man.*

> *And the man said: "This is now bone of my bones, and flesh of my flesh; she shall be called Woman, because she was taken out of Man."*

As Fletcher argues, half of Adam's being was sacrificed in order for there to be a proper "help meet" for him. While many simplify "help meet" to mean mate, that is not consistent to the original text. The Hebrew term is *ëzer K'neg'Dô*. While *neg'D* does translate to counterpart or mate (and also connotes some aspect of opposition), the term ëzer adds the word "aid" to the description. Taken together, it seems that the Woman was created to be mate of Adam that would help him. This is the source of the claim against the Woman for which the Lord God assigns liability.

Adam files a cross claim of breach of contract against the Woman. In essence, in response to the allegation, Adam says "Yes I did it, but it was because she failed to do her duty."

If this is a cross claim, then the Court's judgment against the Woman would have to be for the benefit of Adam. Unlike criminal punishment, which does not have to provide any "benefit" to anyone, a breach of contract claim is for damages from one party to be awarded to the other.[14] The judgment against the Woman was:

> *Unto the woman He said: "I will greatly multiply thy pain and thy travail; in pain thou shalt bring forth children; and thy desire shall be to thy husband, and he shall rule over thee."*

The latter two portions of the judgment seem to clearly meet the requirement that they be for the non-breaching party's (Adam's) benefit. However, why would he ever want the Woman to have increased pain in childbirth?

This seems like a negative consequence to the Woman without any benefit to Adam. I struggled with this idea for a while, but like many times before, Fletcher came riding to the rescue. Fletcher argues that, if Adam was split equally into male and female parts, originally he was androgynous. I think his analysis is inextricably linked to the interpretation that the word "woman" in the text indicates a gender. As discussed above, I believe that gender has no relevance to the term Woman in this "case." If correct, isn't it possible that both Adam and the Woman remained androgynous even after they were split into two parts?

This would solve the benefit to Adam dilemma. The penalty did not increase the pain of child birth, but rather assigns the role of child bearer to one of the two androgynous beings. The laws of nature from the first creation story mandate sexual reproduction

---

14 I have to answer an obvious question raised: Is this a civil case or a criminal case? In the common law tradition of the United States, actions for damages would occur in a totally separate cause of action than criminal charges. The O.J. Simpson murder trial was totally separate from the subsequent wrongful death action brought by Ron Goldman Sr. However, in the inquisitorial model of civil law countries, there is no such line of demarcation. A single court has no problem adjudicating both the government's and the victim's actions against the Defendant. The Lord God follows this inquisitorial model in his proceedings. He is the one that interrogates the witnesses. Like a judge in an inquisitorial system, he has a more active role than the more passive referee and scorekeeper like responsibilities of a judge in the adversarial (common law) model. Since the Lord God is using the inquisitorial method, I have no problem following the civil law tradition of combining civil and criminal causes of action.

for mankind. As they are getting kicked out of Eden, the Lord God will need to assign a sex to each in order for them to reproduce. One of them would have to assume the role of child bearer and suffer the pain of childbirth and the other will not. As part of his damages for breach of contract, Adam gets to avoid the possibility that he will be chosen to be the child bearer.

This appears to be bootstrapping on steroids, however, there is some supportive evidence in the text. First, a difference between the two creation stories is that in the first story, Elohim, creator of the laws of nature, told the male and female mankind to "Be fruitful, and multiply" but in the second creation story the first mention of procreation is in the Woman's penalties.

Next, there is the second naming of the Woman as Eve. The legal interpretation maxim of "*In pari material*" allows us to look at other statues on the same subject matter. Three others are renamed in Genesis. In 17:5 Abram becomes Abraham (Father of many nations). In 17:15 Sarai becomes Sarah (mother of many nations). In 32:29 Jacob becomes Israel (One who prevails over God). In each instance, the name change signifies a change in roles. Two of these are especially relevant to the current discussion because they signify a switch from infertility to fertility. Only after the judgment does Adam call his wife Eve (The Mother of All Living). Significantly, after Adam names her Eve, she is never again referred to as "woman" in Genesis. If "woman" were merely a designation of sex, than she would retain both "woman" and "Eve" thereafter.

One major objection to this line of thought is that it reinforces the misogyny that Fletcher was trying to prevent. It makes females subordinate to men. I believe the text also avoids this problem.

> *"And I will put enmity between thee and the woman, and between thy seed and her seed; they shall bruise thy head, and thou shalt bruise their heel."*

This is a very odd verse. Why does the text mention the woman's seed/offspring? If she is destined to be the sexual partner of Adam, wouldn't they share offspring? Also, why does this appear within the penalties assigned to the serpent and before the Lord God is even addressing the Woman? These caused me to re-evaluate the purpose of this verse.

It is there not just to identify what it includes, but more importantly, what the other penalties do not. Under the legal interpretation of *Expressio unius est exclusio alterius* which translates to "the express mention of one thing excludes all others," the express mention that the enmity with the serpent will also apply to the Woman's offspring means that the other penalties assigned to the Woman will **not** carry to her offspring. Eve shall be ruled by her husband, but her offspring will not.

Finally, remember that the enmity penalty assigned to the offspring is contained within the sentence to the serpent. It does not necessarily follow that this is also a penalty for the Woman or the Woman's offspring. Said another way, the enmity between serpents and humans is far more likely to cause negative consequence to the serpent than the human.

Adam alleged that the Woman breached her contract with Adam to help him. The Court agreed and awarded him the damages of her desire, his dominion over her, and the fact that she would be assigned the female role and bear the pain of childbirth.

D. Reasoning Issue #4 – Do the punishments and penalties assigned to Adam and the Woman apply to their offspring?

As noted above, the interpretation maxim of *Expressio unius est exclusio alterius* supports the idea that, since only the enmity penalty is applied to offspring, the other penalties are not. However, the cursing of the ground would continue to affect offspring as long as it may persist. Further, the denial of access to the garden appears to be a penalty that continues to apply.

This legal conclusion seems to support Fletcher's assertion that the Christian (Catholic) doctrine of original sin is not supported by the text of Genesis. Fletcher finds the idea of original sin to not only be unsupported by the text, but morally repulsive. Any concept of mass punishment of offspring seems legally indefensible, immoral and nonsensical. Further, it seems in direct conflict with Ezekiel 18:20 "*a son shall not bear the iniquity of the father.*"

Fletcher proposes a separation thesis that views the eating of the fruit "...not as a Fall or sin, but as a necessary step in the evolution of God's children." They had to "...grow up and leave the paternal garden." I believe this thesis is supported by the findings, above. For this final portion of the paper, I am setting aside legal interpretation and, instead, looking to see if Fletcher's separation thesis is actually in conflict with the Catholic doctrine of original sin.

Comments

The Comments section of a case brief can be used to talk about how the law from the case at hand relates to other laws. As stated, I am going to use it to evaluate how Fletcher's separation thesis interacts with the doctrine of original sin.

Original sin is certainly at the core of Catholic theology. The Catholic Catechism states that to "...tamper with the revelation of original sin (undermines) the mystery of Christ." This seems to support Fletcher's assertion that the Church started with an axiom that the redemption of Christ was necessary, and then reversed engineered it back to the doctrine of original sin.

Rather than work backwards, let's start with Fletcher's separation thesis and work forward and see if it leads to the possibility of original sin. In the Garden, Adam was so close to God as to be one with him. At that time he had no needs or desires that were not fulfilled. He was not hungry, lonely, or even mortal thanks access to the Tree of Life.

Adam ate the fruit and everything changed. He became separate from God. He had to assume the adult roles of parent and provider. Just like the child that matures, moves out and develops their own family and home, as Adam matured, his separation from his parent would have increased. Each new experience, need, or struggle would increase the gap between them.[15]

Where Fletcher's paternal analogy falls apart is that the relationship between with Yähwè 'Élöhîm and Adam was much closer than that of parent and child. A parent and child never share a consciousness in the manner Fletcher describes the Adam/God relationship. A child would never dream of nor desire to obtain a oneness with their parent. They have always viewed themselves as a separate individual from their parent and they would not want

---

15 Fletcher argues that the gap is so significant that Adam feels naked without the protection of a Covenant.

to sacrifice their individual self.

Instead, this relationship between Adam and God would be more akin to the between Adam and the Woman.

> *"Therefore shall a man leave his father and his mother, and shall cleave unto his wife, and they shall be one flesh."*

This verse describes beings that feel incomplete when separate. Fletcher states that prior to eating the fruit, Adam was not even aware that he was a being separate from God. This describes a unity of consciousness that would dwarf the "one flesh" unity described in the verse. If husband and wife will abandon their parents and cling to each other to end feelings of separation, one can only imagine what Adam would do to regain his oneness with Yähwè 'Élöhîm.

Perhaps a better analogy than a parent is to view Yähwè 'Élöhîm as a continuing life source similar to oxygen. Suddenly, the separation becomes far more negative. Sure, we can eventually be proud of our increased ability to hold our breath and learn to operate without oxygen, but we would never argue that life partially or completely separate from oxygen is the preferred state.

We do not truly appreciate the value of oxygen until we are cut off from it. That would mean that Adam was destined to separate himself from God. Catholicism would argue that even if Adam's decision to separate from the will of God was predictable, inevitable, and a necessary step in our maturation, it was also both a sin and a Fall. It was a sin because it caused separation from God, which is the actual definition of sin provided in Isaiah 59:2. To paraphrase Thomas Wayne and Alfred from the movie Batman Begins, it was a Fall that then enables us to learn how to get back up.

Thus, rather than conflicting with the doctrine of original sin, if we use the definition of sin provided in another statute as "...that which separates us from God," Fletcher's separation thesis provides it an excellent foundation.

Conclusion

As we near the end of this thought exercise, I want to introduce you to one final, perhaps counterintuitive aspect of the case brief: the (historical) truth of the facts in the case is irrelevant. Consider this example. John Doe is charged with robbery. At trial, the two robbery victims both testify that although they were intoxicated at the time, they are certain that it was John Doe who stole their purses while threatening them with a knife. John Doe is found guilty at trial and sentenced to ten years in prison. John Doe appeals claiming that since there was no physical evidence, the testimony of two intoxicated witnesses should not be enough to sustain such a serious conviction. In the published opinion of State v. Doe, the appellate court disagrees and issues an opinion denying the appeal and upholding the conviction. From that point forward, as a matter of law, if a jury uses only the testimony of two drunk witnesses to find a defendant guilty of robbery, that is enough to legally sustain the conviction. Now assume that Jeff Doe, John Doe's identical twin brother, then confesses to the robbery and even provides the two stolen purses to the court. This will probably be enough to set aside John Doe's conviction, but it has no effect on the legal viability of the published opinion in State v. Doe. Even though it turns out that John Doe was innocent, the law that "...two intoxicated witnesses is sufficient evidence to sustain a robbery conviction" is still valid. Thus the lessons we may have gleaned from our case brief analysis of the first three chapters of Genesis do not depend on the historical accuracy of the facts therein.

PART II

The Collective Human Identity

Part II of this volume explores the seemingly paradoxical relationship between Western Individualism and Collective Identity and argues for the Biblical origin of both. It also explores the links between the creation stories in Genesis and the modern legal value of equality.

In the first article in this section, "Punishment, Guilt, and Shame in Biblical Thought", Fletcher explores the identity of the individual and the collective within the framework of guilt. Fletcher identifies (1) guilt as objective pollution, and (2) guilt as a subjective feeling. He notes examples of objective guilt in the stories of the Abraham and Isaac, both of whom deceive a foreign leader into committing, or nearly committing, adultery. The foreign leader victims treat "guilt" as an objective wrong doing that puts a stain upon their kingdoms. In Leviticus guilt is again evoked as a form of "pollution" that can be cleansed via animal sacrifice. Subjective guilt appears in the story of Joseph, whose brothers seem to feel guilty for their collective crime of selling him into slavery. Fletcher concludes the piece by distinguishing guilt from shame, as "people feel shame for who and what they are, and guilt for what they have done." Shame can more often be irrational, and neither in the bible nor in modernity is it linked to punishment for sin.

In a piece titled "Sin, Guilt and Punishment in the Biblical Cultic Sphere", Professor Joel Baden builds on George Fletcher's piece by digging into Leviticus 4-5 in order to show how "cultic" legislation is built around the idea of responsibility, both individually and collectively, with "guilt" serving as a cleansing force against the stains of sin. Baden lays out four forms of punishment: (1) unwitting sins by priests that are then implicated to the people; (2) unwitting sins by individuals; (3) knowing violations by individuals; (4) sins related to defiling a sacred object.

Baden demonstrates that for "unwitting" sins there is a feeling that God's space in the Tabernacle has been soiled, and it can only be cleaned via the proscribed offerings. "It is the fact of sin, not the content of the sin that is problematic within the system." People do not feel emotional guilt for unwitting sin, but take responsibility to cleanse the Tabernacle, or God could otherwise forsake them. When it comes to intentional, or knowing, sins, the required offerings are strikingly similar for a knowing perpetrator as for an unknowing perpetrator, save one key difference: confession. Baden explains that a "brazen sinner," who refuses to take responsibility for the pollution he created, could be exiled or put to death. But the simple act of personal responsibility – via confession – equalized the "penalty" to that of an unknowing sinner.

Finally, Baden explains that the defiling of sacred objects requires a steeper price (i.e. an expensive Ram for offering, plus a surcharge) as a sort of "reparation offering" because in addition to the spiritual pollution in the Tabernacle, real community property has to be repaid for. Baden makes clear that the underlying system for all of these forms of sin and punishment is one of individual responsibility to the larger collective.

In "Collective Guilt and Collective Punishment", George Fletcher builds upon the groundwork laid by "Punishment, Guilt, and Shame in Biblical Thought". He uses the biblical tension between guilt as objective pollution and guilt as a psychological state in order to explore the question of whether collective guilt justifies collective punishment. Fletcher argues that two justifications for collective punishment are complicity in the original (or ongoing) sin and deterrence. He cites the Israeli-Palestinian conflict as a real-world touch point, for both sides of that conflict explicitly use collective guilt and punishment as a means for constant fighting and retaliation against members of the other side. Fletcher notes that in any case of collective punishment, there is a sense of injustice.

Drawing on the same Biblical stories as the earlier piece

to paint guilt as either a form of pollution requiring cleansing (objective guilt) or as a feeling of wrongdoing (subjective guilt). Objective guilt is cleansed via some form of ritual (oftentimes a sacrifice), while subjective guilt is ameliorated by admission of the feeling of wrongdoing, if not of the wrongdoing itself. Fletcher's hope is that modern people in large, collective conflicts, as in Israel-Palestine, can emulate the example of biblical subjective guilt, thereby recognizing past wrongdoings instead of seeking collective punishment for the objective past wrongs committed.

In "Teamwork Makes the Dream Work – Collective Punishment and the Law of Soccer", Professor Doctor Katharina de la Durantaye uses George Fletcher's ideas around collective guilt as a launch pad into the "law of soccer." Specifically, Durantaye argues that the law of soccer does not renounce collective guilt and punishment in ways that most modern legal systems do.

Durantaye points to different forms of sanctions – stadium bans and disqualifications – that act as collective punishment. Stadium bans are issued by club owners against groups of fans, including fans that have committed no harm. Disqualifications are sanctions by leagues against the soccer clubs, imposed for misconduct by club supporters who are not members of the club (i.e. the fans). Stadium bans amount to "liability of fans for other fans," while disqualifications represent a form of "liability of clubs for their fans." Durantaye provides a German case example for each type of sanction, and Durantaye argues that the latter is more problematic than the former. With stadium bans, the property rights of clubs is pitted against the fan's freedom of action, allowing the club's rights to supersede as a preventative measure against potential negative incidents. Club disqualifications, however, assign actual culpability of fans' actions onto a soccer club. Punishment for the bad behavior of another is, Durantaye says, a violation of the principle of culpability.

In the fifth and final Fletcher article, "In God's Image: The Religious Imperative of Equality under Law", he argues that the jurisprudential principle of equality under the law is best grounded in a holistic view of human dignity. He identifies the basis for this value for Western Law within the first creation story within Genesis. Fletcher notes that such a holistic view is superior to an alternative approach that seeks to identify specific traits for defining humaneness or equality. Specifically, Fletcher puts forward the thesis that the text of Genesis (the "first" creation story in particular) provides the roots for the "truth" that "all men are created equal," with its account of a holistic and universal human dignity. He then uses this thesis to offer a new doctrinal principle in American equal protection jurisprudence. This is a significant addition to the foundation of a legal virtue previously defended with merely utilitarian assertions.

Fletcher traces the idea of holistic human dignity from Genesis, on to the secular language of Kant, as well as to The Declaration of Independence, written by Thomas Jefferson, which appealed to the divine as the moral basis for independence if all men are created equal. Abraham Lincoln adapted this religious language of equality for applications to the individual. Lincoln's usage provided a religious and moral argument against slavery, and, later was used similarly by Martin Luther King Jr. and other civil rights leaders. Courts and philosophers in recent years, however, have largely ignored the religious basis of these universal equality principles that are so deeply embedded in American political discourse. The movement away from the biblical text has implications for American Constitutional law in the arena of "equal protection" cases. Fletcher breaks out "equal protection" doctrine into two types of cases: (1) arbitrary legislation cases, and (2) caste-reinforcing discrimination cases. He then proposes that we adopt a "Kantian principle" into our understanding of equality in the form of a "judicial imperative." The judicial imperative is a categorical obligation to eliminate caste-reinforcing policies. In the parlance of equal protection doctrine, these are policies impacting "suspect classes" (e.g. race, nationality, gender).

In the final piece in this volume, "God's Freedom", Professor Arthur J. Jacobson jumps off from George Fletcher's argument that the "first" creation story suggests a deep equality for all people, because all are made in the image of God. Jacobson digs into the distinctions between the first and second creation stories in Genesis, arguing that the second story introduces a fundamental tension between freedom and inequality, played out by God.

In the first creation story, God does not "create" man ex nihilo as a bi-gendered individual. This story is about creating lawfulness out of chaos, with the deity referred to as "Rulers." But the deity is not truly "free" until it "fashions" Adam and Ever in the second story, allowing God to have another being relative to which the deity can exist self-consciously. Eve performs the first act of freedom in the story of eating from the tree of knowledge (about which Jacobson has some interesting interpretive commentary), and God responds to this act by shortening the lifespan of humans. Jacobson suggests that God, here, could be said to commit homicide for the first of many times throughout the bible. This homicidal act, along with the way God plays favorites between Cain and Abel, demonstrate the earliest examples of unequal treatment. Here, they are by the deity itself. God's evolution through the two creation stories, Jacobson argues, thus shows the tension between the virtue of lawful equality and the virtue of freedom, the latter generally leading to inequality.

CHAPTER FIVE

Punishment, Guilt, And Shame In Biblical Thought

George P. Fletcher

The centrality of guilt in the criminal law provides puzzling perspective in the perennial debate on the nature and purpose of punishment. Why is it that all legal systems use this highly charged moral term to refer to an essential component of liability to punishment? This question is not easily answered. The reliance on the concept of guilt in the criminal law is suffused with paradox and mystery.

First, we do not really require guilt in order to punish; we insist only that the defendant be found guilty – that is, in common law systems, that the jury return a verdict of "guilty." The defendant need not feel anything, least of all actual guilt for having committed the crime. Significantly, where we do probe the defendant's sentiments, namely in sentencing, the relevant question is not guilt but remorse or regret. A Virginia jury recently imposed the death penalty on one of the Washington snipers, John Allen Muhammad, and some of the jurors explained their verdict to the press on the grounds that he did not express remorse for the killings.[1] It probably would not have helped him much to say

---

1 James Dao, *Sniper Mastermind Sentenced to Death*, Int'l Herald Trib.,

that he recognized his guilt or that he felt guilty for what he had done. The jurors wanted to hear something more than that which they had already assumed.

We use the language of guilt and blame in the criminal law without actually demanding that anyone feel guilty or that anyone blame anyone else. The defendant must be blameworthy for a wrongful act in order to be found guilty. If the act is committed under conditions of insanity or duress, the actor is not blameworthy. But to say that the actor is blameworthy is not to imply that the judge or jury actually tenders a certain sentiment, a posture of blaming, toward the defendant in the dock. In the same way that the defendant need not feel actual guilt, those condemning him need not tender a feeling of blame. On that particular day, the official actors in the legal system might feel nothing at all. Still they are required, in their roles, to act as though they actually blamed an offender who has no justification or excuse for committing a crime. Obviously, the evidence – not the transient sentiments of the officials – should determine liability to punishment.

Thus, we use the language of guilt and blame in the criminal law without expecting that anyone actually feels guilty or feels the need to blame. It is as though we are watching a production of Hamlet and know that Hamlet is supposed to feel ambivalence about acting, but we do not know whether the particular actor playing Hamlet feels anything of the sort.

Alasdair MacIntyre's notable comment about contemporary moral theory could apply as well to the language of guilt and punishment: "What we possess ... are the fragments of a conceptual scheme, parts which now lack those contexts from which their significance derived."[2] In the field of criminal justice we seem to be living in the afterlife of some other conceptual scheme that was once rich with meaning. My task in this paper is to engage and pursue that hypothetical Eden of meaning by engaging in an archaeological study of the concept of guilt. I will examine the concept in one of its primary sources, the Bible – in particular, the Hebrew Bible and the book of Genesis. These texts are not the only sources of our concept of guilt and punishment, but surely they

---

Nov. 26, 2003, at 5.

2 Alasdair MacIntyre, After Virtue 2 (2d ed. 1984).

must be among the formative texts of Western culture.

Guilt As Pollution And Sacrifice

When we go back to the Hebrew Bible, we have some difficulty pinpointing the exact emergence of the concept of guilt in the narrative of creation and the patriarchs.[3] A good deal depends on the translation of the word "guilt" into Hebrew. Modern Hebrew relies upon the word *"ashma"* to capture the idea of guilt in the criminal law. Variations on the root aleph-shin-mem for *ashma* figure prominently in the biblical text but there is no reason to assume that this is the only way to render the concept of "guilt" in ancient Hebrew. For example, there is considerable dispute about the proper reading of the colloquy between Cain and God after Cain slays his brother Abel and God sentences him to become a solitary wanderer of the earth – a fitting punishment for someone who has slain his brother. Cain intervenes, "My *avon* is more than I can bear." The problem is finding the right translation of *avon* into English or into any other modern Western language.

The King James translation of the Bible popularized Cain's lament as, "My punishment is greater than I can bear."[4] This way of rendering the text demeans Cain into someone who has committed fratricide and is unable to own up to the deed and accept punishment for what he has done. Interpreting Cain's *avon* as punishment fits well with the first murderers initial response to God: "Am I my brother's keeper?"[5] But there are many clues that this translation is incorrect. For one thing, in the modern Hebrew, the word *avon* refers to a misdemeanor, a kind of crime, and not to the punishment for the crime. It would be proper, therefore, to render Cain's statement as: "My sin (crime, iniquity) is greater than I can bear." This would be, in effect, a confession of guilt. For reasons I do not comprehend, translators still gravitate today toward reading

---

3 This article represents a revision of my thoughts as presented in the Storrs Lectures. *Cf.* George P. Fletcher, *The Storrs Lectures: Liberals and Romantics at War: The Problem of Collective Guilt*, 111 Yale L. J. 1499 (2002).

4 Genesis 4:13.

5 Genesis 4:9.

avon as punishment rather than as crime or sin.

In my view, Luther got it right when he translated the verse as: "Meine Sünde ist größer, denn daß sie mir vergeben werden möge."[6] ("My sin is greater than can be forgiven me.") In the current on-line version of the translation, the editor has rewritten Luther's original to conform to the sense of the King James translation. It reads: "Meine Strafe ist zu schwer, als daß ich sie tragen könnte."[7] ("My punishment is greater than I can bear.") The same bias is evident in the scholarship of James Kugel, who concedes that early readers of the text read *avon* as "sin" or "iniquity" but that this reading was, in his view, incorrect. His taking a stand on this delicate issue requires a reasoned argument, which he fails to provide.[8]

The common translation of "guilt" into Hebrew as *asham* or *ashma* makes its first appearance in the biblical narrative in the last of the three tellings of the story of a patriarch entering a foreign land and fearing that the "barbarians" will kill him in order to gain the sexual favors of his wife. The pattern is always the same: Abraham (twice) and then Isaac relive the same deception – each tells the foreign potentate (first Pharaoh and then a king named Abimelech in the land of Gerar) that his wife is in fact his sister. In all three cases something happens to inform the potentate that either he or a man of his court is about to commit adultery.

In the first version, after Abraham passes Sarah off as his sister, Pharaoh takes her into court. Plagues then descend upon "Pharaoh and his household" as a sign that a sexual sin has occurred or is about to occur.[9] Pharaoh quickly realizes that something is wrong in the natural order and confronts Abraham with his lie.

In the second retelling of the same basic story, the truth

---

6 Die Heilige Schrift 1 Mose 4:13 (1967) (Gideon version).

7 Menighetsfakultetet, *Das Erste Buch Mose* (Genesis), *at* http://www. menfak.no/bibelprog/mb?lMO+4,1-5,6&bi=Luther (last visited March 19, 2004) (on file with the Notre Dame Journal of Law, Ethics & Public Policy).

8 *See* James L. Kugel, Thè Bible As It Was 96 (1997).

9 Genesis 12:17 (New International Version).

of sexual sin is realized not by a plague but by God coming to Abimelech in a dream and saying, "You are but a dead man because of the woman that you have taken, for she is a man's wife."[10]

In the third telling, when Isaac passes off Rebecca as his sister, a king also named Abimelech discovers the lie when he sees them engaging in affectionate behavior that would be incest if they were actually brother and sister.[11]

Assuming that they are not an incestuous couple, Abimelech confronts Isaac, establishes the lie, and then says: "What have you done to us? One of the people might have lain with your wife, and you would have brought guilt upon us."[12] The one who is responsible for the situation, the one who lied, is paradoxically not affected by the guilt. Guilt is objective and it affects the entire land where the sin occurs.

An analogy with Oedipus is compelling.[13] As Oedipus brought a plague on Thebes by killing his father and marrying his mother, Isaac brings guilt on the land of Abimelech. The existence of the stain invites reflection about its cause, and the investigation into the cause, of course, provides the structure of Sophocles' play Oedipus Rex. The striking difference between the Greek and the Hebrew story, however, lies in the personal reaction to the incident

---

10 Genesis 20:3. All translations of the Bible are my own, unless otherwise indicated.

11 Genesis 26:8. The assumption that they are engaged in sexual behavior derives from use of the verb Ltsachech to describe their activity. The verb is often translated as "sporting" – a term that also carries a sexual connotation in English. But no one is quite sure what the Hebrew word means. It also used a key term describing Ishmael's offense against Isaac, an offense so egregious that Sarah felt compelled to expel him from the household. Genesis 21:9. In that context it is often translated as "mocking." But why should mocking be regarded as so serious? It is more plausible to think of Ishmael as engaged in some kind of sexual abuse of his younger brother Isaac. In any event, some account is required to explain the use of the same verb to describe what was done to Isaac and later to capture what Isaac and Rebecca were doing in front of Abimelech.

12 Genesis 26:10.

13 Sophocles, Oedipus Rex (R.D. Dawe ed., Cambridge Univ. Press 1982) (c. 429 B.C.).

that brings or threatens to bring the stain on the land. Oedipus puts out his eyes with his wife Jocasta's brooch and goes into voluntary exile. The text tells us nothing about Isaac's feeling for having brought about this situation of potential stain and pollution.

In the second telling of this story, when it is Abraham rather than Isaac who engages in the lie, Abimelech says something similar to Abraham after the deception is revealed to the potentate in a dream: "What hast thou done unto us? And what have I offended thee, that thou hast brought on me and on my kingdom a great sin?"[14] Here the key word is not *asham* but *chataah*, which is conventionally translated as sin.

As between these two references to a stain brought upon the land, there is a good reason for taking *asham*[15] and not *chataah*[16] as the first reference to "guilt." We find the same pattern in the use of the word *asham* as we have already noted in the use of *avon*, namely, a strong conceptual link between the ideas of guilt (or sin or iniquity) and of punishment. Like *avon*, *asham* refers ambiguously both to the deed and the effort to cleanse the world of its stain.

The term *asham* comes into prominence in chapter five of Leviticus, where we encounter the various forms of sacrifice necessary to cleanse the world of its various forms of pollution.[17] *Asham* is the word used in this context to describe a whole range of sacrifices. The prescription is to bring a "guilt sacrifice" to atone for specific sins, and burnt offerings for others. The conceptual merging of the deed and the remedy validates the general biblical pattern. The easy interchange of the negative and the positive, the contamination and the decontamination, reveals a way of thinking totally different from the modern conception of guilt.

Walter Burkert, a distinguished historian of Greek religion and culture, has a different take on this easy association of guilt and punishment in the ancient world. He suggests that those who committed the offense requiring a sacrificial response actually

---

14 Genesis 20:9 (King James Version).

15 Genesis 26:10.

16 Genesis 20:9.

17 Leviticus 5:6 ("And he shall bring his guilt offering to the Lord for the sin that he has sinned.").

tendered personal feelings of guilt and projected these subjective feelings onto the sacrifice.[18] Though I was once skeptical of this thesis as it applied to the book of Exodus, I now think the matter is more complex than I once thought.[19]

The book of Genesis is ambivalent about whether guilt is appropriately accompanied by feelings of guilt or whether there might be feelings of guilt without any external pollution. Adam and Eve might feel shame after they eat of the forbidden fruit and discover their nakedness but there is no sign that they feel guilt for having disobeyed God. Yet when Joseph's brothers learn that the sibling they tried to kill is alive, well, and prospering, they cry in guilt for having ignored his pleas for help.[20] This tension within the book of Genesis reflects a dichotomy that is generally assumed to juxtapose an ancient with a modern understanding of guilt.

Feeling Guilty For Wrongdoing

In the modern approach to guilt, the focus is not on pollution but on the feelings of those who are guilty. The shift has been from its external impact of guilt on the world to the inner, human experience. The disengagement of the inner feeling from reality has led to the supposedly modern phenomenon of free-floating guilt, as exemplified in Kafka's novel, *The Trial*.[21] Joseph K expects to be tried for something, but he does not know what. In another form of disengagement – this time both from the impact of the action and from the actor's sentiment we now acknowledge that a suspect might be guilty even if he does not feel anything and resolutely protests his innocence.

A careful reading of the Joseph story reveals that this way of thinking is not uniquely modern. It is found in the book of

---

18 Walter Burkert, *Greek Tragedy and Sacrificial Ritual*, 7 Greek Roman & Byzantine Stud. 87, 112 (1966) (noting that "the community is knit together in the common experience of shock and guilt" at the time of sacrifices).

19 For my earlier views, see Fletcher, supra note 3.

20 Genesis 42:21.

21 Franz Kafka, *The Trial* (Breon Mitchell trans., Schocken Books 1998) (1925).

Genesis as well. To grasp the alternative model of *asham* or guilt presented in the Joseph story, we should review the first part of the tale in Genesis.[22]

The saga begins with a built-in conflict between Joseph and his ten elder brothers. Jacob, their father, loves Joseph more than the others and the ten are jealous. When some receive more love than others, as Abel was favored by God, we can expect enmity between brothers. The conflict among the sons of Jacob becomes more acute when Joseph relates two dreams, which his brothers interpret as a fantasy of domination over them. As the astute German commentator Claus Westermann points out, this was a startling new political idea – namely, that one brother could acquire a superior political status to his siblings.[23] The brothers throw him into a pit and conspire to kill him, but Reuben, the eldest, protests the plan to kill Joseph and suggests that they merely leave him to die. This they do, and then sit down to break bread, as though they were celebrating Joseph's demise. At that point Judah sees a caravan of Ishmaelites approaching and realizes that it might be better to sell Joseph to the voyagers rather than kill him and conceal their act. Apparently, it does not occur to him that selling their brother into slavery is also a wrong that they would have to conceal from Jacob and others. Before the brothers can realize Judah's plan, a band of Midianites pass by. And some group (the text is ambiguous on this point) lifts Joseph out of the pit and sells him to one of the passing caravans headed for Egypt.

Reuben discovers that Joseph has been taken and tears his clothes in distress. To cover up their crime, the brothers then dip Joseph's coat – Jacob's gift of love – in the blood of a slaughtered goat and take it to Jacob as proof of Joseph's death. The traveling merchants sell Joseph into the service of Potiphar, an Egyptian official.

This is the end of the passage recounting the tale of crime and betrayal. It is worth noting that no one in this story acts as an individual. Only a collective act in throwing Joseph into the pit, and later, in lifting him out. The brothers function as a unit. Even

---

22 Genesis 37, 39-42.

23 Claus Westermann, Die Joseph-Erzahlung: Elf Bibelarbeiten Zu Genesis 37-50, at 24 (1990).

when Reuben protests, he speaks in the first person plural. The next segment of the saga traces Joseph's rise to political power in Egypt. When he meets his brothers again, at least a decade later, he is the "governor over the land."[24] With a famine in Canaan, Jacob sends ten of the brothers, excluding the youngest Benjamin, to find food in Egypt. When they encounter Joseph, the ten bow down to him without recognizing him, but Joseph recognizes them and recalls the dream.[25]

There follows a conversation in Genesis that leads to the brothers recognizing their guilt for the way they committed a crime toward Joseph.[26] The word used for guilt in this context is the same as used in the story of Abimelech and Isaac. The process by which they come to confess their guilt is one of the most remarkable interactions in the corpus of biblical literature. Joseph stages both a conversation and a physical environment that leads his brothers to understand the moral dimension of the way they had treated Joseph.

The first step in the interaction is Joseph's accusing the brothers of being spies. It is hard to know whether Joseph himself believes the charge to be true or whether he is testing his brothers. With his usual political insight, Westermann points out that spying is a characteristic feature of nations, not of families.[27] Joseph himself is acting as the officer of a state; his accusation of spying is designed to find out whether the brothers are also acting on behalf of a state or whether they identify themselves as a family rather than a nation. The brothers defend themselves against the charge by claiming that they are "the sons of one man in Canaan."[28] The Westermann thesis explains this response but it

---

24 Genesis 42:6 (King James Version).

25 Genesis 42:8-9.

26 Genesis 42:9-21.

27 Westermann, supra note 23, at 73. In the first translation of the Bible into German, Martin Luther opted for a different term altogether. He translates the Hebrew term as "*Kundschafter*," which means something like "investigator." *See* Die Heilige Schrift, supra note 6, at 1 Mose 42:9 (1967).

28 Genesis 42:13.

seems strained nonetheless – individuals and informal groups do, in fact, sometimes spy on each other.

A totally different approach to the accusation begins with the motive that Joseph attributes to the spying, namely, "to see the nakedness of the land."[29] The sexual overtones of the word "nakedness" suggest an analogy with the earlier intervention of the brothers, the "sons of Jacob," to reclaim their sister Dinah from the house of Schechem. Whether that rescue was deceitful and improper or not, the brothers thereby demonstrated their loyalty to members of the clan. By suggesting sexual overtones to the mission of his ten brothers, Joseph might be revealing his own yearning that they have to come to take him as they had schemed and fought to hold onto Dinah in Chapter 34 of Genesis.[30]

The problematic aspect of the brothers' response to the spying charge is the seemingly gratuitous addition to their claims to be all the sons of one father: "(T)he youngest is now with his father, and one is absent."[31] This admission gives Joseph the opportunity to stage a dramatic recreation of one brother's being absent. First, he suggests that the brothers send one of their group to fetch their brother Benjamin. And then he immediately makes it impossible for them to act on this suggestion by locking them up for three days. He plants the idea that they deprive themselves of another one of their number by sending him on a mission to Canaan and then he reminds them of what they did to Joseph by throwing them all into confinement.

Then Joseph appears to them and makes a remarkable appeal to moral conscience. He is about to change the proposal but introduces his shift by saying "I fear God."[32] The equivalent one would use today would be, "I am a moral person." Or: "I answer to a

---

29 The French Jewish translator André Chouraqui captures the sexual dimensions nicely in his translation: Vous êtes venus pour voir le sexe de la terre. See La Bible, Entête 42:12 (André Chouraqui trans., 1989). The sexual association is missing in Luther's translation, where the passage is rendered as the "investigators" coming to see "where the land is open." Die Heilige Schrift, supra note 6, at 1 *Mose* 42:12.

30 I am indebted to Rabbi David Silber for this interpretation.

31 Genesis 42:31.

32 Genesis 42:18 (King James Version).

higher power." For example, when the midwives in Egypt refused to obey Pharaoh's command to kill all the male children born to Jewish women, they are described as "fearing God."[33] Joseph implicitly appeals to his brothers to bring to bear their own moral conscience.

As a "moral person," Joseph tell his brothers that they should take grain back to Canaan and fetch Benjamin but that they should leave one brother with him as a surety. At this point the brothers are moved to confess: "And they said to one another: But we are guilty (*asham* in the plural form) concerning our brother."[34] They experience an awakening of conscience. Though they thought they knew what they had done, they appreciate its meaning for the first time.

Moral transformations rarely arise from a finite set of factors. In this case we can point at most to a set that separately or in combination might have generated the brothers' realization that they had committed a great wrong. They are: (1) their spending three days in confinement, which somehow brought home to them the experience of Joseph in the pit, (2) Joseph's invoking the idea of "fearing God," (3) Joseph's playing on their incompleteness as a set of brothers, first by insisting that they bring Benjamin down to Egypt, then suggesting that they send home to fetch him, and finally requiring that one be left behind while the others seek to complete their numbers, and (4) finally, and speculatively, the possibility that Joseph himself planted the seed by expressing a longing to be rescued as Dinah had been. The beauty of the text is enabling us to understand that this human breakthrough could have happened without understanding the process of moral change.

What they do feel guilty about? Reuben suggests that they should feel guilty about having killed Joseph. He says that his "blood must be redeemed," which is a classic biblical formula for punishing homicide.[35] That is what Reuben originally believed and perhaps

---

33 Exodus 1:17.

34 Genesis 42:21.

35 See Genesis 9:6 ("Whoever spills the blood of a human being, by a human being will his blood be spilled."). On the magical significance of releasing the blood of the decedent, see David Daube, Studies In Biblical Law 122-23 (1947).

what the other brothers also believed from the very beginning.[36]

Significantly, however, the other brothers interpret their guilt at a more abstract level. It is not about either throwing him into the pit with the intention of either killing him or of letting him die in the pit. Their guilt attaches to having nominally heard but ignored his cries of anguish: "(T)hat we saw the anguish of his soul and we not hear."[37]

This subtle relocation of the guilt could either be trivial or profound. The trivial version derives from the way the brothers use their declaration of guilt to explain their current misery: Because we ignored his pleas, "our anguish has come over us."[38] Thus, they rationalize their anguish as a response to their ignoring someone else's anguish. This converts their confession of guilt into a tactical mistake about controlling their personal fate.

The more profound interpretation of locating the brothers' guilt in not hearing Joseph brings to bear a refined view of freedom of the will, a view generally associated in contemporary philosophy with Harry Frankfurt.[39] By analogy to the idea of second-order volitions as the mechanism for regulating and resisting first-order impulses, we should think of guilt as a second-order failure to resist our baser impulses. It is understandable that the brothers would want to kill one of their own who sought to rule over them, but they have resisted their base homicidal impulses. Their second-order volition should have been to heed Joseph's appeal for compassion. It does not matter much whether that appeal is implicit in Joseph's humanity or whether it is articulated as cries for help. The point is that the brothers did not hear it.

The metaphor of hearing fits the situation perfectly. We "hear the voice" of conscience rather than read an image of conscience in our mind and thus it makes sense for the brothers to associate hearing with understanding the moral dimension of their

---

36 This assumption would contradict the widely held view that the brothers sold Joseph into slavery. See *Acts* 7:9.

37 Genesis 42:21.

38 Id.

39 See generally Harry G. Frankfurt, The Importance Of What We Care About (1988).

actions. Further, Jewish theology emphasizes hearing over sight in the relationship with God. This is evident in Moses' confrontation with God on Mount Sinai and in the liturgical demand on Israel to "hear" and understand that God is one. By contrast, Christianity emphasizes the sense of sight and the role of images, particularly of Jesus on the cross, in sustaining faith.

The Conflicting Paradigms Of Guilt

In these portions of Genesis, we encounter radically opposed conceptions of guilt. The first view is that guilt is associated with pollution in the objective sphere; the second, with feelings in the subjective realm. Along with this contrast go several others. Guilt-as-pollution is a fixed quantity, the same for everyone; guilt-as-feeling is a matter of degree, different in each person. Although both of these ideas are present in Genesis, only the subjective view has survived in our conscious thinking about criminal liability.

The assumption of modern criminal law is that some people are more guilty than others. Their relative degrees of guilt depend on two factors: first, how much they contribute or how close they come to causing physical harm, and second, their internal knowledge of the action and its risks. The principal who controls the actions leading to harm is more guilty than the accessory who merely aids in execution of the plan. Those who take risks intentionally are worse than those who do so inadvertently. These assumptions about relative guilt are built into the modem way of thinking about crime and punishment.

These shifts from the external to the internal, and from the categorical to the scalar, account for another conceptual reorientation. Guilt-as-pollution was connected with a particular kind of response – the sacrifice of animals in a religious ritual. In the modern, secular understanding of guilt, the linkage is not with sacrifice in the Temple but with punishment prescribed in court. As sacrifice functions as means of cleansing the world of pollution, punishment has the symbolic effect of canceling out the crime. As Michel Foucault put it, punishment reenacts the crime and thus rids the world of the pollution it represents.[40]

This way of thinking about punishment carries forward and transmutes the conception of guilt-as-pollution. It follows that precisely as stains need to be eradicated, the guilty need to be punished. As Oedipus and Abimelech are paradigmatic figures for the theory of guilt-as-pollution, Raskolnikov is the exemplar of the modern man who knows precisely what he has done but fails initially to grasp the moral qualities of his actions.[41] He captures the existential situation of all terrorists and ideological killers who know precisely what they have done but who have yet to discover their guilt for having put their hand to evil. The process of discovery carries with it the sudden explosion of truth. Repression caves in, and truth overwhelms. The reaction can often be violent, as in the case of Oedipus. Or it can be therapeutic and lead to a reconciliation with the victims or with one's self.

The Joseph story is arguably an example of the therapeutic response, a precursor to the Truth and Reconciliation Commission as an alternative to punishment in the transition to democracy. Though Reuben thinks that Joseph's blood must be redeemed by punishment,[42] in fact no blood was spilled and no irreversible harm occurred to Joseph. The narrative leads not to punishment but to reconciliation. Though the brothers are united in the end, those who have wronged Joseph still fear him.[43] Their guilt is never fully expunged.

Shame In Genesis

In the modern approach to guilt, we are more likely to begin with our feelings than follow the pattern of the ancients and infer guilt for a plague or from a vision of God in a dream. As we know from the tale of Joseph, however, it is difficult to rely on feelings of guilt to generate an inference of guilt in fact – the feelings thrive

---

40   Michel Foucault, *Discipline And Punish: The Birth Of The Prison* 45 (Alan Sheridan trans., Vintage Books 1979) (1975).

41   See Fyodor Dostoevsky, *Crime And Punishment* (David McDuff trans., Penguin Books 1991) (1866).

42   Genesis 42:24.

43   Genesis 50:15.

on psychological sources other than actions that might occasion guilt for sins and crimes actually committed.

The centrality of the self in modern thought has led to a general tendency to think about shame in place of guilt. If sin and pollution are the favored foci of the ancients, shame has become the pet theme not only of contemporary psychiatry but of philosophers and social critics attempting to come to grips with crimes of the past.

Some rather simple distinctions hold between shame and guilt. People feel shame for who and what they are, and guilt for what they have done. Shame is felt in the eyes of others, real or imagined, and for that reason is associated with seeing and being seen (recall Oedipus putting out his eyes). Guilt is experienced as the voice of conscience and therefore associated with the hearing. Shame can often be irrational. For example, a hunchback might feel ashamed for the contortions of his body, though there is no suggestion of personal responsibility. You can feel shame about the behavior of other people over which you have no control at all. Guilt, by contrast, has some connection to morality, to right and wrong, to sources of conscience based on rational criteria.

The sense of shame in the biblical context hardly differs from the contemporary understanding. The leading pair of passages frame the eating of the forbidden fruit by Adam and Eve. Before they eat of the fruit, we encounter a negative reference to shame: "And they were both naked, the man and his wife, and were not ashamed."[44] After they eat of the fruit, the reaction seems to be the opposite: "And the eyes of them both were opened, and they knew that they were naked; and they sewed fig leaves together, and made themselves aprons."[45] The text does not tell that they felt ashamed after eating the fruit, but this is seemingly always inferred from their covering their genitals immediately upon becoming aware of their nakedness. The strong connection between the eyes and the sense of shame also supports the reading of shame into the text after the eating of the fruit.

The sentiment that you would expect Adam and Eve to have is not shame but guilt. After all, they had just engaged in radical

44 Genesis 2:25 (King James Version).

45 Genesis 3:7 (King James Version).

disobedience of God's command. In the Christian theory they are responsible for the "Fall" of humankind. They corrupt the species and bring death into the world.[46] This is an occasion for guilt, if anything is. And yet we read exclusively about a reaction of shame.

The core experience of shame is feeling exposed, subject to the gaze of another. There is no suggestion in the text that either Adam or Eve judged each other harshly, blamed each other, felt guilt for anything in particular, but they were aware of each other's eyes. And the first reaction to each other's eyes was to sense the nakedness of that part of the body associated with shame. The response to shame, as to nakedness, is to avoid the gaze. This requires one to cover oneself up, as suggested by the metaphor of clothing oneself in fig leaves.

Shame in individuals, we can conclude, has a sound grounding both in our experience and in our mythology. The feature that makes it different from responsibility and guilt, however, is its non-rational quality. There is nothing logical about feeling shame for one's genitals. And indeed in nudist colonies people can easily overcome their habit of genital shame. Nor is there anything well-reasoned about minorities feeling ashamed of the way they are, with the resulting desire to conceal their origins and stay "in the closet." On the whole, it seems that the practice of coming out liberates people from the strictures of shame. Yet at the same time, a strong sense of shame provides people with sound moral restraints. Feeling ashamed for, say, cheating or committing adultery is a healthy reaction that strengthens our ties with others.

It is not surprising that guilt has played a much greater part in the evolution of legal thinking than is the case with shame. The impulse to pay reparations or to suffer punishment – all of these responses are responses to guilt rather than shame. And though the impulse will arise only if there are feelings or at least a recognition of guilt, the operative feature of guilt in these contexts is not subjectivity but the objective aspect of pollution that we have observed in biblical practices. Reparations and punishment both serve symbolically to cleanse the stains of the past. But these symbolic gestures hardly make sense unless they are read against a biblical history rich in magical events of pollution and cleansing.

---

46 Romans 5:12.

CHAPTER SIX

Sin, Guilt And Punishment
In The Biblical Cultic Sphere

Joel Baden

In his article "Punishment, Guilt, and Shame in Biblical Thought," Prof. Fletcher looks to the narratives of Genesis – the three stories of the endangered matriarch and the Joseph story in particular – as windows into the biblical worldview regarding the notion of guilt and the feeling of guilt, and their related concepts, punishment and shame. In this essay, I would like to extend Prof. Fletcher's inquiry, and look more closely at the biblical passages that most directly and specifically treat the questions of sin, guilt, and punishment: the cultic legislation found in Leviticus 4-5. It is in these chapters that we find a fully developed concept of what constitutes an offense; what the different types of offense are, depending on the mental state of the offender; what punishments fit which offenses; and how the realization of having done wrong – guilt – may, in fact, mitigate some punishments.

The cultic laws of Leviticus are perhaps the densest and least easily accessible texts of the Old Testament; certainly it is safe to say that they are among the most frequently skipped over by those attempting to read the Bible from start to finish. The abundance of technical terms, the repetitiveness, and the cultural distance we feel from a text that is grounded entirely in the value and necessity of bloody animal sacrifice all make Leviticus as a whole, and these chapters in particular, as foreign to the modern-day reader as any biblical text could possibly be.

Nevertheless, for those willing to commit to the detailed examination of these chapters, willing to enter into the world of the ancient Israelite cult and its priesthood, Leviticus is in fact a remarkable text: a fully thought-out, complex, communally-encompassing theological statement to which there are in fact few parallels elsewhere in biblical literature. Many of the values that we take for granted in biblically-dependent societies today – which includes all Western ones – are encoded in these cultic laws. Included among those values are the notions of sin, guilt, punishment, and individual and collective responsibility.

It is necessary first to understand the narrative context of these laws, and thereby the underlying concept to which they are addressed. In the final chapters of the book of Exodus (chs. 35-40), the Israelites, under the direction of Moses and his chief architect, Bezalel, construct the Tabernacle, according to God's precise instructions from earlier in the book (chs. 25-31). The Tabernacle is not just a sanctuary; it is the abode of God, called in Hebrew *mishkan*, which literally means "dwelling-place." This is not figurative language, nor is it metaphorical. It is as literal as could possibly be imagined. In the Tabernacle, in its innermost sanctum, there, above the ark, between the wings of the cherubim (winged lions, not winged pudgy babies), "I will meet with you and I will speak with you" (Exod 25:22). When the structure is finally completed at the end of Exodus 40, "the glory of the Lord filled the Tabernacle" (40:34). From this point forward, God will dwell in this space, in the tent Tabernacle that stands in the very center of the Israelite wilderness camp.

It is from within this divine abode, as noted above, that God will communicate with Moses and the Israelites. The cultic laws that follow in Leviticus are spoken not on Mount Sinai, but at the foot of the mountain, from within the Tabernacle (Lev 1:1). The first three chapters are regulations concerning those sacrifices that are offered freely: whether in celebration, or in hope of divine favor, or in fulfillment of a vow, etc.

In the fourth chapter of Leviticus, however, the Israelites

receive instruction regarding involuntary sacrifices: those that are required to be brought under certain circumstances. The first such circumstance is described in Lev 4:2: "When any person unwittingly sins regarding any of the Lord's commandments about that which is not to be done, and does one of them..." The situation envisioned here is ignorance: the violation of prohibition due to lack of knowledge. Precisely what is unknown in this scenario is not said. It could either be ignorance of the law itself, or, perhaps more likely, the lack of realization that the given situation was relevant under the law – e.g., thinking that it was Sunday rather than Saturday, thus working and violating the Sabbath law. In any case, the violation is unwitting.

And yet, despite being unwitting, this violation receives the label "sin," Hebrew *khatta*. Although the word has a wide range of meanings outside of the cultic legislation, including wickedness and general wrongdoing, here in Leviticus it is fairly well restricted to violations of divinely-given, usually cultic, instruction. According to the biblical authors here, one can "sin" without even being aware of having done anything wrong at all, a notion that is far less common in contemporary theology. "Sin" is a technical term, and is not used only for major violations; one can make any number of exceptionally minor mistakes, and still have sinned. Within the category of unwitting or unintentional sins, there are no hierarchical distinctions.

With the general circumstance established, the law goes on to enumerate the various persons who might sin in this unintentional way, and the sacrificial offerings that they must bring in order to make amends (more on that in a moment). The first such person is the high priest, who, as the representative of all the Israelite people before the deity, can, through his own personal error, implicate all of Israel. Thus we are told, "If it is the anointed priest who has sinned (*khatta*), such that the people are rendered guilty (*asham*)..." (Lev 4:3). Here we are introduced to a new concept, at least within Leviticus: the idea of guilt, *asham*.

Key to understanding this verse is the recognition that the high priest can bring guilt on the people by unwittingly giving them false instructions. Again, a scenario regarding the Sabbath is helpful here: if the high priest fails to offer the specific Sabbath sacrifices on behalf of the people, then the people as a whole –

via the high priest as their cultic representative – have violated a divine commandment, despite the fact that they individually did nothing wrong.

The people, in this scenario, having nothing to feel guilty about, on the emotional level. They have not erred at all. For the same reason, they are not exactly guilty on the legal level either. But their representative has implicated them. Notably, despite the "guilt" devolving onto the people as a whole, it is the representative, the high priest, who is required to provide the sacrifice that is required after such a sin.

More interesting, perhaps, are the three categories below that of the high priest: the congregation of Israel as a whole (Lev 4:13-21); the chieftain of the community (Lev 4:22-26); and the individual (Lev 4:27-31). For each of these categories, similar (though never identical) phrasing is used: "If it is x who sins unwittingly by doing any of the Lord's commandments regarding that which is not to be done" – so much very like the law regarding the high priest – "and x *asham*," as a verb. There is some question as to what the verbal form of *asham* means: is it "to be guilty," as an objective state of having committed a violation? is it "to feel guilty," as an emotional state of feeling bad about said violation? Neither of these, in fact, is probable. For the text goes on: "or the sin which he has committed is made known to him." As this is presented as the equal alternative to *asham*, we can draw a reasonable equation: another person making the sin known to the sinner is equivalent to the sinner doing *asham*. In short, it is neither to be guilty in the objective sense – after all, whether the person actually committed the violation is, in this scenario, never in question, and thus he was "guilty" in the legal sense instantaneously – nor to be guilty in the emotional sense; it is, rather, "to realize one's guilt," or, perhaps better, "to realize one's responsibility." Or, given the legal context, "to realize one's liability" may be best of all.

The logic here is clear: because the context is an unwitting sin, the sinner can hardly begin making amends until he has realized – or had it brought to his attention by others – that indeed he did commit a violation. At that point, he has a remedy ready to hand: the sacrificial offering, the details of which are then laid out in full.

It is here that the presence of the deity in the Tabernacle

comes into play. For the sacrifice offered upon realizing that one has committed an unwitting violation is not mere penalty. In fact, it is not really a penalty at all. The name of the offering is *khatta't*, just like the word for "sin." But the function of this offering, despite the common rendering in translations, is not to "atone" for the sin, as if by paying the price of this animal the sinner has restored his good standing. The function, rather, is to purge – *kipper* – the Tabernacle of the sin.

When an Israelite sins, even unwittingly, the sin – which is considered a very real, tangible, though invisible, miasma-like substance – is attracted by and travels into the sanctuary, where it sticks to God's holy space and objects. This is a very bad thing: no one likes a dirty house, and especially not God. Should the divine abode become too dirty, too contaminated with the accumulated sins of the Israelite people, then God will simply move. He will abandon his Tabernacle, his *mishkan*, and no longer dwell in the midst of the Israelites. This is, needless to say, undesirable in the extreme. (Though if details are required, they may be found in the curses of Leviticus 26.)

Thus the purpose of the sacrifice is to remove that sin from the sanctum – not from the sinner, but from God's abode. The sacrifice works not because the sinner has given up something of value (our modern meaning of the word "sacrifice"), but rather because it is only by killing the animal that one can gain access to its blood – and the blood of the sacrificial animal acts as the ritual detergent to cleanse the sanctuary of the sin. It is for this reason that the blood of the offering is ritually sprinkled upon the altar or, depending on the severity of the sin, upon the interior of the Tabernacle. And it is for this reason that it is only after the blood has been sprinkled, and the sanctuary cleaned, that the sinner is forgiven. He has, through his sacrificial offering, undone the damage to the divine abode caused by his act.

The law made refer to the individual: it is the individual who commits the unwitting violation, and it is the individual who brings the offering as a result, upon realizing his responsibility. Yet the potential danger averted as a result of the sacrificial offering is not the danger that was posed by the violating act itself – no one is injured when another person erroneously works on the Sabbath – but rather the danger posed by the existence of a violating act at all. It is the fact of sin, not the content of the sin, that is problematic within this system. And it is not the individual who will suffer if his sin, when realized, is not ritually purged from the sanctuary; it is, rather, the entire community that is in danger, for God's departure from his abode would affect every individual, sinner or not.

This is why *asham* in this case is much more about responsibility, the responsibility of the individual on behalf of the community, and far less about the taken-for-granted notion of legal guilt or the entirely irrelevant notion of emotional guilt. These biblical authors had already developed the idea of the good of the collective, of a society in which individuals are responsible for their neighbors, and in which sin or crime is bad not because anyone is necessarily hurt, but for its own sake.

When we turn to Leviticus 5, we find a chapter in two parts. The first part presents a situation different from those of the unwitting violations that we encountered in Leviticus 4. Here we are faced with a series of potential scenarios involving violations, the first one of which is telling: "If a person sins: having heard a public demand for testimony, and he is able to testify or saw or heard or knew about the issue, but he does not speak up, so that he bears his *avon*..." This is, quite simply, a case of a witness who is unwilling to testify. There is nothing unwitting about this scenario; this is a conscious act of disobedience. Hence the concluding phrase "he bears his *avon*," using the Hebrew word for iniquity, slightly stronger, perhaps, than *khatta*.

(As an aside, and in direct response to Prof. Fletcher's treatment of this word, in which he wonders why it is that translators seem attached to the translation "punishment" at times, rather than the seemingly more straightforward "iniquity": he is almost certainly correct. This tendency to sometimes render the word, and its synonyms, as "punishment" is an unfortunate result of centuries of misunderstanding of the mechanisms of sin and "atonement.")

The scenarios that follow this initial one of witness recalcitrance all share two basic features: the sin involved is one of omission, rather than commission, and the sinner is fully aware of having done wrong. What is added in the subsequent cases, however, is the notion that the sinner was aware at the time of having violated a commandment, but has since forgotten about it (or ignored it), and therefore hasn't brought the appropriate sacrifice to make amends.

A reasonable question would be: what is the appropriate means to make amends for a sin that is not unwitting, but rather conscious? Such a situation has not yet been dealt with; indeed, it is here at the beginning of Leviticus 5 that it is treated for the first time. The answer is perhaps unexpected: "When he realizes his guilt in any of these matters, he will confess regarding his sin," and he will then bring the same *khatta't* offering as the one who sinned unwittingly. The only difference between the cases of the unwitting sinner and the intentional sinner is the act of confession required for the intentional sinner. Yet that confession is all-important.

An intentional sin can go in one of two directions. A person who sins intentionally and never thinks that he has done anything wrong – never takes responsibility for having polluted the Tabernacle and brought the community into danger – is what is known as a brazen sinner, and the punishment is extreme: he is excommunicated, and perhaps even put to death (Num 15:30-36). Such a person must be eliminated from the community, for he has decided that the rule of law simply does not apply to him. Were he to go unpunished, it would be clear that the laws are of no value, and the danger posed by the increasingly contaminated divine abode would grow far too quickly.

But a person who sins intentionally and does eventually accept liability – as in the cases described in Leviticus 5 – has demonstrated respect, both for the law in and of itself and for the community of which he is a part. The confession is the proclamation of that respect, of that realization of personal and communal responsibility. And with that confession, the intentional sin is in a sense downgraded to the category of unwitting sin, at least in terms of the sacrificial ritual required to purge the sanctuary of it.

The biblical legislators thus provide the Israelites with a rather lenient mechanism for maintaining the wholeness of the community and the divine presence therein. There is no extra penalty for those who sin intentionally, even if they avoid their responsibility for a period. As long as the rule of law is respected, and the responsibility of each individual for the preservation of the community recognized – in the public confession, which reinforces these social standards – there is no need, according to these laws, to inflict any special punishment. Or, to put it the other way, and in a manner that is more relevant perhaps to current legal norms: the act of public confession mitigates the expected punishment for intentional sins. Confession – the open acceptance of responsibility, of liability, of guilt – is a guaranteed way to reduce one's sentence.

The final set of cultic laws to be investigated here are those in the second half of Leviticus 5. Here we again encounter the term *asham*, though in a slightly different (yet still related) manner. These laws return to the issue of unwitting sin, but of a particular nature: those actions by which one unintentionally touches or otherwise mistreats a sacred object, something belonging to God. An easy example of this would be the unintentional touching of the altar (which stood in the outer court of the sanctuary, accessible, though prohibited, to any Israelite); a less obvious example is that of unwittingly bearing false witness, since acting as witness involved taking an oath by the name of the Lord, and thus bearing false witness involves desecration of the Lord's name – which is considered God's property as much as the altar or the ark.

In such scenarios, the sinner is required to bring a ram – a quite expensive animal – plus twenty percent of the ram's value, as symbolic payment for the sacred object that has been defiled. Yet the ritual involved remains the same: the blood is sprinkled, the sanctuary is cleansed, and the sinner is forgiven. This offering of the ram is not called a *khatta't*, however; it is, rather, known as an *asham* sacrifice. And here, once again, we can see how the word *asham* in this cultic legislation is more properly about the liability and responsibility associated with "guilt" than it is about the fact of the crime or the emotion of remorse. With the ram and the extra twenty percent surcharge, the offerer takes responsibility for the property damage he has done. This offering, so often translated as "guilt offering," is much better rendered as "reparation offering," at least as far as the title represents the function of the ritual.

There are indeed narratives that deal with the question of guilt: those that Prof. Fletcher treated in his article, and others as well. But the laws of Leviticus provide the most fertile ground for investigation of this topic, insofar as it is here, and only here, that a full picture of how sin, guilt, and punishment are interwoven – at least according to this particular biblical author – is provided. What we find in these chapters is a system that understands the individual almost exclusively as part of a community. The laws and rituals exist not for the purpose of punishing the individual, but rather for the purpose of enforcing the individual's responsibility for the larger collective. The individual's sin does indeed affect the community as a whole, by potentially driving the deity out of the divine abode. But far more important is that the individual is given the opportunity, through the sacrificial system, to take responsibility for his actions. Whether this system has any relevance to our own contemporary judicial system – its aims and its methods – I leave to the legal experts.

CHAPTER SEVEN

Collective Guilt
And Collective Punishment

George P. Fletcher

In the Middle East, it is difficult to be seen as an individual, as someone who is simply doing his thing not as an Arab or Jew, as a Muslim, Christian, or black-hatted Jew, but simply as a solitary man or woman who happens to live in this part of the world. There are many parts of the world that reveal a similar group consciousness – India and Pakistan, Northern Ireland – and they stand in sharp contrast to the liberal idea that the only true units of action in the world are individuals, not groups. In the Middle East, it is difficult to kill a member of the "other" side simply on grounds of personal hatred. Every killing implicitly invokes a confrontation between Palestinians and Jews, or between Islamists and settlers, or between terrorists and civilians.

This phenomenon makes the Middle East the proper arena for reflecting on the issues of collective guilt and collective punishment. When a suicide bomber attacks Israeli children, the Jews consider the entire Palestinian population guilty, directly or indirectly. When Jews move into the West Bank, establishing new settlements, Palestinians accuse the entire Jewish nation of "taking"

Palestinian land and creating facts-on-the-ground that render a Palestinian state less feasible. This reciprocal perception of the other side's collective guilt fuels the endless cycle of violence that has tragically dispelled dreams of peace in the region. The two nations – Jews and Palestinians – are reduced metaphorically to single agents struggling against each other.

Under the pressure of the second Intifada beginning in September 2000, many otherwise sober and rational American Jews lost their sense of proportion and began advocating collective punishment for Palestinians. On the assumption that it takes an entire village to create a suicide bomber, Alan Dershowitz started proposing various ways of penalizing the entire village – including destruction of all the houses in the area. In his own words:

> Israel's first step in implementing this policy would be to completely stop all retaliation for five days. Then it would publicly declare precisely how it would respond in the event of another terrorist attack, such as destroying empty houses in a village used as a base for terrorists, and naming the village in advance. The next time the terrorists attack, the village's residents would be given 24 hours to leave, and then the Israeli troops would bulldoze the houses.[1]

Dershowitz's colleague, Washington lawyer Nathan Lewin, has gone further and proposed the death penalty for the entire family of the suicide bomber. Lewin brazenly invokes the precedent of Amalek as a biblical warrant for collective punishment.[2] Both of these sophisticated, liberally-trained lawyers sense that their proposals seem outrageous to others, and therefore, both guard their flanks with some traditional legal arguments of individual responsibility.

Dershowitz shifts subtly from collective punishment to punishment for complicity in the acts of terrorists. There is no

---

1 Alan Dershowitz, *Why Terrorism Works: Understanding the Threat, Responding to the Challenge* 177 (2002).

2 Nathan Lewin, *Deterring Suicide Killers*, Sh'ma: A Journal of Jewish Responsibility, May 2002, at 11-12.

doubt that particular individuals who aid and abet the commission of terrorist acts – by providing money or weapons, counseling or encouragement – should be guilty as accessories to the murder. As to the handlers, who convince young men and women that by killing innocent children they acquire a place in Heaven, the maximum punishment would be appropriate. But it is not clear how far we should stretch the idea of complicity to sweep up the "good Palestinians" who implicitly endorse suicide bombings but take no active steps to facilitate the attacks.

To buttress his argument for Palestinian complicity, Dershowitz relies heavily on a case (the Fall River rape case, well-known from the film *The Accused*) in which men in a bar who cheered on the rapists are presented as potentially complicitous in the rape itself. Dershowitz says that in a case like this, there is nothing wrong with thinning out the criteria of complicity so long as "the consequences imposed on the (accessories) are proportional to their complicity."[3] That is, if you actually raped the victim, you might get 20 years; if you held her down, 10 years; and if you merely cheered on the primary offenders, you might get a year in a jail. This is absolutely correct, even though the American and many other legal systems hold that all aiders and abettors may be punished to the same degree as the actual perpetrators are punished.

The law of complicity is firmly grounded in liberal criteria of individualized justice. It has nothing to do with collective punishment. The latter comes into play when an entire village might suffer the destruction of its houses whether the residents were directly complicitous in a particular act of terror or not. And even if they are theoretically supportive of a suicide bomber in their midst, Dershowitz hardly envisions a time-consuming, individualized trial of each person who might lose his or her home under the plan. The leap from the collective guilt of the village to its collective punishment would be automatic.

To alleviate the obvious injustice of punishing the innocent individuals as well as the guilty, Dershowitz claims that the prior warning generates a new basis for blaming those who suffer:

The policy and its implications will be perfectly

---

3 Dershowitz, supra note 1, at 176.

clear to all the Palestinian people: whenever terrorists blow themselves up and kill Israeli citizens, they also blow up a house in one of their villages. The destruction is entirely their own fault, and it is entirely preventable by them.[4]

Note the moves made in this argument. First, the intervening agency of the Israeli Army drops out of the picture. The image is one of self-destruction. The criminal becomes the agent of his own punishment. But here the "criminal" consists of many different people who may or may not be the same as those who suffer the destruction of their homes. Thus Dershowitz's argument becomes plausible – if it is plausible – by collapsing an entire nation into a single actor and then eliminating the Israeli Army as the intervening agent. In the rhetoric of self-destruction, "terrorists" choose the punishment of their fellow nationals.

Ultimately, the argument for collective punishment in this scheme is not justice but deterrence.[5] The same is true of Lewin's rage-filled fantasies of hanging entire Palestinian families. Leave aside the Kantian argument condemning deterrence as a violation of human dignity, as the use of the condemned person merely as a means to the end of social protection. There is no evidence that the violent reprisals on the West Bank have had much of a deterrent impact on terrorists and suicide bombers. On the contrary, punishment perceived to be unjust has the effect of increasing the solidarity and resentment of those who suffer and, ultimately, the effect of augmenting resistance rather than decreasing it.

. But neither the argument of complicity nor the shift to deterrence can assuage our sense of injustice about blaming and punishing the collective for crimes actually carried out by individuals. This leads one to suspect that behind all these rationalizations for collective punishment there lurk deeply-held sentiments of collective guilt. The proponents of collective punishment assume that Palestinians are guilty as a collective for nurturing a culture that takes pride in suicide bombers. This not an unreasonable assessment of the way in which the entire culture

---

4 Id. at 177.

5 Id. at 179.

contributes to the actions of a few.

To round out the picture, we should consider the way in which Palestinians attribute collective guilt to Jews and Israelis and how they then justify the collective punishment of all Jews as a proper response. The Hammas and other right-wing Palestinian terrorist groups regard all Israelis, and probably all Jews, as guilty for the great sin of settling the country and defeating the combined Arab armies in the War of Independence. The continued presence of the Jews on Palestinian "ancestral land" recreates the crime in every generation and seems to represent an ongoing humiliation to Arab honor. It is not surprising that the Muslim world has become a fertile market for all the lies ever manufactured against the Jews – from early Christian myths to the latter-day *Protocols of the Elders of Zion*. Israel's partnership with the United States only exacerbates the image of Jews as exercisers of uncanny powers – able not only to kill the Son of God, but to conquer and manipulate the world's media and financial systems.

The idea that Jews act as a corporate body obviously has its origins in the *Book of Matthew*, where the Roman Governor Pontius Pilate decides to deliver Jesus to his death, and yet as a Roman and as an individual, he is able to wash his hands of guilt and attribute the entire decision to the Jewish crowd: "And all the people answered and said, His blood be on us and on our children." (*Matthew* 27:25.) However large this crowd might have been, it surely did not include all the Jews then living, not to mention the Jews of future generations, and yet all the Jews then living and not yet born are implicitly held accountable as a corporate entity for the behavior of this crowd outside the palace of Pontius Pilate. The words of the crowd "and on our children" are fashioned to entail liability for future generations.

Holding the Jews liable as a corporate body is no different from the way Jews hold Amalek guilty across the generations for some mythical crime committed against Moses in the desert – attacking from the rear, according to *Deuteronomy* 15:16. Fortunately, we no longer know who the members of the tribe of Amalek are. If we did, those who take the commandments of the Bible seriously would face an embarrassing moral problem as to whether they were under a duty to continue to wage war against "the Amalek."[6]

The example of Amalek illustrates the important difference between collective guilt and a declaration of perpetual war. In the case of the Jews, the statement "His blood be on us" seems to be a self-attribution of guilt. There is no declaration of war against the Jews in *Matthew*, merely an ideological foundation for holding Jews forever guilty, both collectively and individually, for "Christ-killing." But the notion of guilt is not used in connection with Amalek.[7] This is a case of a war declared in perpetuity, never subject to a peace agreement.[8]

In practical effect, collective punishment punishes very much like perpetual war: Witness Lewin's invocation of Amalek to justify his claim of collective punishment. And recall Oliver Wendell Holmes, Jr.'s analogy between the criminal walking to the gallows and the soldier sacrificing his life in war: both die, per Holmes, for the sake of the greater good.[9] The superficial resemblance of war and capital punishment is that in both, some people feel justified in killing other people. Of course, there are different reasons for taking life. In the case of punishment, state officials execute offenders because they are guilty of capital offenses under pre-announced legal standards. In the case of war, soldiers kill "enemy" soldiers in order to further the ends of the armed conflict.

The Thesis: Separating Guilt From Punishment

For the purposes of this paper, I will assume that collective guilt is a plausible, widely-shared, and sometimes healthy response to collective wrongdoing. I know that this idea disturbs liberal individualists, who think that individuals are the only conceivable unit of action. Elsewhere I have argued at length against this liberal postulate in favor of the view that the ideas of collective action,

6 Exodus 17:16: "(T)he Lord will have war with Amalek from generation to generation."

7 A possible exception in *Numbers* 24:20: Amalek is described as a first among the nations but with a fate of "everlasting perdition."

8 I am indebted to Dr. Zvi Blanchard for this point.

9 Oliver W. Holmes, The Common Law 43 (1881) (Dover Publications 1991).

collective intention, and collective guilt all have a sound grounding in Western culture.[10] There is no need to rehearse those arguments here. Rather I wish to focus in this article on the specific question of whether collective guilt justifies collective punishment.

There are many who think that the recognition of personal guilt entails a craving to be punished. The paradigm for this view is Raskolnikov's moral breakthrough in Dostoevsky's *Crime and Punishment*. Having killed an old lady in order to rob her, Raskolnikov is fully aware of his deed but surely aware that society regards his action as wrong. Yet he feels no guilt. When he does recognize his guilt, he feels the need to be punished. This connection between guilt and punishment comes through in part in the German association between *Schuld* (guilt) and *Verschulden* (debt). There is a similar association in Hebrew between *chaiyav* (liable) and *chov* (debt). The suggestion is that someone who is guilty owes a debt. He or she must make amends, must do something to repair the damage. It is not so clear how one negotiates the transition from "making amends" to "craving punishment," that is, between a feeling of the necessity of doing something oneself and the sense that others must impose punishment in retaliation for the wrongdoing. But this conceptual leap – or something like it – is necessary to support the claim of a necessary connection between guilt and punishment.

Another tradition in Western thought supports the possibility of confessing one's crimes without necessarily incurring a debt to suffer punishment. The exemplar of this alternative approach are Truth and Reconciliation Commissions, which, most notably in South Africa, promise immunity from punishment in return for a public confession of wrongdoing (with or without a confession of guilt).[11] According to this alternative tradition, an entire group could recognize its guilt without thereby incurring a debt – at least not a debt to suffer punishment.

The striking feature of these conflicting conceptions of guilt – one linked to punishment and the other not – is that both have

---

10 George P. Fletcher, *The Storrs Lectures: Liberals and Romantics at War: The Problem of Collective Guilt*, 111 Yale L.J. 1499 (2002).

11 *Details Announced of Commission to Probe Apartheid Abuses*, Agence France Presse, July 29, 1994, Int'l News Section.

strong roots in narratives of Genesis. In the bulk of this paper, I will attempt to explain, on the basis of a close reading of the biblical text, how both have come to resonate in our thinking about guilt and punishment. The first is rooted in the textual sources that treat guilt as a form of pollution requiring a mode of cleansing or expiation. The second derives from Chapter 42 of Genesis, in which ten of Joseph's brothers come to the collective conclusion that they are guilty for having ignored their brother's cries of pain. Joseph's brothers behaved like ancient predecessors to Raskolnikov. They threw Joseph into a pit without water, fully expecting him to die. They planned to cover up their deed by soaking his coat in animal blood. Thus they evidently knew that they were doing something wrong, but do not experience a sense of guilt until many years later in Egypt, when, unbeknownst to them, they come under the power of Joseph. I shall refer to the first strand in this interweaving conception of guilt as guilt-in-pollution; the second strand is aptly called guilt-in-feeling. One is external and tends toward a conception of collective guilt; the other is internal and more closely associated with individual sentiments, though nothing prevents a group of people, like Joseph's brothers, from experiencing this sentiment collectively.

Guilt As Pollution

In this study of guilt in the Bible, I take the Hebrew term *asham* to be equivalent to the English term "guilt." The word is so used in modern Hebrew, and there is every indication in the biblical text – as we shall see – that this is the appropriate translation from the biblical Hebrew. When we first encounter *asham* in Genesis, the concept is both collective and objective. The term appears in a story told in three different versions in the lives of two of the Patriarchs. The pattern is always the same: One of the forefathers of the Jewish people is about to enter a foreign land where he suspects that the "barbarians" will kill him and take his wife. Therefore, Abraham twice and Isaac once relive the same deception: each tells the foreign potentate that his wife is in fact his sister. In all three cases something happens to inform the potentate that either he or a man of his court is about to commit adultery.

In the first version, Abraham (then called Abram) passes

Sarah (then called Sarai) off as his sister to the Egyptian Pharaoh, who takes her into court. Plagues then descend upon "Pharaoh and his household" as a sign that a sexual sin has occurred or is about to occur.[12] Pharaoh quickly realizes that something is wrong in the natural order and confronts Abram with his lie. In the later retelling of the same basic story (with Abram renamed Abraham and the potentate named Abimelech), the truth of sexual sin is realized not by a plague but by God coming to the King in a dream and saying, "You are to die because of the woman that you have taken, for she is a married woman."[13] In the third telling, when Isaac passes off Rebecca as his sister, a king also named Abimelech discovers the lie when he sees them engaging in affectionate behavior that would be incest if they were actually brother and sister. Assuming that they are not an incestuous couple, Abimelech confronts Isaac, establishes the lie, and then says, "What have you done to us? One of the people might have lain with your wife, and you would have brought guilt (*asham*) upon us."[14]

This is how the notion of guilt makes its appearance on the biblical stage. In those places where you would expect to find it – after Adam and Eve eat of the forbidden fruit, after Cain kills Abel, after Ham abuses his father Noah – the concept is absent. Adam and Eve feel shame, and Cain complains that his sin – *avon*, sometimes translated as punishment – is too great for him to bear.[15] But none of these leading characters in the biblical narrative mention their possible guilt for their misdeeds.

As it appears in the story of Isaac and Abimelech, that guilt (*asham*) is understood as something like a stain, a form of pollution on the people. The stain afflicts the entire nation of Pharaoh or Abimelech. In the second telling of this recurrent mythical confrontation, when God comes to Abimelech in a dream

---

12 Genesis 12:17.

13 Genesis 20:3.

14 Genesis 26:10.

15 Some translations of the Bible translate *avon* as "punishment"; others as "sin" or "crime." The problem is well summarized in Etz Chayim (Tree of Life): Torah and Commentary 27 n.13 (David Lieber ed., 2001) (hereinafter Etz Chayim) (comment on the editor's choice of the word "punishment").

to warn him of the impending adultery, Abimelech responds that he is personally innocent in his heart (she told him that she was his sister) and pleads, therefore, not only for himself but for his entire "righteous nation."[16] Similarly, in the third telling, Abimelech accuses Isaac of bringing guilt "upon us," on our own people – implicitly not just on Abimelech and apparently not at all on Isaac or Rebecca.[17] The guilt arises not from the culpability or deed of the offender but solely from the consequence: the participation in adultery. And the guilt attaches collectively to the entire nation represented by the person who engages in sinful intercourse with a married woman.

In the first recitation of this tale, Pharaoh learns of the guilt not from a dream but from the plague that descends on him and his house, reminiscent of the plague that descends on Thebes as the first sign that Oedipus has engaged in an act contrary to the natural order.[18] The plague is evidence of pollution, of contamination generated by human action. The idea that guilt is pollution bears several features that can only jar our modem sensibilities. The guilt is collective, it is objective, and it is the same for everyone. Also at odds with our contemporary thinking is the total irrelevance of fault or blameworthiness. The men prepared to sleep with Sarah or Rebecca have no idea that she is married and that the union would be adulterous. Nonetheless, they bring a plague on the land, and they bring "guilt" on the people. The sins of adultery and incest inhere in the act itself, regardless of personal culpability.

The remedy for guilt, in the sense the term is used in the Hebrew Bible, is to bring a sacrifice. The sacrifice cleanses the stain. Remarkably, the word used repeatedly in Chapter 5 of *Leviticus* to describe a whole range of polluting events and the appropriate

---

16 Genesis 20:4.

17 Genesis 26:10.

18 Sophocles, Oedipus Rex (Stanley Appelbaum ed. & George Young trans., Dover 1991). The text is not clear whether the pollution derives primarily from the patricide or the incest. The following lines of the Chorus suggest that the incest is at least a major factor: "Time found thee out. Time who sees everything. Unwittingly guilty; and arraigns thee now consort ill-sorted, unto whom are bred sons of thy getting, in thine own birthbed. 0 scion of Laius's race." Id. at 43.

sacrificial response is also *asham*.[19] These are sacrifices, called "guilt" sacrifices, to atone for polluting events such as touching an unclean animal.[20] The prescription is to bring a guilt sacrifice to atone for guilt – the same word used both for the cleansing act and the stain. The interplay here between the remedy and the deed recalls the controversy about translating the word that Cain uses in his complaint that something about his fratricide is too difficult to bear. Some think that he is referring to the punishment, others to the crime itself.[21] This easy interchange of the negative and the positive, the contamination and the decontamination, reveals the tight conceptual connection between the two.

The hypothesis seems safe that the Ancient World understood these concepts in a way different from our own understanding. In contemplating whether Oedipus feels guilt or shame for his fated patricide and incest, it is often said that the Greeks at the time of Sophocles did not distinguish between the two concepts.[22] There are signs of both in the play. When Oedipus discovers his crime, he craves punishment as though he were guilty in the modem sense, but the method of his self-inflicted punishment – putting out his eyes and going into exile – resonates with shame. He cannot bear to see others looking at him.

While the ideas of guilt and shame are interwoven in Athens, they are distinct in Jerusalem. The biblical text recognizes a culture of shame in the story of Eden and a distinct understanding of guilt and guilt sacrifices in *Leviticus*. Even in Athens, there are clear differences between Sophocles and Aristotle, who was born a century later than the playwright; and *The Nicomachean Ethics* continues to be a guide to the general theory of responsibility and enables us to understand the concept of guilt as it is used in the modern sense.[23]

But the ancient sense of guilt as pollution is still with us.

---

19 Leviticus 5:6, 15-16, 18-19, 25.

20 Leviticus 5:2.

21 See supra note 15.

22 Bernard Williams, Shame and Necessity 88-89 (1993).

23 3 Aristotle, The Nicomachean Ethics 1110-111 lb2 (D. Ross trans., London: Oxford Univ. Press 1925).

It is expressed in the idea of a conceptual connection between contamination and decontamination. The form that this connection takes today is the belief that a guilty act requires punishment, and the metaphors that we use to discuss retributive punishment carry forward the principle of decontamination. We share the Hegelian faith that punishing a wrongdoer vindicates the Right against the Wrong or validates the norm against those who would undermine it. In this way of thinking, the crime pollutes the moral order and the punishment serves to restore the law and the world as it should be.

Guilt As Consciousness Of Wrongdoing

In the modern approach to guilt, the focus is not on pollution but on the feelings of those who are guilty. The shift has been from its external impact on the world to the inner, human experience of guilt. The disengagement of the inner feeling from reality has led to the supposedly modem phenomenon of free-floating guilt, as exemplified in Kafka's novel *The Trial*. Joseph K. expects to be tried for something, but he does not know what. In another form of disengagement – this time both from the impact of the action and from the actor's sentiment – we now acknowledge that a suspect might be guilty even if he does not feel anything and resolutely protests his innocence.

A careful reading of the Joseph story reveals that this way of thinking is not uniquely modem. It is found in the book of Genesis as well. To grasp the alternative model of *asham* or guilt presented in the Joseph story, we should review the first part of the tale in Genesis 37, 39-42.

The saga begins with a built-in conflict between Joseph and his ten elder brothers. Jacob, their father, loves Joseph more than the others, and the brothers are jealous. When some brothers receive more love than others, as Abel was favored by God, we can expect enmity between brothers. The conflict among the sons of Jacob becomes more acute when Joseph relates two dreams, which his brothers interpret as a fantasy of domination over them. As the astute German commentator Claus Westermann points out, this was a startling new political idea – namely, that one brother could acquire a superior political status to his siblings.[24] The brothers conspire to kill him and then throw him into a pit. Reuben protests the plan to kill Joseph and suggests that they merely leave him to die. This they do and then sit down to break bread, as though they are celebrating Joseph's demise. At that point, Judah sees a caravan of Ishmaelites approaching and realizes that it might be better to sell Joseph to the voyagers than kill him and conceal their act. Apparently, it does not occur to him that selling their brother into slavery is also a wrong that they would have to conceal from Jacob and others. Before the brothers can realize Judah's plan, a band of Midianites passes by. One of the groups (the text is ambiguous on this point) lifts Joseph out of the pit and sells him to one of the passing caravans headed for Egypt. Reuben discovers that Joseph has been taken and tears his clothes in distress. To cover up their crime, the brothers then dip Joseph's coat – Jacob's gift of love to him – in the blood of a slaughtered goat and take it to Jacob as proof of Joseph's death. The traveling merchants sell Joseph into the service of Potiphar.

This is the end of the passage recounting the tale of crime and betrayal. It is worth noting that no one in this story acts as an individual. A fraternal collective act in throwing Joseph into the pit and, later, in lifting him out. The brothers function as a unit. Even when Reuben protests, he speaks in the first person plural. The next segment of the saga traces Joseph's rise to political power in Egypt. When he meets his brothers again, at least a decade later, he is the "governor of the land." With a famine in Canaan, Jacob sends ten of the brothers, excluding the youngest Benjamin, to find food in Egypt. When they encounter Joseph, the ten bow down to him without recognizing him, but Joseph both recognizes them and recalls the dream.

There follows a conversation in Genesis 42:6-21 that leads to the brothers' recognition of their guilt for the way they conspired to kill and abandon their brother. This is one of the most remarkable interactions in the corpus of biblical literature. Joseph stages both a conversation and a physical environment that lead his brothers to understand the moral dimension of facts that they had long known.

---

24 Claus Westermann, Die Joseph-Erziihlung: Elf Bibelarbeiten zu Genesis 24, 37-50 (1990).

The first step in the interaction is Joseph's accusing the brothers of being spies. It is hard to know whether Joseph himself believes the charge to be true or whether he is testing his brothers. With his usual political insight, Westermann points out that spying is a characteristic feature of nations, not of families.[25] Joseph himself is acting as the officer of a state; his accusation of spying is designed to find out whether the brothers are the same or whether they identify themselves as a family rather than a nation. The brothers defend themselves against the charge by claiming that they are "the sons of one man in Canaan." The Westermann thesis explains this response, but it seems strained nonetheless: individuals and informal groups do, in fact, spy on each other.

A totally different approach to the accusation begins with the motive that Joseph attributes to the spying, namely, "to see the nakedness of the land."[26] The sexual overtones of the word "nakedness" suggest an analogy with the earlier intervention of the brothers, the "sons of Jacob," to reclaim Dinah from the house of Shechem. Whether that rescue was deceitful and improper or not, the brothers thereby demonstrated their loyalty to members of the clan. By suggesting sexual overtones to the mission of his ten brothers, Joseph might be revealing his own yearning that they have to come to take him as they had schemed and fought to hold onto Dinah.[27]

The problematic aspect of the brothers' response to the spying charge is the seemingly gratuitous addition to their claims to be all the sons of one father: "the youngest is now with his father,

---

25 Id. at 73. In the first translation of the Bible into German, Martin Luther opted for a different term altogether. He translated the Hebrew term as *"Kundschahfter,"* which means something like "investigator." Die Heilige Schrift, 1 Mose 42:9 (Gideon ed. 1967).

26 The French Jewish translator André Chouraqui captures the sexual dimensions nicely in his translation: *Vous tes venus pour voir le sexe de la terre.* La Sainte Bible, Entete 42:12 (André Chouraqui trans., 1989). The sexual association is missing in Luther's translation, where the passage is rendered as the "investigators" coming to see "where the land is open." Die Heilige Schrift, supra note 25, at 42:12.

27 I am indebted to Rabbi David Silber for this interpretation.

and one is absent." This admission gives Joseph the opportunity to stage a dramatic recreation of one brother's being absent. First, he suggests that the brothers send one of their group to fetch their brother Benjamin. This proposal seems never to be pursued. Instead, after holding them three days in custody, Joseph suggests that they leave one of their collective in Egypt and return, as a group of nine, to fetch Benjamin.

At this point the brothers are moved to confess: "And they said to one another. But we are guilty (*asham* in the adjectival plural form *ashemim*) concerning our brother." (Genesis 42:21.) Great moral insights rarely arise from a finite set of factors. In this case we can point at most to a set that separately or in combination might have generated the brothers' realization that they had committed a great wrong. They are: (1) their spending three days in confinement, which somehow brought home to them the experience of Joseph in the pit; (2) Joseph's playing on their incompleteness as a set of brothers, first by insisting that they bring Benjamin down to Egypt, then suggesting that they send home to fetch him, and finally requiring that one be left behind while the others seek to complete their numbers; and (3) finally, and speculatively, the possibility that Joseph himself planted the seed by expressing a longing to be rescued as Dinah had been. The beauty of the text is enabling us to understand that this human breakthrough, this moral transformation, could have happened.

Now what do they feel guilty about? It is not about the supposed death of Joseph, not about their act of throwing him into the pit with the intention of either killing him or letting him die. Their guilt attaches to having heard and ignored his cries of anguish. Thus the guilt is displaced from the pollution to the act causing the pollution and, finally, to the victim's pleas to avoid committing the act. This subtle relocation of the guilt could either be trivial or profound. The trivial version derives from the way the brothers' use their declaration of guilt to explain their current misery: "We saw the anguish of his soul when he pleaded with us and we did not grasp it, and therefore our anguish has come over us."[28] Thus they rationalize their anguish as a response to their ignoring someone else's anguish. Emphasizing the latter part of the

---

28 Genesis 42:21.

passage converts their confession of guilt into a tactical mistake about controlling their personal fate.[29] It would be like regretting not having given money to a beggar on the street because the stock market crashed in the days following.

The more profound interpretation of locating the brothers' guilt in not hearing Joseph's cries brings to bear a refined view of freedom of the will, a view generally associated in contemporary philosophy with Harry Frankfurt.[30] By analogy to the idea of second-order volitions as the mechanism for regulating and resisting first-order impulses, we should think of guilt as a second-order failure to resist our baser impulses. It is understandable that the brothers would want to kill one of their own who sought to rule over them, but they should have resisted their base homicidal impulses. Their second-order volition should have been to heed Joseph's appeal for compassion. It does not matter much whether that appeal is implicit in Joseph's humanity or whether it is articulated as cries for help. The point is that the brothers did not hear it.

The metaphor of hearing correlates with actions producing guilt. We "hear the voice" of conscience rather than read an image of conscience in our mind, and thus it makes sense for the brothers to associate hearing with understanding the moral dimension of their actions. Further, Jewish theology emphasizes hearing over sight in the relationship with God. This is evident in Moses' confrontation with God on Mount Sinai and in the liturgical demand on Israel to "hear" and understand that God is one. By contrast, Christianity emphasizes the sense of sight and the role of images, particularly of Jesus on the cross, in sustaining faith.

Admittedly, there is a problem in understanding collective guilt as a second-order failure by a group to regulate its first-order group impulses. It would be hard to ascribe a conscience to a collective such as the brothers. Yet the brothers do react as a group to Joseph's dreams and have the impulse, as a group, to rid

---

29 Some English translations unfortunately translated *ashem* as "punished" simply because, as we noted, when guilt is understood as pollution, the decontaminating sacrifice is also called *asham* or guilt. Etz Chayim, supra note 15, at 260 n.21.

30 See Harry G. Frankfurt, The Importance of What We Care About 20 (1988).

themselves of him. Their confession occurs as a collective event, as evidenced by their speaking to each other before they declare their collective guilt. The impact of the brothers' confession appears to dispense with the need for punishment, for Joseph hears them and he cries. (Genesis 42:24.) The confession itself prepares the group for the reconciliation that occurs several chapters later.

It is arguably difficult to speak of guilt in this situation, because, in fact, no blood was spilled and no irreversible harm occurred to Joseph. At most, the brothers were guilty of a reckless attempt to sell him into slavery (assuming that it was Ishmaelites who lifted him out and sold him to the Midianites). In the biblical and Talmudic materials, there is no recognized crime of attempt, not to mention reckless attempt, which is not considered a crime even in modem legal systems.

It is worth noting Reuben's distinctive view on their collective guilt. He tried to separate himself from the group by assessing the brothers as not having "heard" his admonition not to sin against the boy. If Reuben is speaking sincerely, then he has a limited conception of sin indeed, for he did advocate leaving Joseph to die. Now, he asserts, Joseph's "blood must be redeemed." (Genesis 42:22: "Damo nidrash.") This reference to redemption of the blood takes us back to the view of guilt as pollution. We also encounter this idea in the biblical story most similar to the tale of enmity between Joseph and his brothers, namely, Cain's jealousy and subsequent fratricide of Abel: "And God said, What have you done? The voice of your brother cries to me from the ground." (Genesis 4:10.) The view eventually prevails that capital punishment is necessary to release the blood of the victim.[31] If this were the view of Joseph's brothers about their guilt, it would be difficult to take this story as establishing an alternative to guilt as pollution. But Reuben's views, based as they are on false assumptions, are exclusively his own and serve to contrast the traditional view with the modern conception of guilt as form of consciousness.

---

31 See Genesis 9:6 ("Whoever spills the blood of a human being, by a human being will his blood be spilled."). On the magical significance of releasing the blood of the decedent, see David Daube, Studies in Biblical Law 122-23 (1947).

Politics And Collective Guilt

The conception of collective guilt explicated in the Joseph story might lead one to a fantasy of reconciliation in the Middle East. Jews would discover and confess guilt for having displaced Palestinians from their lands in 1948, and Palestinians would discover and confess guilt for their nearly sixty-year campaign of delegitimation and terrorism against Israel and its citizens. By recognizing the wrongs they had committed, both sides would concede their guilt, but would not incur any debt to be punished. They would be in the position of Joseph's brothers, who could achieve reconciliation without punishment for their wrong.

Would that this fantasy were politically feasible. It is not because neither side would trust the other to resist exploiting the confession under the supposed rationale that guilt entails punishment and the punishment they have in mind would be subject to execution by their respective military organizations. The most I can claim for this argument based on biblical sources is that in fact there is no necessary connection between guilt and punishment and that – in theory, at least – confessions of collective guilt are possible without an implied justification for punishment in response.

CHAPTER EIGHT

Teamwork Makes The Dream Work: Collective Punishment And The Law Of Soccer

Katharina de la Durantaye[1]

A. Kickoff

Sport stadiums are today's cathedrals.[2] They are destinations of Sunday family outings, and it is there that people of different cultural and educational backgrounds pilgrimage to sing and pray,

1 I thank my team, especially Sebastian J. Golla, Judith Hackmack, Patrick Neu and Simon Scharf, for wonderful input and excellent research assistance.

2 Often, this sentence is literally true. Nowadays, soccer stadiums tend to have chapels where priests of the Lutheran faith, as so called "stadium priests" marry people and baptize children. *See only* Thomas Leißer, *Gott im Stadium? Die Kapelle auf Schalke*, 2006 ZGP Vol. 2, 22. The Protestant Church in Germany has identified sport as one of the most important fields of interaction between religion and culture, and is even hosting a website on questions of church and sport (www.kirche-und-sport.de). Even the term fan has a religious undertone. It is derived from the Latin word *fanaticus* which means divinely inspired.

and to be part of something that transcends social status and wealth. Some of the traditions they practice seem ancient, and so does, to a certain extent, the law that governs the sport they come to watch.

The paradigmatic example for this is soccer, the sport most played and loved around the world:[3] While modern legal systems renounce notions of collective guilt and collective punishment, often in their constitutions,[4] the law of soccer does not seem to be free from them. Even *Sepp Blatter*, the notorious former President of FIFA (*Fédération Internationale de Football Association*, the international soccer association) and a man known to have a rather flexible approach to rules, criticized some of the sanctions under the law of soccer as "disproportionately collective punishment."[5] He is not alone in his opinion.

Members and/or functionaries of regional and national

---

3 In 2006, an estimated 265 million people played soccer around the world, more than any other sport, see FIFA, *265 Millionen spielen Fußball*, Fifa Magazin, July 2007, at 10, http://de.fifa.com/mm/document/fifafacts/ bcoffsurv/gmaga_9471.pdf. *See* also Henning Vöpel & Max Steinhardt, Wirtschaftsfaktor Fußball 5 (2008), http://www.hwwi.org/fileadmin/ hwwi/Publikationen/Partnerpublikationen/HSH/Fussballstudie_14_B. pdf.

4 In German constitutional law, the principle of culpability (*Schuldprinzip*) is derived from the rule of law (*Rechtsstaatsprinzip*, Grundgesetz (GG) (Constitution) art. 20 (3)) as well as from the right to human dignity (*Menschenwürde*, GG art. 1 (1)) and the right to personality (*Allgemeines Persönlichkeitsrecht*, GG art. 2 (1)). See, e.g., Bundesverfassungsgericht (BVerfG) (Federal Constitutional Court), Entscheidungen des Bundesverfassungsgerichts (BVerfGE) 45, 187 (259-260); BVerfGE 110, 1 (13) as well as Tatjana Hörnle, *Strafzumessungslehre im Lichte des Grundgesetzes*, in Das strafende Gesetz im sozialen Rechtsstaat 105, 107-109 (Eva Schumann ed., 2010).

5 Sepp Blatter, *Sporting sanctions, not shut stadiums*, The FIFA Weekly 23, Apr. 17, 2014, available at http://www.fifa.com/mm//Document/AF-Magazine/FIFAWeekly/02/32/03/81/LowRes_Weekly_26_en_Neutral. pdf. *Blatter* was referring to matches played behind closed doors, i.e. matches to which no spectators are allowed (in German, they are called *Geisterspiele* (ghost matches)), and renounced them as an "extremely dubious instrument."

soccer associations, clubs and fan groups all have labeled different sanctions of the law of soccer as collective punishment.[6]

Collectivization of responsibility is inherent in team sports such as soccer. Every action by a player influences the team's chances of winning. Only very rarely, if ever, can a goal be attributed to one individual player alone. Players always rely on their teammates to deliver the ball, or simply to distract opponents and keep them busy. Even if a goal were an individual accomplishment, its benefits would be collective; goals are scored for the team.

Similarly, if one player violates the laws of the game, the effects will be felt by the team as a whole: FIFA's as well as regional and national laws of the game state that if a player commits one of eleven offenses, a referee awards a free kick or a penalty kick – both of which are good scoring opportunities – against the offender's team.[7] Only one of these offenses requires intent on the part of the

---

6 The rejection of these forms of (perceived) collective punishment is especially strong among fans, see, e.g., Christoph Ruf, *Schutz oder Schikane?*, Bundeszentrale für politische Bildung (bpb), Mar. 4, 2013, http://www.bpb.de/gesellschaft/sport/160774/unsicher-der-streit-um-die-sicherheit; The Members of the Committee of FSE & The Respect Fans! Campaigning Group, 100,000s of Supporters from Across Europe Address UEFA in Open Letter, Football Supporters Europe, http://www.fanseurope.org/en/news/news-3/1265-100-000s-of-supporters-from-across-europe-address-uefa-in-open-letter-en.html; Spiegel Online, *Fan-Netzwerk fordert Umdenken der UEFA*, Spiegel Online, Feb. 2, 2016, http://www.spiegel.de/sport/fussball/fannetzwerk-football-supporters-europe-fordert-uefa-reformen-a-1079040.html. For reports about discussions among functionaries, *see, e.g..*, Express, *Diskussion über Kollektivstrafen: Darf man die Fans in Sippenhaft nehmen?*, Express, Jan. 24, 2013, http://www.express.de/fussball/diskussion-ueber-kollektivstrafen-darf-man-die-fans-in-sippenhaft-nehmen-,3186,21540468.html; Lutz Wöckener, *DFB führt Bewährungsstrafe für Rot-Sünder ein – Interview mit Hans E. Lorenz*, Die Welt, July 20, 2013, http://www.welt.de/sport/fussball/article118231314/DFB-fuehrt-Bewaehrungsstrafe-fuer-Rot-Suender-ein.html.

7 *See* only FIFA, *Laws of the Game 2016/2017*, at 81, Law 12. Such an offense is committed if a player kicks, trips or strikes an opponent (or tries to do so), if he charges, jumps at, pushes, tackles, challenges, or holds

player,[8] two offenses can be committed without any fault.[9]

While such collectivization raises little, if any, doubts when taking place during a match and on the field of play, things become more complicated when actions off the field are concerned. Under the law of soccer – national as well as regional and international – clubs are liable not only for how their team's players (or coaches) behave during a match but also for actions by their members or supporters before, during and after a match, inside the stadium or outside of it.[10] The clubs are sanctioned by either national soccer associations (to which the respective club is a member) or by international soccer associations (to which the club's national soccer association is a member). These sanctions, such as the disqualification of a club from a competition, do indeed evoke associations of collective punishment: a club is "punished" for the misbehavior of people who might not be its members and whose behavior might be very hard for the club to control.

---

an opponent, impedes an opponent with contact, spits at an opponent or deliberately handles the ball. Cf. also Deutscher Fußball Bund (DFB), *Fußball-Regeln 2015/2016,* at 81, Regel 12 (Law 12). Union of European Football Associations (UEFA), *Disciplinary Regulations 2016,* art. 3 (2) refers to the *Laws of the Game* as issued by the International Football Association Board (IFAB).

8 That offense is the deliberate handling of the ball. Cf. Ulrich Haas & Julia Jansen, *Die verbandsrechtliche Verantwortlichkeit für Zuschauerausschreitungen im Fußball,* 2008 Zeitschrift für Sport und Recht (SpuRt) 129, 142. One might argue that a player who spits at an opponent acts intentionally as well. However, intent is not (expressly) required.

9 Holding an opponent and impeding an opponent with contact do not require any fault, the remaining seven offenses have to be committed carelessly, recklessly, or with excessive use of force.

10 Cf., e.g., FIFA Disciplinary Code art. 67 (Liability for spectator conduct), FIFA Disciplinary Code art. 58 (Discrimination), UEFA Disciplinary Regulations art. 8 (Responsibility), UEFA Disciplinary Regulations art. 16 (Order and security at UEFA competition matches), UEFA Disciplinary Regulations art. 14 (Racism, other discriminatory conduct and propaganda), DFB Rechts- und Verfahrensordnung (DFB-RuVO) (DFB Code of Law and Procedure) § 9a (Responsibility of Clubs), DFB-RuVO § 9 (Discrimination and Similar Offenses).

However, soccer associations are not the only ones whose sanctions seem problematic. Sometimes, clubs issue stadium bans against fan groups for violent behavior of some of their members. In Germany, such sanctions have recently led to a number of court cases where clubs, fan groups or fans claimed that they were subjected to (unconstitutional) collective punishment.[11]

In this article, I will examine whether such sanctions really do constitute instances of collective punishment. German criminal law prices itself for its systematic coherence. And yet, when it comes to sports law, said coherence reaches its limits, and the interplay between criminal and private law is particularly rich. Soccer associations and clubs are private entities, and, as such, they enjoy the freedom of association.[12] The criminal law concepts of (collective) guilt and punishment do not really fit, even if soccer associations are so powerful that a club's decision of whether to become a member is only of a hypothetical nature.

I will analyze three kinds of sanctions, all of which are being vividly discussed in courts and German academic literature – stadium bans, fines and disqualifications.[13] These sanctions are

---

11 For the facts at stake, *cf. only* Andrej Reisin, *Anhänger-Problematik bei Braunschweig: Eintracht sperrt linke Ultra-Gruppe aus*, SPIEGEL ONLINE, Sept. 27, 2013, http://www.spiegel.de/sport/fussball/eintracht-braunschweig-belegt-linke-ultra-gruppe-mit-stadionverbot-a-925014. html. *See also* Marc Heinrich, *Eintracht-Fans von zwei Spielen ausgeschlossen*, FAZ.NET, Jan. 21, 2016, http://www.faz.net/aktuell/ sport/fussball/bundesliga/dfb-sportgericht-harte-strafe-fuer-eintracht-frankfurt-14026812.html. That same incident prompted Hermann Schaus, head of the State of Hesse's parliamentary group of DIE LINKE, to issue a press release in which he criticized the sanctions as grossly disproportionate, cf. Hermann Schaus, *Fußball-Fans sind keine Verbrecher: Kollektivstrafen gegen ganze Fanszenen sind vollkommen unverhältnismäßig*, Apr. 27, 2016, http://www.linksfraktion-hessen.de/ site/fraktion/abgeordnete/hermann-schaus/pressemitteilungen/2765-fußball-fans-sind-keine-verbrecher-kollektivstrafen-gegen-ganze-fanszenen-sind-vollkommen-unverhältnismäßig.html.

12 *See* GG art. 9 (1).

13 A different but related sanction is a partial stadium closure. It will not be covered in this article. That sanction was used in a case which occurred in March 2014: After four fans of FC Bayern Munich had displayed a

based on different bodies of substantive law and highlight different aspects of a possible collectivization of liability. Stadium bans have their basis in the clubs' ownership of the stadium's premises. If they are issued against fans because of their membership in a certain fan group out of which crimes have been committed, fans may be held liable for conduct by other fans. Fines and disqualifications, by contrast, are ordered by soccer associations against individual clubs based on their membership in the association, and they may lead to clubs being held liable for the conduct of their supporters. Because of that, the article distinguishes between liability of fans for the behavior of other fans (B.I.), and liability of clubs for their fans (B.II.).

Along the way, I will make use of a category which George P. Fletcher uses in his article on collective guilt and collective punishment. Therein, he describes "two conflicting concepts of guilt,"[14] both of which he finds rooted in Genesis. Under the first one, guilt is a form of pollution which can befall a whole nation, independently of fault, and which requires cleansing. While "guilt as pollution" thus is linked to punishment, the second concept, "guilt as consciousness of wrongdoing," is not. It, too, can befall multiple people, as long as they act and feel in common, such as Joseph's brothers in Genesis, the example Fletcher uses to make his point. Here, the acknowledgment of guilt vindicates the crime; no further action is needed.

In its pure form, neither of the two can be found in modern Western legal system. And yet, traces of both ways of thinking have survived in our concepts of individual punishment. Those who

---

homophobic banner during the club's Champions League round of 16 home match against Arsenal London, UEFA ordered that the section inside the stadium where the four had been seated would be kept empty during the club's quarter final home match against Manchester United. It did so based on UEFA Disciplinary Regulations art. 14 – a partial stadium closure is the minimum "punishment" the norm provides for. *Cf. only* Martin Zips, *Bayern Fans zahlen Geldbuße wegen homophoben Banners*, Süddeutsche Zeitung, May 14, 2014, http://www.sueddeutsche.de/sport/champions-league-bayern-fans-zahlen-geldbusse-wegen-homophoben-banners-1.1960714.

14 George P. Fletcher, *Collective Guilt and Collective Punishment*, 5 Theoretical Inquiries in Law 166, 169 (2004).

speak about punishment in terms of retributive justice consider crimes as a disturbance of the law, a pollution of sorts, which has to be washed away in order for the law to be reinstalled; Fletcher speaks of contamination and decontamination.[15] And: while guilty acts require punishment independently of whether the perpetrator feels guilty or not, his or her admission of guilt does have a bearing on the sentence imposed. Guilt as an outspoken acknowledgment of wrongdoing lowers the need for external punishment.

I am not attempting to solve all legal problems involved in the problem of collective punishment and the law of soccer. Rather, I would like to raise sensitivity for the issues at stake, and to distinguish different layers worth thinking about. The article will show that, despite attempts to label sanctions under the laws of soccer as sanctions under private law, they verge on the border of collective punishment. As such, they raise questions of constitutional law. This is particularly true for disqualifications. The article will also show that the idea of "guilt as pollution" can be found in the law of soccer.

B. Laws Of The Game

The sanctions[16] which may be constitutionally problematic can roughly be broken down into two categories – those where fans of soccer clubs incur sanctions because of past behavior of other fans, and those where clubs are sanctioned because of what their fans did. Stadium bans which are issued against fans who might be somehow connected to riotous fans (e.g. by being members of the same fan club) but who have themselves not broken any rules belong to the first group. If, instead, a club is disqualified from a competition because of past fan behavior, its fans will be unable to watch the matches and will thus be affected by the decision as well. However, it is the club that is the immediate addressee of the sanction and the one to feel it most strongly. The disqualification from a major soccer event may, depending on the club's success in

---

15 Fletcher, supra note 13, at 172.

16 The term "sanction" is not meant to imply that the measures are ones of criminal law. Rather, the term comprises of private, criminal and other sanctions and includes both liability under private law and punishment.

the competition, lead to losses of several million Euros.[17]

Before going into detail, let me say a word on the law of soccer in general. It is a multilayered affair. In its Laws of the Game as well as in its other regulations (such as the Disciplinary Code, the Regulations on the Status and Transfer of Players and many more),[18] FIFA sets the global standard. FIFA's members, regional soccer associations like the Union of European Football Associations (UEFA), incorporate FIFA's rules. UEFA and its counterparts then oblige its members, national soccer associations such as the *Deutscher Fußball Bund* (DFB) in Germany, to accept their incorporation of these rules. The national associations, in turn, require their member clubs to accept their terms and conditions.[19]

---

17 DFB's Sports Court estimated that Dynamo Dresden's disqualification from the Cup Competition (see below at II.) will "not have considerably stronger economic effects for the club than two matches played behind closed doors" (*"wirtschaftlich nicht härter oder wesentlich härter als bei der Verhängung von zwei Geisterspielen"*), DFB-Sportgericht (DFB Sports Court), docket number 85/2012/2013, Dec. 10, 2012, in 2013 SpuRt 83, 84. *Eintracht Frankfurt*, a soccer club from Frankfurt am Main, estimates the costs of a ghost match to be between three and five million Euros, *see* Jan Christian Müller, *Die Kosten eines Geisterspiels*, Frankfurter Rundschau, Apr. 17, 2013, http://www.fr-online.de/eintracht-frankfurt/eintracht-frankfurt-die-kosten-eines-geisterspiels,1473446,22391690.html

18 For an overview, *see* the various documents at FIFA, Laws and Regulations, http://www.fifa.com/aboutfifa/officialdocuments/doclists/laws.html.

19 On September 20, 2016, Germany's Federal Court of Justice (*Bundesgerichtshof*) held that rules by such associations are only binding on the association's members and on those who actively accept them. In the case in question, FIFA had forced the association which organizes one of the forth-highest divisions in Germany, the so-called regional league (*Regionalliga*), to relegate a soccer club to a lower league. The organizers had enforced FIFA's ruling even though their statutes did not contain the relevant parts of FIFA's rules. Since soccer clubs are only members of the association which organizes the league they play in, the court held the enforcement to be unlawful.
See BGH, Sept. 20, 2016, docket number II ZR 25/15, available at https://dejure.org/dienste/vernetzung/rechtsprechung?Gericht=BGH&Datum=20.09.2016&Aktenzeichen=II%20ZR%2025%2F15.

Because of this pyramid-like structure, with FIFA on top and national clubs at the bottom, the law of soccer is almost uniform throughout the world. Apart from small variations concerning, for example, the question of whether video evidence is permitted in order to determine whether a goal was valid or not, soccer is played according to the same rules across the globe. Even the sanctions for fan behavior outside the field and/or stadium are similar. In the following, I will concentrate on the situation in Germany but will, where appropriate, make comparisons with cases elsewhere, mainly in Europe.

I. Liability Of Fans For Other Fans

A safe way of making sure that the peace inside the stadium and during the match is maintained is to prevent troublemakers from entering the stadium's premises altogether. Clubs do so based on their right as stadium owners to decide whom to grant admission to their property. A club may not only issue a ban for its own stadium.[20] DFB's Guidelines on the Uniform Treatment

See Jan. F. Orth/Martin Stopper, *Entscheidungsvollzug in der Verbandspyramide und Ausbildungsentschädigung*, 2015 SPURT, 51, 52.

20 A sanction with a similar effect as a stadium ban is a ticket ban. Unlike stadium bans, ticket bans are usually not issued by clubs out of their own volition. Instead, the police orders a soccer club to issue a ticket ban for a certain match in order to prevent expected violent behavior by fan groups – the home team may not give the usual quota of tickets to the visiting team. This happened, for example, in April 2012, when FC St. Pauli was to receive Hansa Rostock for a match of Germany's *Zweite Bundesliga* (Second National League). The day for which the match was scheduled was the last day of *Hamburger Dom*, a funfair that took place right next to FC St. Pauli's stadium. Because of this and since fans of both teams had in the past had several violent encounters, the police ordered FC St. Pauli not to give any tickets to Hansa Rostock, and declared its order to be immediately enforceable. Every Hansa Rostock fan was thus deemed potentially dangerous, independently of whether he or she had ever been involved in violent activities, or were associated with any fan groups that advocated violence. FC St. Pauli's attempt to receive preliminary relief failed both at the Administrative Court of Hamburg and at the Hamburg Administrative Court of Appeals, Verwaltungsgericht Hamburg (VG Hamburg) (Administrative Court Hamburg), Apr. 2,

of Stadium Bans (Guidelines on Stadium Bans) specify that DFB and its member clubs consent to accepting nationwide bans issued by each other.[21] As a consequence, a ban issued by one club immediately becomes effective throughout the country. In 2016, 1.621.of these nationwide bans were in effect in Germany.[22]

One such case is pending at the Federal Constitutional Court.[23] In all likelihood, it will be decided by the end of 2016.[24] The case concerns a nationwide stadium ban issued against the appellant, a fan of FC Bayern Munich.[25] After a match played in

---

2012, docket number 15 E 756/12, *available at* http://justiz.hamburg.de/contentblob/3360790/data/15-e-756-12-vom-02-04-2012.pdf; Oberverwaltungsgericht Hamburg (OVG Hamburg) (Administrative Court of Appeals Hamburg) in 2012 Neue Juristische Wochenschau (NJW) 1975, 1975. *See also* Christof Wieschemann, *Schuld und Sühne – Die Haftung der Fußballvereine für das Verhalten ihrer Anhänger*, 2013 Kölner Schrift zum Wirtschaftsrecht (KSzW) 268, 272.

21 DFB, *Richtlinien zur einheitlichen Behandlung von Stadionverboten* (Guidelines on Stadium Bans) §§ 1(4)(3), 2(2). For a general examination of nationwide stadium bans Marius Breucker, *Zulässigkeit von Stadionverboten*, 2005 Juristische Rundschau (JR) 133, 134; Jan F. Orth & Björn Schiffbauer, *Die Rechtslage beim bundesweiten Stadionverbot*, 2011 Rechtswissenschaft (RW) 177-217.

22 See Landesamt für Zentrale Polizeiliche Dienste, Polizei Nordrhein-Westfalen, Jahresbericht Fußball Saison 2015/16, 27, https://www.polizei.nrw.de/media/Dokumente/Behoerden/LZPD/ZZZZ-160908-1(ZIS-Jahresbericht_bis_2015-2016,_Stand_06.10.2016,_15.00_Uhr).pdf. The previous year, 2.218 such bans were in effect.

23 BVerfG, docket number 1 BvR 3080/09.

24 It should be noted, though, that every year since 2014, the court has announced its intention to decide the case before the year was over. For 2016, *see* BVerfG, Übersicht über die Verfahren, in denen das Bundesverfassungsgericht anstrebt, im Jahre 2016 unter anderem zu entscheiden, http://www.bundesverfassungsgericht.de/DE/Verfahren/Jahresvorausschau/vs_2016/vorausschau_2016_node.html (last visited Nov. 1, 2016).

25 FC Bayern Munich is Germany's most successful soccer club and biggest brand in German sports and, as such, strongly disliked by many fans from other parts of the country. The club won a record-breaking 26 national titles, 18 national cup titles (DFB Cup) as well as five times the Champions

Duisburg, a group of about 100 members of FC Bayern Munich's notorious fan club *Schickeria* München had clashed with supporters of the appellee, the host club MSV Duisburg. At least one person was injured, and one car was damaged.[26] Since the appellant was a member of *Schickeria* München, local police arrested him;[27] prosecution started a preliminary investigation regarding a possible breach of the peace (*Landfriedensbruch*).[28] The appellant acknowledged having been among the 100 members involved in the turmoil but claimed that he, personally, had not committed any crime.

Soon thereafter, MSV Duisburg issued a nationwide stadium ban against him. The ban was to be valid for two years.[29] The club did so in accordance with the Guidelines on Stadium Bans. They

League (which was called European Champion Clubs' Cup until 1992). 14 of its players played in the 2014 World Cup, 7 of which for the German team (which won the Cup). In the season 2014/15, the Bayern Munich AG had an annual turnover of €4785.6 million, *see* https://de.statista.com/themen/186/fc-bayern-muenchen/ (last visited Nov. 1, 2016). As of April 20, 2016, Forbes estimated the value of Bayern Munich's team at $2,678 million, Forbes, *Soccer Team Valuations*, http://www.forbes.com/teams/bayern-munich/ (last visited Nov. 1, 2016).

26 Bundesgerichtshof (BGH) (Federal Court of Justice), Oct. 30, 2009, docket number V ZR 253/08, para. 1, available at http://juris.bundesgerichtshof.de/cgi-bin/rechtsprechung/document.py?Gericht=bgh&Art=en&nr=49956&pos=0&anz=1.

27 *Schickeria München* is known for its riotous behavior. Following disturbances after a match between FC Bayern Munich and FSV Mainz 05 on August 22, 2009, 81 of its members obtained stadium bans. *See* Wolf-Dieter Walker, *Zivilrechtliche Reaktionsmöglichkeiten auf Gewalt im Sport*, in Sport und Gewalt 51, 67 (Wolfram Höfling & Johannes Horst eds., 2011). Over the past few years, though, *Schickeria's* image has changed. In 2014, it received DFB's Julius Hirsch Preis, an annual award given to people and/or initiatives dedicated to combat anti-Semitism, racism and violence in soccer, *see* Florian Fuchs & Sebastian Krass, *Revolution beim FC Bayern*, Sueddeutsche.de, Aug. 27, 2014, http://www.sueddeutsche.de/sport/begnadigte-ultras-revolution-beim-fc-bayern-1.2106266.

28 Strafgesetzbuch (StGB) (Criminal Code) § 125.

29 See BGH, supra note 25, para. 2. The maximum length of a stadium ban in Germany is 60 months, i.e. 5 years, Guidelines on Stadium Bans § 5(3).

provide for such a ban if the prosecution has begun a preliminary investigation regarding a set group of offenses, including breach of the peace.[30]

When the charges were dropped because of the insignificance of the offense,[31] the appellant asked that the ban be revoked. According to the Guidelines on Stadium Bans, a club is only obliged to do so if the banned person was found not guilty, or if charges were dropped for lack of evidence.[32] If they were dropped for other reasons, clubs should only reconsider the ban.[33] In the case in question, MSV Duisburg ultimately decided against lifting it, basing its decision on the evidence gathered by the police and which showed that the plaintiff had been part of the fan group out of which crimes had been committed.[34] Unhappy with the outcome, and under the impression that he was being punished for crimes committed by others, the appellant brought suit.

Just as the lower courts,[35] the German Federal Court of Justice (*Bundesgerichtshof*, BGH) ruled against the appellant. It held that the stadium ban was a measure of private law, and based on the stadium owners' right to, as a rule, "freely decide whom they allow to enter their property, and whom they do not" (*Hausrecht*).[36]

---

30 Guidelines on Stadium Bans §§ 1(1), (5); 4(3), (4). Local stadium bans, by contrast, are issued for lesser offenses, Guidelines on Stadium Bans §§ 1(4); 4(2).

31 Cf. Strafprozessordnung (StPO) (Code of Criminal Procedure) § 153.

32 Guidelines on Stadium Bans § 7(1) with reference to StPO § 170 para. 2.

33 Guidelines on Stadium Bans § 7(2).

34 BGH, supra note 25, para. 23: *„Der Kläger ist nicht zufällig in die Gruppe, aus der heraus Gewalttaten verübt worden sind, geraten, sondern war Teil dieser Gruppe."*

35 Amtsgericht Duisburg (AG Duisburg) (Magistrate's Court Duisburg), Mar. 13, 2008, docket number 73 C 1565/07; Landgericht Duisburg (LG Duisburg) (Regional Court Duisburg), Nov. 20, 2008, docket number 12 S 42/08.

36 BGH, supra note 25, para. 11: *„Es ... (das Hausrecht) ermöglicht seinem Inhaber, grundsätzlich frei darüber zu entscheiden, wem er den Zutritt zu der Örtlichkeit gestattet und wem er ihn verwehrt."* See also Breucker, supra note 20, at 135.

The BGH did, however, acknowledge that this *Hausrecht* is limited for organizers of sport events, such as soccer clubs, since they generally do contract with everybody.[37] These organizers, the court held, are under a constitutional obligation not to arbitrarily preclude individual fans from attending matches. They could only do so if, "based on objective facts and not subjective worries, there is a danger that the people in questions could, in the future, create disturbances."[38] As a rule, the BGH held, stadium bans are lawful if they comply with the Guidelines on Stadium Bans; the court deemed them to be a balanced set of rules.[39]

In the case in question, the court saw reason for exclusion. The BGH ruled that the burden of proof should not be set too high,[40] given that organizers of sport events are under an obligation to protect peaceful spectators from violent ones, and that the sanction in question was one of private and not of criminal law: "While there (in criminal law), a person may, according to the principle *in dubio pro reo*, not be punished if a crime is not proven, stadium bans can only reasonably fulfill their preventative function if they may also be issued against visitors who are not convicted of a crime but whose past behavior gives reason to worry that they might disrupt safety during future matches."[41] As such, it was enough

---

37 BGH, supra note 25, para. 13.

38 BGH, supra note 25, para. 17: *„ein sachlicher Grund für ein Stadionverbot besteht daher, wenn aufgrund von objektiven Tatsachen, nicht aufgrund bloßer subjektiver Befürchtungen, die Gefahr besteht, dass künftige Störungen durch die betreffenden Personen zu besorgen sind."* Cf. also BGH, supra note 25, para. 16: *„Konkret geht es darum, potentielle Störer auszuschließen, die die Sicherheit und den reibungslosen Ablauf von Großveranstaltungen wie einem Liga-Fußballspiel gefährden können."*

39 BGH, supra note 25, para. 27.

40 BGH, supra note 25, para. 17.

41 BGH, supra note 25, para. 19, quoting Amtsgericht Freiburg (AG Freiburg) (Magistrate's Court Freiburg), SpuRt 2005, 257: *„Während insoweit (im Strafrecht) nach dem Grundsatz in dubio pro reo eine Bestrafung unterbleibt, wenn keine Tat bewiesen ist, können Stadionverbote einen nennenswerte präventive Wirkung nur dann erzielen, wenn sie auch gegen solche Besucher ausgesprochen werden, die zwar nicht wegen einer Straftat verurteilt sind, deren bisheriges Verhalten aber besorgen lässt,*

that the plaintiff belonged to a group out of which crimes had been committed. His membership of that group justified the assumption that he surrounded himself with a violent environment, and that he may cause violence in the future.[42]

The decision received mixed reviews,[43] and it is the interplay between private and criminal law that forms part of the critique. The Guidelines on Stadium Bans provide that clubs base their decision on that of the police and the prosecution; if criminal charges are brought, a (private) stadium ban is to be issued.[44] The Guidelines do not, however, foresee the same automatism if charges are dropped. The ban is to be revoked automatically only if the person against whom it had been issued was found innocent, or if charges were dropped for lack of evidence. If charges were dropped for other reasons, it is at the club's discretion whether or not to lift a ban.

This interdependence between initial criminal proceedings and stadium bans is problematic because of police and prosecutorial practices, and because of certain features of German criminal procedure: First, where crimes are committed out of a group, the prosecution often starts investigating against the group as a whole.[45]

---

dass sie bei künftigen Spielen sicherheitsrelevante Störungen verursachen werden."

42 BGH, supra note 25, para. 23.

43 DFB and local police welcomed the ruling, see Diethelm Klesczewski, *Anmerkung zum Urteil des BGH vom 30.10.2009, Az.: V ZR 253/08*, 2010 Juristenzeitung (JZ) 251, 252. *See also* Herbert Geisler, *Besorgnis künftiger Störungen als ausreichender sachlicher Grund für die Verhängung eines Stadionverbotes*, in juris PraxisReport BGH-Zivilrecht (jurisPR-BGHZivilR) 25/2009, Anm. 4; Martin Nolte, *Gefahrenabwehrrechtliche Fragen im Kontext gewaltträchtiger Sportveranstaltungen*, in Sport und Gewalt 37, 48-49 (Wolfram Höfling & Johannes Horst eds., 2011). For critical remarks, see Peter W. Heermann, *Entscheidungsanmerkung*, 2010 NJW 534, 537; Orth & Schiffbauer, supra note 20, at 217; Thomas Marzahn, *Entscheidungsbesprechung, Fans im Fokus – Zivilrechtliche Reaktionen auf ein soziologisches Phänomen*, 2010 Zeitschrift für das Juristische Studium (ZJS) 428, 433.

44 Guidelines on Stadium Bans § 4(3).

45 According to the principle of legality enshrined in StPO § 160 para. 1,

Anyone who finds him- or herself in the middle of a group of soccer fans that commit crimes such as a breach of the peace does thus not only face criminal investigations but will also be banned from attending soccer matches. Secondly, after having initiated criminal proceedings (and thus once the stadium ban is in effect), the prosecution often does not go through the burdensome process of determining whether they have, in fact, enough evidence to go to trial. Rather, in cases like the one at issue where the damage was rather minor, the prosecution sometimes takes the easy way out and drops charges because of the insignificance of the (supposed) crime, thereby avoiding any statement as to whether a crime was actually committed.[46]

The accused has no judicial recourse against that decision. He or she cannot, for example, force the prosecution to keep investigating in order to get the opportunity to prove his or her innocence, or to make the prosecution realize that it lacks the evidence it needs in order to go to trial.[47] If he or she could do so, he or she would not only bring the criminal case to an end but could, at the same time, force the soccer club to revoke the stadium

the prosecution is obliged to investigate the facts and to begin preliminary investigations once it learns that a crime has been committed.

46 In 2014, prosecutors in Germany worked on 4,696112 preliminary investigations. Only 441234 led to charges. 2,701767 cases were dismissed; only 1.319,171of them for lack of evidence (StPO § 170 para. 2). *Cf.* Statistisches Bundesamt, Rechtspflege – Staatsanwaltschaften 26 (2014), https://www.destatis.de/DE/Publikationen/Thematisch/ Rechtspflege/GerichtePersonal/Staatsanwaltschaften2100260147004. pdf;jsessionid=584385E34CD5FBEEDC062E99CE88490B.cae2?__ blob=publicationFile (last visited on Nov. 1, 2016). Of the 186 cases that were tried for breach of the peace, 16 ended a verdict of non-guilty, and 43 in a dismissal (*Verfahrenseinstellung*) Cf. Statistisches Bundesamt, Rechtspflege – Strafverfolgung 60-61 (2014), https:// www.destatis.de/DE/Publikationen/Thematisch/Rechtspflege/ StrafverfolgungVollzug/Strafverfolgung2100300147004. pdf;jsessionid=0E7CA30CA6A682DC88FC76CB3C734AAC.cae4?__ blob=publicationFile.

47 The only thing he or she may do is to access the case files (see StPO § 147) in the hopes of gathering exculpating information which he or she may then pass on to the club.

ban. Instead, if the Federal Constitutional Court will uphold BGH's verdict, fans will, in the future, not only have to prove that the facts on which the club based its decision are wrong. In addition, they will carry the burden of proof that the club's prognosis for their future behavior was erroneous, a task which is not easy to fulfill.[48]

And yet, despite the fact that stadium bans are usually issued in reaction to possible criminal behavior,[49] they ultimately do not constitute instances of (collective) punishment but, in their worst cases, excesses of a stadium owner's *Hausrecht*. The main purpose of a stadium ban is to prevent future violence; the Guidelines on Stadium Bans expressly classify them as a "preventative measure of civil law."[50] The ban's purpose is to ensure the safety of the match. The relevant legal question is whether the measure the club took was proportionate, and, as the BGH put it, "based on objective facts."[51]

While it is debatable whether that requirement was, in the case in question, indeed fulfilled, the principle of culpability (*Schuldprinzip*) does not play a significant role in this legal determination. This is true not so much because of the practical consideration that "stadium bans can only reasonably fulfill their preventative function if they may also be issued against visitors who are not convicted of a crime but whose past behavior gives reason to worry that they might disrupt safety during future matches."[52] Rather, the reason is more principled: the principle of culpability, as enshrined in the Constitution, does not apply to measures which do not constitute punishments in a technical sense.[53] The possible lack of culpability on the part of the appellant is not a question of the applicability of the principle of culpability but one of proof and of the excessive use of the so-called *Hausrecht*.

It is no wonder, then, that the appellant did not allege a violation of said principle when he appealed to the Federal

48 Cf. also Marzahn, supra note 42, at 433.

49 Cf. Orth & Schiffbauer, supra note 20, at 186-189.

50 Cf. Guidelines on Stadium Bans § 1(2).

51 BGH, supra note 25, para. 17.

52 BGH, supra note 25, para. 19.

53 Cf. Dörte Poelzig, Normdurchsetzung und Privatrecht 341-342 (2012).

Constitutional Court. Rather, he is trying to make a case for an even stricter limitation of the *Hausrecht* for organizers of sport events: According to him, their freedom of contract should be limited in a way similar to that of companies which supply essential goods – he thus essentially claims a "basic right to physically attend a soccer match."[54]

This might sound strange, but: Because the basic rights enshrined into the GG do have indirect effects between private individuals and thus do not only apply between the state and its citizens, the Federal Constitutional Court will have to balance the property rights of soccer clubs[55] and their negative freedom of contract[56] against the appellant's personality rights (*allgemeines Persönlichkeitsrecht*)[57] and his right to equal treatment[58] as well as the general freedom of action and the right to physical integrity of other spectators.[59]

In doing so, the court may very well find that past or ongoing criminal investigations are a suitable criterion for evaluating future danger, as long as the individual facts of a case are given due consideration.[60] In the case in question, the BGH tried to distinguish the set of facts from those of other cases. It underlined that the appellant had not been part of the violent group by accident but that he was a member of *Schickeria* München; it could thus be

---

54 Very critical as to the existence of such a right Geisler, supra note 42, Anm. 4. The claim is based on BGB §§ 826, 249, according to which a refusal to contract can be a "willful, immoral injury" (*vorsätzliche sittenwidrige Schädigung*). In determining whether an action is "immoral", courts have to take into account the GG and the basic order it creates. Cf. Breucker, supra note 20, at 136.

55 This right is guaranteed in GG art. 13 and 14.

56 This right is enshrined in GG art. 2 (1).

57 This right is derived from GG art. 2 (1) in conjunction with art. 1 (1).

58 This right is found in GG art. 3 (1).

59 For an in-depth analysis of the constitutional issues involved in such cases, see Linus Schmitt, Das bundesweite Fußball-Stadionverbot 131-149 (2013).

60 Schmitt, supra note 58, at 149 favors this solution.

assumed that he generally approved of their actions.[61]

And yet, the BGH has created a slippery slope.[62] In 2016, Dresden's Court of Appeals upheld a stadium ban which a Leipzig soccer club had issued in 2007 against a functionary of the National Democratic Party (NPD).[63] The NPD is a party on the extreme right which, from 2004 until 2014, formed part of the Parliament in the State of Saxony where Leipzig (and Dresden) are located. Currently, the German Constitutional Court is – for the second time[64] – examining whether the party's purpose is to impair or destroy the German democratic constitutional order,[65] a finding of which would render the NPD unconstitutional.[66]

The Dresden Court based its decision not on any reprehensible behavior of the plaintiff as a soccer fan – inside the stadium or outside of it. Instead, it relied on the person's role within the NPD. The court held that a functionary of said party can be expected to surround himself with violent people and that he himself might cause disruptions in a soccer stadium which could endanger third people.[67]

---

61 BGH, supra note 25, para. 23.

62 Several courts have since applied the BGH's ruling. See only Amtsgericht München (AG München) (Magistrate's Court Munich), Oct. 22, 2014, docket number 242 C 31 003/13, 2015 SpuRt 37.

63 Oberlandesgericht Dresden (OLG Dresden) (Court of Appeals Dresden), March 11, 2016, docket number 2 OLG 21 Ss 506/15.

64 The first case ended in a disaster for the Federal Government: The proceedings brought to light that some of NPD's highest officials were, as informants, on the government's payroll. Therefore, the Federal Constitutional Court dismissed the case on procedural grounds, *see* BVerfGE 107, 339 (docket number 2 BvB 1/01).

65 BVerfG, docket number 2 BvB 1/13.

66 *See* GG art. 21 (2), BVerfGG artt. 13 no. 2, 43 ff. The judgment will be pronounced on January 17, 2017, see Bundesverfassungericht, *Press Release No. 79/2016: Proceedings Concerning the Prohibition of the National Democratic Party of Germany (NPD)*, Nov. 3, 2016, http:// www.bundesverfassungsgericht.de/SharedDocs/Pressemitteilungen/ EN/2016/bvg16-079.html.

67 OLG Dresden, March 11, 2016, docket number 2 OLG 21 Ss 506/15,

In both the case pending at the Federal Constitutional Court and the one decide by the OLG Dresden, the fans in question were banned not because of individual culpability but because of their membership in a group. Because the courts found that group reprehensive, membership of that group "polluted" the fans and made them "guilty."

To be sure, there are differences between these instances here and the Biblical cases in which *Fletcher* finds "guilt as pollution." In the Biblical stories, a whole group is being punished because individual members' violations of divine laws while in the sports law cases, individuals rather than a group are banned from a stadium. In addition, membership of a fan group or a political party is a voluntary act while membership of a people is not.

The heart of the problem, though, is similar: Even though the stadium bans were issued against individuals, they were issued against these individuals as members of a group, and because of their membership. In both instances, the plaintiffs were not the only ones targeted – the whole group was targeted but they were the ones who brought suit. And even though membership of a fan group or a political party is voluntary, the freedom to become a member is constitutionally protected unless the group is forbidden.[68] This is especially true for party membership. A party is constitutional unless and until the Federal Constitutional Court holds otherwise. Basing a sanction against an individual solely on his membership of a lawful group thus seems highly problematic.

II. Liability Of Clubs For Their Fans

Soccer associations, be they national, regional or international, are not open to individuals; their membership

---

para. 13: „(V)ielmehr war Anknüpfungspunkt für die Verhängung des Stadionverbots gegen ihn der Umstand, dass er der Vereinsführung als (aktiver) NPD-Funktionär bekannt und damit die Annahme gerechtfertigt war, dass er sich bei Fußballveranstaltungen in einem zu Gewalttätigkeiten neigenden Umfeld bewegte und von ihm deshalb künftige, Dritte gefährdende Störungen zu besorgen sind." Very critical Christian Rathgeber, *OLG Dresden: Eigenschaft als NPD-Funktionär rechtfertigt Stadionverbot*, FD-Strafr 2016, 377127.

68 GG Artt. 9 (1); 21 (1).

consists of soccer clubs and/or associations. Since fans are not members of soccer associations, associations cannot sanction riotous fans directly. Instead, they have taken to sanction the clubs which these fans "support." The associations do so in the hopes that the clubs may – at least in cases where they are fined – then try to identify and ultimately sue the troublemakers, or that the clubs will double their efforts to appease them and/or to prevent them from entering the stadium. The DFB expressed "perpetrator-oriented sanctions" as their "medium-term goal."[69]

On the German national level, the arsenal of sanctions is enumerated in an article of DFB's Charter (*DFB Satzung*) with the title "The Association's Power to Punish, and Forms of Punishment" (*Strafgewalt des Verbandes und Strafarten*); the individual sanctions are termed "punishments" (*Strafen*).[70] These "punishments" include fines up to € 250,000.00, exclusion from the use of DFB's establishments, matches played behind closed doors, deduction of points, and disqualifications from competitions.[71]

1. Fines

Fines are usually issued against a club whose fans illegally used pyrotechnics within a stadium's premise.[72] Over the past few

69 See DFB, 9-Punkte-Papier
(Verfolgung und Ahnung Zuschauerfehlverhalten), 2014, Nr. 2,
http://www.dfb.de/fileadmin/_dfbdam/55113-9-Punkte-Plan.pdf:
„Entsprechend dem zentralen Leitgedanken der Beschlüsse des DFB-Bundestages 2013 zur Bewährungsstrafe und Auflagenverhängung bei Zuschauerfehlverhalten sollen der DFB-Kontrollausschuss und die DFB-Sportgerichtsbarkeit ihre Arbeit vorrangig „täterorientiert" ausrichten, d.h. die Ermittlung der verantwortlichen Täter durch den Heim- und den Gastverein und deren Bestrafung bzw. Inregressnahme durch die Vereine und dadurch die Verhinderung zukünftiger Ordnungsverstöße sind das primäre Ziel des sportstrafrechtlichen Handelns der DFB-Rechtsorgane. Mindestens mittelfristig werden effektive Tataufklärung, Täterermittlung und zivilrechtliche Inregressnahme der Täter durch die Vereine (general-)präventive Wirkung haben!"

70 DFB Satzung § 44.

71 DFB Satzung § 44 (2).

72 See the list of recent fines at Faszination-Fankurve.de, Strafenkatalog,

years, clubs have doubled their efforts to identify the individual fans who used fireworks, and to bring suit.

Recently, the BGH sanctioned that practice.[73] According the court, a contract between a spectator and a club as the organizer of a soccer match includes the spectator's obligation to take account of the club's legal interests, such as not getting fined by the DFB.[74] If a spectator violates his obligation, the club may claim damages if it can prove the spectator's individual responsibility.[75]

The court remanded the case and did not decide whether a club may completely pass on a fine which is unusually high because the club in question is, under DFB's rules, treated as a repeat offender.

In a similar case, Rostock's Court of Appeals had held that a club may indeed do so.[76]

In general, the court's ruling is laudable: Since the DFB cannot fine fans directly, fining a club is the only recourse it can take. By enabling clubs to pass fines on to individual offenders, the court allows for an individualization of a sanction's effect. When a club passes on a fine, personal responsibility and the duty to carry its financial consequence are being aligned. This only holds true, however, if a fan is obliged to pay but those parts of a fine which reflect the offense in question. Clubs should not be able to take recourse for premiums which are due because of prior offenses

---

Sep. 05, 2016, http://www.faszination-fankurve.de/index.php?head=%E2%80%8BPyrostrafen-fuer-Muenster-Osnabrueck-amp-Chemnitz&folder=sites&site=news_detail&news_id=13596.

73 BGH, Sept. 22, 2016, docket number VII ZR 14/16.

74 In such cases, the basis for liability is BGB § 280 para. 1, sometimes in conjunction with § 241 para. 2.

75 BGH, Sept. 22, 2016, docket number VII ZR 14/16. The reasoning has not yet been published, the press release is available at http://juris.bundesgerichtshof.de/cgi-bin/rechtsprechung/document.py?Gericht=bgh&Art=en&sid

76 Oberlandesgericht Rostock (OLG Rostock) (Court of Appeals Rostock), Apr. 28, 2006, docket number 3 U 106/05: *„Die straferhöhende Vorbelastung des Vereins setzt deren Schadensersatzpflicht nicht herab."*

in which the fan in question did not take part.[77]

2. Disqualifications

Fines are not the only way in which a club can be held liable for the behavior of its fans. Even matches played behind closed doors, the sanction that *Sepp Blatter* recently, and famously found problematic, are not the strictest sanctions soccer associations may order. An even stricter one, in terms of financial consequences, is the disqualification of a club from a competition. This is what happened to Dynamo Dresden, a club with a fraction of fans who famously like, in more ways than one, to play with fire.[78] In 2012, in an away match against Hannover 96, they repeatedly lit fireworks and other pyrotechnics. In addition, and after having lost in a penalty shootout, about 200 fans invaded the field of play. They had to be pushed back by police. As this was not the first instance of its kind, DFB's Sport Court (*Sportgericht*) disqualified Dynamo Dresden from the DFB National Cup Competition for the following season.[79] DFB's National Court (*Bundesgericht*) upheld the decision.[80]

---

77 If they were, clubs would be disincentivized from taking preventative measures against such offenses. This was one of the major arguments against allowing clubs to pass on fines to spectators at all,
see Bernhard Pfister, *Kein Regress des Vereins gegen Fans wegen einer Verbandsstrafe!*, 2014 SpuRt 1, 10, 11-12.

78 On the international arena, UEFA's Control, Ethics and Disciplinary Body (CEDB) recently issued a suspended disqualification against the Russian team from the 2016 European Championship because of "crowd disturbances, use of fireworks and racist behavior," UEFA, Sanctions imposed on Russian Football Union, June 14, 2016, http://www.uefa.org/mediaservices/newsid=2376811.html.

79 DFB-Sportgericht, docket number 85/2012/2013, Dec 10, 2012, in 2013 SpuRt 83.

80 DFB-Bundesgericht (DFB Federal Court), docket number 5/2012/2013, Mar 28, 2013, in 2013 SpuRt 214. A similar case, in a European contest, involved *Feyenoord Rotterdam n.V.*, a club whose supporters had on multiple occasions proven disruptive. After Feyenoord's fans had created riots during a match at and against *AS Nancy Lorraine*, where they threw stadium seats at police officers and onto the field of play, creating such

The case was especially controversial because the match had taken place in Hannover, and Hannover 96 had control over who entered the stadium and whether these people carried fireworks. DFB's National Court conceded that Dynamo Dresden had indeed not been at fault – the club alleged that it had, to no avail, informed Hannover 96 about possible safety risks[81] – but that it was liable nonetheless because Dynamo's supporters had caused the disruptions.[82] Hannover 96, by contrast, was sanctioned comparatively lightly – the club had to pay €70,000 in fines.[83]

The court based its decision on § 9a no. 1, 2 of DFB's Code of Law and Procedure (*DFB Rechts- und Verfahrensordnung*, DFB-RuVO), a norm that provides for strict liability for soccer clubs. According to it, clubs are not only responsible for what their players, officials, members and employees do but also for behavior of supporters and spectators, be they club members or not. As such, the home club and the visiting club (and their respective affiliates) are liable for incidents of any kind that take place before, during and after a match, both inside and around the stadium. Thus, what is relevant is not where an incident takes place but whose

turmoil that the match was disrupted for 34 minutes, UEFA's Appeals Body fined the club CHF 100.000,00 and barred it from participating in the 2006/2007 UEFA club competition. The Court of Arbitration for Sport (CAS) upheld the judgment and stated: "(H)ooliganism needs to be eradicated from sport. It has nothing to do with football, and the UEFA, as other football associations, has consistently fought against this phenomenon. The panel is of the opinion that clubs showing constant disorder in relation to hooliganism deserve severe sanctions." CAS 2007/A/1217 – *Feyenoord Rotterdam v. UEFA*, para. 12.9. Cf. also Robert C.R. Siekmann, Introduction to International and European Sports Law 338-341 (2012); Ivan Cherpillod, Peter T. M. Coenen & Juan de Dios Crespo Pérez, *Hooliganism*, in CAS and Football: Landmark Cases 181, 188-200 (Alexander Wild ed., 2012).

81 Cf. Wieschemann, supra note, 19, at 269.

82 DFB-Sportgericht, docket number 85/2012/2013, Dec 10, 2012, in 2013 SpuRt 83, 83.

83 Cf. *Fußball-Club Dynamo Dresden von DFB-Pokal ausgeschlossen*, Focus, Dec. 10, 2012, http://www.focus.de/sport/fussball/dfbpokal/dresden-wird-fuer-fan-randale-bestraft-fussballklub-dynamo-dresden-von-dfb-pokal-ausgeschlossen_aid_878836.html.

supporters/spectators have caused it.[84] Neither RuVO nor FIFA's
or UEFA's regulations on which the norm is based do define the
term "supporter."[85]

Dynamo Dresden appealed to the Permanent Neutral
Court of Arbitration for Clubs and Corporations of National
Soccer Leagues (*Ständiges neutrales Schiedsgericht für Vereine
und Kapitalgesellschaften der Lizenzligen*),[86] alleging the illegality
of § 9a DFB-RuVO, given that it provides for punishment without
fault. Under German law, associations, especially such powerful
ones as the DFB, may punish its members only if they respect the
principle of culpability.[87]

---

84 FIFA Disciplinary Code (2011) art. 67 and UEFA Disciplinary
Regulations (2016) art. 8, 16 no. 1, 2 set up a very similar system for the
international arena. This is not surprising, given that FIFA Disciplinary
Code (2011) art. 146 obliges national soccer associations to "adapt their
own provisions to comply with this code for the purpose of harmonizing
disciplinary measures."

85 The CAS explicitly sanctioned this lack of precision in UEFA's analogous
provision: „The Panel has no doubt that it is UEFA's deliberate, and wise,
policy not to attempt to provide a definition for "supporter." (...) The only
way to ensure (...) responsibility (of soccer clubs) is to leave the word
"supporter" undefined so that clubs know that the Disciplinary Regulations
apply to, and that they are responsible for, any individual whose behavior
would lead a reasonable and objective observer to conclude that he or she
was a supporter of that club," CAS 2007/A/1217 – *Feyenoord Rotterdam
v. UEFA*, para. 11.6.

86 DFB's Charter, like that of many powerful associations in Germany,
provides that, once the remedies within the association are exhausted,
the case will be decided by a court of arbitration instead of a state court,
see DFB Satzung § 17 no. 1. See also Ständiges neutrales Schiedsgericht für
Vereine und Kapitalgesellschaften der Lizenzligen, Schiedsgerichtsvertrag
(Permanent Neutral Court of Arbitration for Clubs and Corporations of
National Soccer Leagues, Arbitration Contract).

87 See only Jan F. Orth, *Gefährdungshaftung für Anhänger?*, 2009 SpuRt
10, 11-12; Volker Röhricht, *Probleme des Beweisrechts im Sport –
Verbandssanktionen bei Doping und Zuschauerausschreitungen*, in
Sportrecht damals und heute 15, 39 (Württembergischer Fußballverband
ed., 2001). See also Frank Thumm, *Verbandsrechtliche Haftung von
Vereinen bei Zuschauerausschreitungen auf nationaler Ebene*, in
Verantwortlichkeiten und Haftung im Sport 9, 18 (Württembergischer

The court did not decide this question head-on. It referred to the principle of culpability but held – without much explanation – that said principle only applied to punishments while the disqualification constituted a preventative measure.[88] Where the primary target is "the prevention of future unsportsmanlike behavior by supporters" (*die Verhütung künftigen unsportlichen Verhaltens der Anhänger*), the court held, § 9a DFB-RuVO is in accordance with general principles of German law.[89] Since the association was lacking practical and legal means to influence violent fans, the norm would help raise the pressure on soccer clubs to make fans change their behavior, and it would put clubs in a position to sue its fans and thereby shift the financial burden onto those who have caused the incidents.[90]

Because of the constitutionally granted freedom of association,[91] and since the norm dealt with situations specific to sport events, the court held that § 9a DFB-RuVO did not have to be similar to general concepts of private law.[92] Even though, the court deemed the norm to be akin to private law concepts such as strict liability for (potentially) dangerous activities (*Gefahrveranlassung*), and held that the norm did not violate principles of equity and good faith (*Treu und Glauben*, § 242 BGB); the term "supporter" was sufficiently specified, and the means was proportionate to the end it was designed to achieve.[93]

Fußballverband ed., 2012). So far, courts have mostly decided this question with regard to cases involving doping, *cf. only* Oberlandesgericht Frankfurt a.M. (OLG Frankfurt a.M.) (Court of Appeals Frankfurt a.M.), May 18, 2000, docket number 13 W 29/00, para. 58; OLG Hamm, Sept. 19, 2001, docket number 8 U 193/00, para. 39.

88 Ständiges neutrales Schiedsgericht für Vereine und Kapitalgesellschaften der Lizenzligen, decision May 14, 2013, in 2013 SpuRt 200, 202.

89 Id. at 202.

90 Id. at 202-203

91 GG art. 9 (1).

92 Ständiges neutrales Schiedsgericht für Vereine und Kapitalgesellschaften der Lizenzligen, decision May 14, 2013, in 2013 SpuRt 200, 203.

93 Id. at 204.

Interestingly, the court does not make much use of the language of DFB's Charter even though the language of its § 44 (Power to Punish and Forms of Punishment) strongly indicates that a disqualification constitutes punishment, and not a preventative measure.[94]

The same is true for the purpose the sanction serves: According to the court, § 9a DFB-RuVO is lawful if the measure in question does not primarily serve a "purpose of atonement" (*Sühnezweck*) and/or entails a "verdict of unlawfulness" (*Unrechtsurteil*).[95] However, the DFB Bundesgericht had rightly held that the disqualification entailed a verdict that what had happened violated the rules of the game and should be condemned, and that it was not only a measure of special prevention but, more importantly, one of deterrence.[96] Deterrence, though, is one of the core purposes of punishment.[97]

In this respect, stadium bans and disqualifications differ significantly: the former are designed to ensure that a match may be played without interruptions. They do so by keeping possible troublemakers outside of the stadium's premises. The latter, however, do not ensure the safety of a match. Instead, they prevent the match from happening at all.

In addition, the measure does not seem well suited to achieve a preventative goal:[98] It could help fans to cool down if the DFB National Cup Competition was the main event in German

---

94 See also Jan F. Orth, *Von der Strafe zur Maßnahme – ein kurzer Weg!*, 2013 SpuRt 186, 187.

95 Ständiges neutrales Schiedsgericht für Vereine und Kapitalgesellschaften der Lizenzligen, decision May 14, 2013, in 2013 SpuRt 200, 202 *See also* Orth, supra note 93, at 188.

96 *„Bei einer Abwägung (...) erschien der Pokalwettbewerbsausschluss (...) ein weiteres generalpräventives Signal"*, Jan F. Orth, supra note 93, at 188 *citing* DFB-Bundesgericht, docket number 5/2012/2013, Mar. 28, 2013, in 2013 SpuRt 214, 214-216.

97 See also Orth, supra note 93, at 188.

98 Compare Id. at 189. *Contra* Wolf-Dietrich Walker, *Verschuldensunabhängige Verbandssanktionen gegen Sportvereine für Zuschauerausschreitungen*, 2014 NJW 119, 122; according to him, fines do not serve any preventative purpose while disqualifications do.

soccer's annual calendar.[99] In reality, however, the *Bundesligen* (National Leagues) are the more important (and lucrative) competitions for professional teams, and Dynamo Dresden was not to be excluded from participating in them, giving its fans a chance to gather (and kindle with fire) every week.

What is more, the court's declaration that the norm was reasonable because it lacked an alternative is far from being convincing. For once, practical considerations of that kind cannot render constitutional principles inapplicable. Second, the association would, even if it did not abandon the principle of culpability, have means to make clubs influence their fans: Clubs are under an obligation to take measures which ensure that its fans either have no access to the stadium or behave well once inside it – both the DFB National Court and the Court of Arbitration mention them.[100] If a club failed to fulfill these duties, it would itself be at fault and could thus be held liable without any violation of the principle of culpability.[101] If it did not, there would be no basis for liability.

The Court of Arbitration should thus have, in line with DFB's Charter, viewed the disqualification as a form or punishment. Had it done so, it might have struck the measure down as an unlawful instance of collective punishment and, as such, a violation of the principle of culpability.[102]

---

99 Orth, supra note 93, at 189.

100 For a list of measures, see DFB-Bundesgericht, docket number 5/2012/2013, Mar 28, 2013, in 2013 SpuRt 214, 215. As to the Court of Arbitration, see Orth, supra note 93, at 189.

101 Id. at 190 suggests that the DFB could shift the burden of proof and thus to force soccer clubs to produce evidence that they did, indeed, do all that was possible in order to prevent fan violence.

102 Dynamo Dresden, unhappy with the Court of Arbitration's decision, requested that it be nullified; since it violated the principle of culpability, the club alleged, the decision violated *ordre public* (Zivilprozessordnung (ZPO) (Code of Civil Procedure) § 1059). The OLG Frankfurt a.M. held that the club's petition was admissible but without cause, OLG Frankfurt a.M., June 13, 2013, docket number 26 SchH 6/13, para. 4. See also Jan F. Orth, *DFB-Pokal: Wie geht es weiter mit Dynamo Dresden? – Eine rechtliche Analyse*, June 20, 2013, at 8, http://www.janforth.de/wordpress/wp-content/uploads/2013/09/dynamodresden.pdf.

C. Final Score

Fines, stadium bans and disqualifications have multiple goals. They each aim at punishing past behavior as well as preventing future disturbances. And yet, they are not only based on different bodies of law – property rights vs. charters established based on freedom of association – but also raise different legal problems.

Fines are the least problematic of the three sanctions. Since clubs may pass fines on to individual spectators, their effect is felt by the perpetrator, and not by the club whose team the individual is rooting for.

In determining the legality of stadium bans, courts have to balance the constitutional rights of the banned person against those of the club that issued the ban as well as those of other visitors. An individual stadium ban may be a disproportionate use of a club's *Hausrecht*, and as such, it might be illegal. Hence, stadium bans which are not based on individual deeds but solely on a person's membership of a (lawful) group and thus on a concept akin to Fletcher's "guilt as pollution," give rise to concern. However, as preventative measures, they do not violate the principle of culpability.

With respect to disqualifications, courts have to balance the association's freedom of association against the principle of culpability. Where a sanction by an association is a punishment, the latter trumps the former, and the principle of culpability applies. Where a sanction, by contrast, constitutes a preventative measure, associations may sanction without having to give regard to the principle of culpability.

Disqualifications arguably fall under the first group – not only because DFB's Charter names them as such, but because the purpose it serves is the punishment for past behavior, and not so much the prevention of future disturbances. Instead of ensuring the safety of a match, a disqualification eliminates a match from a competition's calendar. Therefore, DFB's practice of disqualifying clubs from competitions, and § 9a DFB-RuVO, the norm on which this sanction is based, are highly problematic.

CHAPTER NINE

In God's Image: The Religious Imperative Of Equality Under Law

George P. Fletcher

The claim that all people are entitled to equal treatment under the law leads a double life. It is assumed to be true and, at the same time, treated with persistent skepticism. The claim is beyond controversy in the sense that one could hardly imagine a modern constitution that did not commit itself to some version of equality under the law. The form of this commitment might resemble the American Fourteenth Amendment, which prohibits the States from denying any person within their jurisdiction "the equal protection of the laws." Or it might be akin to the straightforward declaration in the German Basic Law of 1949 that "all human beings are equal under the law" (Alle Menschen sind vor dem Gesetz gleich).[1] Admittedly, there are some variations on this basic commitment, such as the approach of the European Convention on Human Rights, which defines basic rights in its first thirteen articles and then, in Article 14, prohibits discrimination on the basis of any one of a number of listed characteristics, including race, gender, national origin,

---

1 Grundgesetz (Constitution) art. 3(1) (F.R.G.).

and the catch-all expandable phrase "other status."[2] Some recent constitutional provisions even anticipate the problem of affirmative action and hold, as does section 15(2) of the Canadian Charter of Rights and Freedoms, that the commitment to equal protection of the law "does not preclude any law, program or activity that has as its object the amelioration of conditions of disadvantaged individuals or groups . . . ."[3] Of course, in states in which the matter is left open in the constitutional text, the issue of affirmative action raises fundamental questions about the meaning of equal treatment under the law. This difficult problem aside, however, unity prevails in contemporary Western democracies that equal treatment is an indispensable premise of the rule of law, as we now understand it.

At the same time, skeptical voices multiply about whether the concept of equality has any independent content. Peter Westen's influential article has convinced many that equality is an empty concept, that it merely restates an independent conclusion about whether two categories or persons should be treated alike or differently.[4] Joseph Raz pursues the same theme of equality's redundancy by arguing that the only relevant question is what each group of people deserves on its own merits. His suspicious posture becomes clear: "Rhetorical egalitarian slogans are used by all, and serve to mask deep differences in the sources of one's concern for social improvement."[5]

The strongest critique of equality as a principle of justice is that it is circular. Suppose the question is whether women should be admitted to a state military academy traditionally restricted to training male officers.[6] The central issue is whether women and

---

2 European Convention for the Protection of Human Rights and Fundamental Freedoms, Nov. 4, 1950, art. 14, Europ. T.S. No. 5, 213 U.N.T.S. 221.

3 Can. Const. (Constitution Act, 1982) pt. I (Canadian Charter of Rights and Freedoms), §15(2). See also Grundgesetz art. 3(3) ("No one may be prejudiced or favored because of his sex, his parentage, his race . . . .").

4 See Peter Westen, The Empty Idea of Equality, 95 Harv. L. Rev. 537, 546-47 (1982).

5 Joseph Raz, The Morality of Freedom 233 (1986).

6 This is the problem posed in United States v. Virginia, 518 U.S. 515

men are essentially alike. They are clearly not alike with regard to the ability to give birth, but they may be alike in most other respects. The inquiry into similarity and difference cannot be answered, it is claimed, without specifying the purpose of making the comparison. The specific issue is whether women and men are alike with respect to their suitability for military careers. If they are alike for this purpose, then it is hardly much of an inference to conclude that women should be admitted to an exclusively male military academy. The conclusion is anticipated in the premise that they are equally suited for military careers. In general terms, if two groups are alike or are equal for purposes of treatment X, then both should receive treatment X. It is only camouflage, the argument goes, to add some abstract claim about all persons being created equal or treating like cases alike.

One way to avoid circularity in the claim that like cases ought to be treated alike is to develop a standard for affirming human equality that is logically prior to the particular context for allocating some mode of treatment. The argument would then run: People are intrinsically equal and *therefore* must be treated equally in this particular context. This "therefore" has force only if two conditions are met. First, the premise of equality must be established independently of the question of how the two groups should be treated in a particular situation. Second, the reason for affirming the equality of all people must be sufficiently strong to warrant the inference that they should be treated alike for a specific purpose. For example, men and women are alike in the sense that they are both mortal. Mortality does not imply that men and women should have equal opportunities to pursue military careers. A claim of intrinsic equality would elicit something among human beings that would compel us to conclude that they should receive equal treatment under the law.

Some philosophers have tried to analyze human equality by searching for some single factor by virtue of which we are equal. We might all be equal because we can use language and say things like, "I am as good as you are."[7] We might all be equal in the sense

(1996) (holding that denying women admission to the Virginia Military Institute violated equal protection).

7 See Bruce A. Ackerman, Social Justice in the Liberal State 56 (1980).

that we feel pleasure and pain.[8] Or we might be equal because, in principle, we can act both rationally and reasonably.[9] All these arguments suffer from the same objection. Suppose someone could not speak, would he not be equal to other human beings? Suppose she could not feel pleasure or pain, would that put her outside the human community? If he were not rational, would he not be one of us? None of these criteria alone could be an adequate test of equality unless it was accompanied by a theory that explained why that factor, and that factor alone, was sufficient to generate the strong sense of human equality – the same strong sense in which Lincoln claimed that Americans were dedicated to the proposition that all men are created equal.[10]

Even if we could isolate the single factor that explained human equality, we would run into another problem: reasoning from the premise of human equality to equality under the law. Suppose that the intended discrimination has nothing to do with the single feature that makes us equal. If that single feature is, let us say, the ability to speak, that feature is not called into question by discriminating against children born out of wedlock. If confronted with a charge of unfair discrimination, a legislator could respond, "Yes, we recognize that you are equal with respect to the ability to speak, but you are not equal with respect to the marital status of your parents." We end up, therefore, with a version of Westen's argument that the concept of equality requires filling out the purpose for which we make the inquiry.[11]

The only way to generate a sound premise of intrinsic equality, I submit, is to find a concept of equality that is holistic in nature. It must apply to every person merely because he or she is a person, and therefore it must be independent of particular criteria and particular purposes. There must be something about us as equal persons that requires our equal treatment. The desiderata,

---

8 See Jeremy Bentham, An Introduction to the Principles of Morals and Legislation 11-12 Q.H. Burns 8c H.L.A. Hart eds., 1970).

9 This is one way to characterize John Rawls's intense commitment to human equality. See John Rawls, A Theory of Justice 504-12 (1971).

10 See infra note 13 and accompanying text.

11 See Westen, supra note 4, at 577-92.

therefore, are two. The conception of equality must be categorical and holistic, and it must assert a basis for inferring that equally situated persons require equal treatment. The question is whether any theory of equality could possibly meet these two requirements.

I

The first question on the agenda, then, is what kind of intrinsic claims of equality are available to us. One answer might be that all individuals are of infinite human dignity (equal in being unbounded in value) and therefore deserve the same or equivalent treatment. This response appeals to the German liberal, tradition drawing primarily on the moral philosophy of Immanuel Kant. In the American context, the foundational text is the resonant claim of the Declaration of Independence that all men, all persons, are created equal. Behind those *created* equal stands a Creator, who is the source of our inalienable rights "to life, liberty, and the pursuit of happiness."[12] If God has made men equal, then the implication must be that God has invested all human beings with sufficient value to entail a duty of government to accord to each person the same, or at least equivalent, rights and duties. We might call this the "individualist reading" of the Declaration of Independence.

The fact is, however, that when human equality was first proclaimed in 1776, the gist of the argument was primarily collectivist rather than individualist. The purpose of the Philadelphia resolution was to argue that all nations had an equal right to determine their form of governance. This primary sense becomes obvious on reading the passage as a whole:

> We hold these truths to be self-evident, that *all men are created equal*, that they are endowed by their Creator with certain unalienable Rights, that among these, are Life, Liberty, and the pursuit of Happiness. That, to secure these *rights*, Governments are instituted among Men, deriving their just Powers from the *consent of the governed*. That, whenever any form of government becomes destructive of

12 The Declaration of Independence (1776), reprinted in American Legal History: Cases and Materials 66 (Kermit L. Hall et al. eds., 1991) (1776).

these ends, it is *the Right of the People to alter or to abolish it, and to institute new Government,* laying its foundation on such Principles and organizing its Powers in such form, as to them shall seem most likely to effect their Safety and Happiness.[13]

The four critical states of the argument, highlighted in italics, are first a recognition that all men are *created equal* and, second, the inference that, as equals, they are endowed with certain *inalienable rights.* Third, the purpose of government is to secure these *rights.* And finally, if government fails to respect *the inalienable rights* of men, then it will not merit the consent of governed, and the people will have the right *to institute new government.* Thus, the case for independence flows directly from the claim that all men are created equal. A simpler version of the same syllogism would go like this: "All men are created equal. Therefore, Americans as a nation are equal to the British and, consequently, can decide for themselves how they wish to be governed." However the premises are configured, the import of the argument is not that all individuals are created equal but that all nations (all men in this collective sense) are of equal status in their right of self-governance. In light of the Declaration's tolerance toward slavery and the leading craftsman of these lines, Thomas Jefferson, himself a slave owner, a more radical claim of individual equality would have been hard to reconcile with the circumstances of 1776.

In the course of time, however, the subsidiary meaning – that all individuals are equal in the sight of God – clearly did emerge. The abolitionists of the 1830s and 1840s relied heavily on the Declaration of Independence. And Abraham Lincoln memorialized the individualist meaning forever when he reminded us that the American nation was "conceived in Liberty, and dedicated to the proposition that all men are created equal."[14] The same theme reverberates through Martin Luther King's classic speech delivered a century minus a few days after the Gettysburg Address:

---

13 Id. (emphasis added).

14 Abraham Lincoln, Gettysburg Address (Nov. 19, 1863), reprinted in *Abraham Lincoln: His Speeches and Writings* 734 (Roy P. Basler ed., 1969).

I still have a dream . . . that one day this nation will rise up and live out the true meaning of its creed – *we hold these truths to be self-evident, that all men are created equal.* I have a dream that one day on the red hills of Georgia, sons of former slaves and sons of former slave-owners will be able to sit down together at the table of brotherhood.[15]

Lincoln's reinterpretation of the Declaration of Independence and the resonance of the Creator in American consciousness now dominate the American conception of equality under law. It would be difficult to find an equally explicit theme of the religious imperative of equality in other legal cultures. Nothing quite like "all men are created equal" is ever cited in the German jurisprudence of equality[16] or, so far as I know, in any other legal culture of the world.[17]

There might be many groundings for a commitment to equality under law. The argument might be that, as a matter of practical politics, it is better to treat people as equals than to run the risk of disenchantment, demoralization, and defiance in large segments of the population. The argument might be that, as brothers in the nation, we should act out of a sense of solidarity and loyalty to our fellow residents in the land. Another consideration might be that the rule of law requires the enactment

---

15 Martin Luther King, "I Have a Dream" Speech Delivered at the Lincoln Memorial (Aug. 28, 1963), reprinted in *A Testament of Hope* 217, 219 (James M. Washington ed., 1986) (emphasis added).

16 Equivalent claims do crop up, however, in areas outside the explicit discussion of equality. For example, for German constitutional theory, the protection of human dignity fulfills a function parallel to doctrine based on the principle that "all men are created equal." See the extensive treatment of this theme in Susanne Baer, Würde oder Gleichheit (1995) and discussion at text accompanying infra note 61.

17 A Lexis search in the English and Canadian materials reveals no references in the case law to the phrase "created equal" in the sense Lincoln intended. The rhetoric of the Declaration of Independence apparently had little influence outside the United States. At least it does not seem to figure into the argument for equal treatment under law in other English-speaking countries.

of non-discriminatory laws and the non-arbitrary execution of these laws by the executive and judiciary. These factors influence American thinking, but we also have a distinctive theological foundation for our commitment to equality. It may be that the religious theme has become so important because of the enormity of the task we have faced in redeeming our jurisprudence from the sin of radical inequality. The struggle to convert the descendants of slaves into fully equal participants in the life of the nation has required a grounding in sources as deep as the theology of creation.

My concern in this Essay is to explore the religious foundations for the commitment to equality, probe their ramifications, and assay whether the current jurisprudence of the Supreme Court has been faithful to its theological inspiration.

II

One of the peculiar features of American political theory is the way in which committed egalitarians totally ignore the theological foundations of American thinking about equality. John Rawls,[18] Ronald Dworkin,[19] and Bruce Ackerman[20] all write as though the religious view of the world were totally irrelevant to their egalitarian projects. Their disregard for the theological theme proves very little, however. If there is indeed a strong conceptual connection between Western religious thought and the principle of human equality, that connection can persist as a background philosophical assumption, even though we no longer refer to the arguments that lead us to regard the assumption as self-evident.

True, there have been great secular moments in our national history and in the crystallization of our values. Our founding documents, the Constitution of 1787 and the Bill of Rights of 1791, recognize no power higher than the will of "We the People" and no historical mission more compelling than the creation of a "more

---

18 See Rawls, supra note 9.

19 Dworkin writes repeatedly about "equal concern and respect" and denies the relevance of the religious point of view to any of his arguments. For his systematic effort to reinterpret religious concepts as secular values, see Ronald Dworkin, Life's Dominion (1993).

20 See Ackerman, supra note 7.

perfect Union." It is also true that these great tributes to the secular mind sidestep the problem of human equality. The Constitution did reject the hereditary class distinctions known so well in the mother country, and that was a major step forward toward an egalitarian society.[21] Yet tolerance of slavery and the accepted hierarchy between men and women prevented more serious attention to the issue of equality as a constitutional principle.

It is no surprise, then, that speaking at the dedication of the burial ground in Gettysburg on November 19, 1863, Lincoln skips over the secular Constitution and returns "(f)our score and seven years" to the Declaration of Independence.[22] Here he finds language more suitable to his religious and egalitarian temperament: "We hold these truths to be self-evident, that all men are created equal ..."[23] The laws of nature and of nature's God entitle every people to "a separate and equal station," and this is the basis for the claim that no government may rule without consent. The end of the Philadelphia Declaration resonates with another invocation of a higher power: "(w)ith a firm reliance on the Protection of Divine Providence, we mutually pledge to each other our Lives, our Fortunes and our sacred Honor."[24]

The abolitionist movement drew heavily on the Bible, but so did the other side. As Lincoln said in his Second Inaugural Address: "Both read the same Bible, and pray to the same God; and each invokes His aid against the other."[25] The Bible certainly did not determine whether one was on the side of equal humanity or on the side of visiting the sin of Ham on all his descendants who lived in the land of Kush (Africa).[26] Everything depends on how one approaches the limited words of scripture. Lincoln held to a moral

---

21 See U.S. Const. art. I, § 9, cl. 8; art. I, § 10, cl. 1 (neither the federal government nor the states may grant any "Title of Nobility").

22 See Lincoln, supra note 14.

23 Declaration of Independence, supra note 12.

24 Id. at para. 32.

25 Abraham Lincoln, Second Inaugural Address (Mar. 4, 1865), reprinted in Abraham Lincoln: His Speeches and Writings, supra note 14, at 793.

26 The biblical argument for slavery, or generally for inferior treatment of Blacks, derives in part from the interpretation of the sin of Ham, Noah's

perspective on slavery that ran deeper than the biblical text. As he continued in the Second Inaugural: "It may seem strange that any men should dare to ask a just God's assistance in wringing their bread from the sweat of other men's faces; but let us judge not that we be not judged."[27] He did not completely mean "let us not judge," for the prosecution of the war represented a rather clear statement of moral conviction.

The Bible no more determines the analysis of human equality than it resolves the debate about the origins of the universe. Yet the foundational texts of Western religion have offered those of an egalitarian disposition material to bolster their convictions. The text of Genesis is, in fact, the beginning of the thread favoring equality that binds the earliest legends of creation together with Lincoln's reformulation of the Declaration of Independence. The foundations of equality emerge in the book of Genesis; they are restated in a secular idiom in Kant; and they come into modern political discourse as an unquestioned assumption of the liberal pursuit of justice. My view is that, if we look carefully at the text of Genesis, we will find the roots of those truths that today we hold to be "self-evident."

The major source of wisdom on human worth lies in the story of creation itself. In the first reference to the creation of Adam in Genesis 1, the text reads:

> And God said, we will make man (Adam) in our own image after our likeness: and they shall have dominion over the fish of the sea, and over the fowl of the heaven, and over the beasts, and over every creeping thing upon the earth. So God created the man in God's own image, in the image of God created God it; male and female created God them.[28]

This richly ambiguous text plays easily between the singular

---

son, in uncovering his father's nakedness. See Genesis 9:22-27. Ham fathered a series of tribes that in biblical geography are associated with the land south of Suez or Africa. See Genesis 10:6-20.

27 Lincoln, supra note 25, at 793.

28 Genesis 1:26-27 (author's translation).

and the plural. God created a singular Adam. God created it – Adam. Yet "male and female" God created them. The nagging question is whether God created one being or two. I use the neuter pronoun "it" to refer to the singular Hebrew pronoun *oto*, which is usually mistranslated from Genesis as "him."[29] I have studiously avoided gender particularity in this passage, either in references to Adam or to God. For, as will become clear, I believe that the preferred reading of this passage is that a gender-neutral being called God created another gender-neutral being called Adam.

Admittedly, this reading of Genesis 1 stands in uneasy tension with the famous story of Genesis 2, which pictures a male figure – Adam – dwelling alone in the Garden of Eden. He cannot find a helpmate among the animals and therefore God brings a sleep over him, removes a rib (as the Hebrew term *tsela* is usually translated), and fashions the rib into a woman.[30] It might be possible to reconcile the two stories in the following way. In Genesis 1, God creates a singular being that is both male and female. Rashi, the medieval Jewish commentator, raises the possibility that Adam is to be understood as a single bi-gendered being with two sides, a male side and a female side.[31] In Genesis 2, God separates the single being into two, thus simultaneously creating a male Adam and a female later to be called Eve. The Hebrew word translated as "rib" (*tsela*) could be read as referring to a whole side of the hermaphrodite being.[32]

A longer history of critical scholarship supports the distinct origins of the two stories of creation. The first story belongs to the so-called priestly tradition of the "E" text, in which God is referred to as simply *Elohim*. Genesis 2, beginning with verse 4, belongs to the "J" tradition, in which God is referred to by the pair of titles: *Adonai Elohim*.[33] These Hebrew terms are usually rendered in English as "Lord" and "Lord God." The word "God" translates the

---

29 In his new translation of the Bible, Everett Fox agrees with the use of "it" to refer to the gender-neutral creation of the first human being. See Everett Fox, The Five Books of Moses 15 & n.27 (1995).

30 See Genesis 2:18-23.

31 See Rashi, Commentary, *in* Chumash 7 (A.M. Silbermann trans., 1934).

32 See id. at 12.

33 See The Anchor Bible: Genesis 3 (E.A. Speiser trans., 1964).

Hebrew Tetragrammaton *Yud-Heh-Vav-Heh*, also known in English as Jehovah, thus the use of the letter "J" to denote the texts that refer to the dual name "Lord God." This difference in the title of God, the primary actor in the story, should alert us to the possibility of even more profound disparities.

The most radical difference between the two stories is, in fact, the way in which God acts in the process of generating Adam. In the first, God *creates* Adam, which is understood to mean that God creates *ex nihilo*;[34] in the second story, God *fashions* Adam from the dust of the ground and then *fashions* Eve from Adam's rib or side.[35] Even more significantly for our purposes, in Genesis 1, God creates Adam in his own image. Whatever this very suggestive term "image" (*tselem*) means, it clearly sets the first story apart from the second, for when God fashions Adam from the soil, God has no model or image to guide His reworking of the raw material. In Genesis 2, we search in vain for the idea that the Adam made from the ground, the Adam from which Eve is extracted, was made in the image of God.

Both of these ideas of Genesis 1 – the act of creation ex nihilo and the principle of creation in the image of God – are central to understanding the moral force of the proposition that all men are created equal. How these links are forged requires some explanation, for the connection between the Genesis tradition and the principle of human equality is hardly obvious. If we follow the legend of Genesis 2, with the resulting expulsion from the Garden of Eden, we encounter the basis for patriarchy that John Locke and many contemporary readers find objectionable.[36] Eve is cursed for having induced Adam to eat of the fruit; she is told in Genesis 3:16, "your desire shall be for your husband and he shall rule over you."[37] This and other stories in Genesis readily support

---

34 The Hebrew root is Bet-Resh-Aleph. This is the same verb that is used in the first line of Genesis to describe God's creation of the world.

35 The Hebrew root is Yud-Tsadik-Resh and implies a previous object from which the new thing is fashioned.

36 See John Locke, Two Treatises of Government 174 (Peter Laslett ed., 1988) (1698) (arguing that Genesis should not be interpreted as giving authority to men over women).

37 Genesis 3:16.

patriarchal institutions.

For several reasons, an exponent of human equality should attribute greater authority to Genesis 1 than to Genesis 2. It is only when we trace ourselves to a single entity – "in the image of God created God it, male and female created God them" – that we can seriously believe that we are all created equal.[38] If we have two original beings – one male and one female – there is no reason to believe that they are of equal status. And if the tale of their creation omits all reference to the dignifying unifying image of God, then we should not be surprised that the legend of the Garden issues an injunction of hierarchy between men and women. To overcome the bias of race, gender, and all the other distinctions that separate us, we must find our source in a single image of humanity, a single entity that partakes of the highest value that we can express.

The ideological enemies of universal human equality are several. One is the legend of multiple original beings, such as Adam and Eve in Genesis 2, with the ever-present possibility that one of the original beings will be regarded as superior to the others. Another enemy of human equality is the doctrine of karma and reincarnation – namely, the belief that a prior life of merit or demerit accounts for our station in the present life. As suggested in Hinduism and Buddhism, the karma of our prior lives explains the rampant inequality that we observe all around us.[39]

Though one could imagine other religious traditions supporting a conception of innate equality, there is no doubt that the assumption of equality in the West has its most plausible source in the myth that we trace to Genesis 1.[40] We are descendants of a

---

38 Genesis 1:27. Samson Hirsch, a nineteenth-century commentator, argued that Genesis 1 suggests that only both sexes, in equal dignity, can solve humanity's problems. See Menachem Kasher, Encyclopedia of Biblical Interpretation 66 (H. Freedman trans., 1953).

39 For a discussion of karma in Buddhism, see Rebecca Redwood French, The Golden Yoke: The Legal Cosmology of Buddhist Tibet 36, 63-64 (1995). For a discussion of karma in Hinduism, see generally Karma: An Anthropological Inquiry (Charles F. Keyes 8c E. Valentine Daniel eds., 1983).

40 The Koran appears to support the view of Genesis 1, explaining that men and women were created simultaneously from the same source:

single being made in the image of God; since we all share a common origin, we can understand the rhetoric that we are all brothers and sisters and that we share a single universal humanity.

The only problem with this thesis is that Genesis itself contains no explicit assertion of human equality. The imperative to treat all human beings equally never emerges explicitly as a commandment either of the Noahite covenant applicable to all peoples or in the covenant with the Hebrews at Mount Sinai. Nevertheless, creation in the image of God carries implications that lead to the thesis of human equality as we understand it in the West.

Let us take Genesis 1 as our point of departure and assume that a single hermaphrodite being was created in the image of a gender-neutral God. What follows from this special attribute of the single being created in Genesis 1? Somehow this special quality of replication of the divine image is passed to all of Adam and Eve's offspring, whether male or female. We know this to be the biblical message, for later, in Genesis 9:6, a few chapters after Cain killed Abel, we encounter the image of God again, this time to explain why it is wrong for one human being to kill another: "Whoever sheds man's blood by man shall his blood be shed; for in the image of God he made Adam."[41]

What is it about being made in the image of God that makes homicide so clearly wrong? What is, after all, an image of God? We know what an image is not – it is not a photograph, not a copy, not a precise replica, not an interpretation. But an image does bear some significant relation? ship to the original, and in this context the point seems clear that human beings partake of the ultimate value associated with the Creator of the Universe.

There can be no higher being on earth than that which

"Men, have fear of your Lord, who created you from a single soul. From that soul He created its mate, and through them He bestrewed the earth with countless men and women." Koran 4:1 (NJ. Dawood trans., Penguin Books 1990); see also Azizah al-Hibri, Islam, Law and Custom: Redefining Muslim Women's Rights, 12 Am. U. J. Int'l L. 8c Pol'y 1, 26 (1997) (arguing that the Koran "states clearly and repeatedly that we were all created from the same nafs (soul)"). For a further discussion of the status of women in Islam and the Koran, see Asghar Ali Engineer, The Rights of Women in Islam (1992).

41 Genesis 9:6.

partakes of the divine. Therefore, no one can claim that he is superior to his intended victim. Thus we can begin to see in the prohibition against killing innocents the roots of theories of both human dignity and human equality. The potential killer and his victim are of equal dignity, and therefore neither can justify killing the other. Self-defense becomes possible only because aggressors themselves challenge the equality of their intended victims and thus become subject to violent repression.[42]

The same basic structure of thought is found in Kant's moral theory. Each innocent human life has a dignity beyond price.[43] The humanity in each of us is of infinite value, and this explains why we must respect the humanity of others as we respect the humanity in ourselves. We cannot use another person merely as a means to an end,[44] and we may commit neither homicide nor suicide.[45] It follows that no human life could be more valuable than any other and that all human beings are perforce of equal value. As this argument is developed in the *Prolegomenon to the Metaphysics of Morals*, Kant does not explicitly assert the essential equality of human beings. Yet, the entire argument that we must respect the dignity of others as well as ourselves is instinct with the assumption of human equality. Significantly, Kant developed this argument in 1785 – contemporaneous with both the Declaration of Independence and the French Revolution. It is as though philosophy was struggling to keep up with the equality-inspired rebellions against George III and Louis XVI.

---

42 The religious rationale for permitting homicide in self-defense is, in fact, not so simple. One problem is whether the rationale for killing in self-defense should be treated as official punishment, subject to all the rules governing courts that impose punishment. For the rabbinical response to this problem, see George P. Fletcher, Punishment and Self-Defense, 8 L. & Phil. 201 (1989) (contrasting the assumption of Jewish duty-oriented and Western rights-based criminal jurisprudence); George P. Fletcher, Self-Defense as a Justification for Punishment, 12 Cardozo L. Rev. 859 (1991) (discussing sources of self defense in Jewish law, particularly the duty to use force to rescue a third party or resist an intruder into one's home).

43 See Immanuel Kant, Foundations of the Metaphysics of Morals 52-53 (Robert P. Wolff ed., Lewis W. Beck trans., Bobbs-Merrill Co. 1969) (1785).

44 See Id. at 54.

45 See Id. at 45, 54.

The structure of Kant's thinking closely parallels the reasoning of Genesis. Kant's idea of universal humanity functions as the secular analogue to creation in the image of God. Both premises generate the strict prohibition against killing innocent non-aggressors. The prohibition against killing, in turn, permits the inference that the potential killer and victim are of equal value. This equality is possible because both are of infinite value, and because no human being could be superior to any other, it follows that we are all created equal.

No particular feature of our existence renders us equal in the image of God or in our universal humanity. The theory of equality turns out to be not analytic, but holistic. We recognize our innate equality not because we value the intelligence, the memory, the capacity for language, or any other particular feature of other human beings. We recognize each other as human, and our equality as humans, because we grasp our non-analyzable resemblance. We relate not by partaking of a single feature that distinguishes us from animals but by way of sharing a common image. There is probably no better expression of this holistic sense of humanity than that which we find in Shylock's pleas for recognition. Challenging Antonio's contempt for him, Shylock inquires:

> And what's his reason? I am a Jew. Hath not a Jew eyes? (H)ath not a Jew hands, organs, dimensions, senses, affections, passions? (F)ed with the same food, hurt with the same weapons, subject to the same diseases, healed by the same means, warmed and cooled by the same winter and summer as a Christian is? If you prick us, do we not bleed? If you tickle us, do we not laugh? (I)f you poison us, do we not die? – And if you wrong us, shall we not revenge?[46]

The composite renders Shylock human. It is not a particular feature, but the whole, the verbal image in which we cannot but recognize ourselves. One could imagine this speech recast in a debate between an abolitionist and a slave holder: "Hath not a slave eyes? If you prick him does he not bleed?" There is no better

---

46 William Shakespeare, The Merchant of Venice act 3, sc. 1.

case for equality than Shakespeare's art. It is effective precisely because it speaks in an image of a complex being. It does not strain the quality of humanness by reducing it to a single feature that we can reject or ignore. Rather, it allows the humanity of the other to ease by our defenses, as the wave breaks and flows past any barrier that we place in its way.

The holistic approach to the "image of God" is critical to the prohibition of homicide. If a single feature defined the quality of humanness that precluded the intentional killing of human beings, we might have endless debates about whether the prohibition extended to people of low intelligence, to those without speech, to those in comas, to those with no enjoyment of life. We would have the same debate about homicide that many proponents of easy abortion propose with regard to fetuses that lack some supposedly essential feature of "personhood."[47] The only reason that the universal prohibition against homicide survives is that we refuse to engage in the chimerical pursuit of the single observable feature that makes us human.

The holistic approach to humanity reflects a romantic sensibility. It favors a situational response over the analysis of factors and reduction of wholes to parts. It favors innate human understanding over scientific formulae. And here we encounter a major paradox in modern legal thought. The romantic sensibility runs through the legal culture, yet we are loath to recognize its presence. When it suddenly asserts itself in legal opinions, as in Justice Stewart's famous remark that he knows pornography when he sees it,[48] we smile politely. We think, mistakenly, that the methodology of images lacks precision. It is wanting in legal virtue. We crave the scientific, the analytic, a litmus test for critical concepts. Nothing could be further from the nature of the problem of recognizing and valuing humanity.[49]

---

47 See the embarrassing analysis by Dworkin that fetuses have no claim to protection prior to developing the ability to feel pain, which may be indicated by electrical brain activity, in Dworkin, supra note 19, at 17. However the debate about abortion is resolved, the status of the fetus should not depend on the pursuit of some single magical component of humanity.

48 See Jacobellis v. Ohio, 378 U.S. 184, 197 (1964) (Stewart, J., concurring).

49 The romantic method runs through many of my articles, but I have

III

The foundation of our jurisprudence of equality, therefore, is the proposition of the Declaration of Independence: "All men are created equal." Yet the Justices of the Supreme Court rely, much less than one would expect, on these truths that the Drafters of 1776 took to be self-evident.

The Supreme Court has cited the proposition in only twenty-three cases, and twelve of those citations are in dissenting opinions.[50] Each time the Court invokes equality in God's image,

---

never managed to analyze the approach systematically. See, e.g., George P. Fletcher, Fairness and Utility in Tort Theory, 85 Harv. L. Rev. 537 (1972) (arguing that the use of metaphors and imagery represents a style of reasoning that may be necessary to protect innocent victims from socially useful risks); George P. Fletcher, The Metamorphosis of Larceny, 89 Harv. L. Rev. 469 (1976) (describing how the classic definition of larceny – conduct conforming to a collective image of acting like a thief – would require eighteenth-century courts to accept unanalyzed perception as a source of law). A good account of the romantic method under the label "ordinary observing" is to be found in Bruce Ackerman, Private Property and the Constitution 88-112 (1977).

50 The Supreme Court has cited the full phrase "all men are created equal" or the modern version "all persons are created equal" in the context of precisely twenty-three cases, appearing in either an opinion of the Court, a concurring opinion, or a dissenting opinion. The first citation to the phrase, surprisingly, was in the notorious Dred Scott case, Scott v. Sandford, 60 U.S. 393, 410 (1856), in which Chief Justice Taney cites the Declaration of Independence only to argue that those who signed it could not possibly have meant to include slaves within the scope of "all men." But see id. at 574-75 (Curtis, J., dissenting) (challenging Chief Justice Taney's arguments).

Subsequently, three Justices account for the remaining twenty-two citations. First, the great advocate of this rhetoric of equality-in-creation is Justice Stevens, who has cited the phrase seven times in dissent, either in opinions under his own name or in opinions he has signed. See Agostini v. Felton, 521 U.S. 203, 244 (1997) (Souter, J., dissenting); Adarand Constructors, Inc. v. Pena, 515 U.S. 200, 249 n.6 (1995) (Stevens, J., dissenting); Cruzan v. Director, Mo. Dep't of Health, 497 U.S. 261, 330 n.1 (1990) (Stevens, J., dissenting); Bowers v. Hardwick, 478 U.S. 186, 218 (1986) (Stevens, J., dissenting); Wygant v. Jackson Bd. of Educ, 476 U.S. 267, 316 (1986) (Stevens, J., dissenting); Fullilove v. Klutznick, 448

however, its simple affirmation has a startling rhetorical effect. A good example is the dissent of Justices Stevens, Marshall, and Brennan in Matthews v. Lucas, upholding discrimination against children born out of wedlock. The Social Security Act prescribes that for the purposes of awarding survivor benefits,

---

U.S. 448, 533 n.1 (1980) (Stevens, J., dissenting); Mathews v. Lucas, 427 U.S. 495, 520 n.3 (1976) (Stevens, J., dissenting). Second, Justice Brewer worked the phrase into three of his opinions for the Court at the turn of the century. See Cotting v. Kansas City Stock Yards, 183 U.S. 79, 107 (1901); Gulf, Colorado 8c Santa Fe Ry. Co. v. Ellis, 165 U.S. 150, 160 (1897); Church of the Holy Trinity v. United States, 143 U.S. 457, 467 (1892). Third, Justice Bradley is credited with the first positive invocation of this phrase in his dissent in The Slaughter-House Cases (Slaughterhouse I), 83 U.S. 36, 116 (1873) (Bradley, J., dissenting) and his concurrence in Butcher's Union Slaughter-House and Live-Stock Co., v. Crescent City Live Stock Landing & Slaughter-House Co. (Slaughterhouse II), 111 U.S. 746, 762 (1884) (Bradley, J., concurring).

A total of twelve of the twenty-three references appear in dissent. In addition to the eight dissents associated with Stevens and Bradley, five more were registered. See Regents of the Univ. of Cal. v. Bakke, 438 U.S. 265, 326 (1978) (Brennan, J., dissenting in part); id. at 388 (Marshall, J., dissenting in part); School Dist. of Abington Township v. Schempp, 374 U.S. 203, 317 (1963) (Stewart, J., dissenting); McGowan v. Maryland, 366 U.S. 420, 563 (1961) (Douglas, J., dissenting); In re Anastaplo, 366 U.S. 82, 99 n.2 (1960) (Black, J., dissenting); Senn v. Tile Layers Protective Union, 301 U.S. 468, 487 (1937) (Butler, J., dissenting).

The remaining cases in which "all men are created equal" appears are Lee v. Weisman, 505 U.S. 577, 606-07 (1992) (Blackmun, J., concurring) (invoking the phrase for an unusual thesis: "A government cannot be premised on the belief that all persons are created equal when it asserts that God prefers some"); City of Richmond v. J.A. Croson Co., 488 U.S. 469, 528 (1989) (Scalia, J., concurring); Illinois v. Allen, 397 U.S. 337, 348 (1970) (Brennan, J., concurring); Bell v. Maryland, 378 U.S. 226, 286 (1964) (Goldberg, J., concurring); Allgeyer v. Louisiana, 165 U.S. 578, 589 (1897).

It is worth noting that only a slim majority of these twenty-three decisions raise equal protection issues: *Adarand, Croson, Wygant, Fullilove, Bakke, Mathews, Bell, Senn, Cotting, Allgeyer, Ellis, Slaughterhouse II,* and *Slaughterhouse I.* The second most common theme is freedom of religion, to which the rhetoric of being "created equal" had relevance in five cases: *Agostini, Lee, Schempp, McGowan,* and *Church of the Holy Trinity.*

the administrator could permissibly presume that "legitimate children" were financially dependent on their decedent-parent, but that children born out of wedlock were not. In response to the challenge that this presumption unfairly discriminated against so-called illegitimates, the Supreme Court upheld the statute. The dissent of the three justices begins with a simple affirmation of human equality:

> The reason why the United States Government should not add to the burdens that illegitimate children inevitably acquire at birth is radiantly clear: We are committed to the proposition that all persons are created equal.[51]

The argument is compelling in this context but out of place in others. The typical case of equal protection analysis responds to some seemingly arbitrary legislative classification, say, permitting optometrists but not opticians to perform eye examinations.[52] It would be slightly ludicrous to begin an argument about whether opticians should have the same professional privileges as optometrists by recalling that all men are created equal.

The appropriateness of affirming the intrinsic equality of all people in some equal protection disputes but not in others enables us to clarify a fundamental cleavage between two radically different kinds of legal problems. In one form of contested discrimination – call it "caste-reinforcing discrimination" – the legislative decision reflects a culturally-rooted differentiation between the privileged and the disadvantaged. If we are comparing whites and blacks, men and women, citizens and aliens, "legitimate" and "illegitimate" children, heterosexuals and homosexuals, we have no doubt about whether in American society one of these pairings has traditionally carried greater privilege. The same could be said for distinctions common in other cultures – between aristocrats and commoners in Britain, between Brahmin and untouchables in India, between ordinary citizens and Eta (descendants of those who once slaughtered animals) in Japan, and between women with

---

51 Mathews, 427 U.S. at 516 (Stevens, J., dissenting).

52 See Williamson v. Lee Optical Co., 348 U.S. 483 (1955).

children and barren women in the biblical culture. In all these cases, the very existence of the distinction implies privilege. The roots of this superiority may be cultural or religious, and because they are widely supported in the society, they are likely to be reflected in legal arrangements that reinforce the indigenous assumptions of hierarchy.

In other cases – let's call them simply "arbitrary legislation" – the statutory law invokes a new categorization that comes across as haphazard or arbitrary. A statute that imposes sterilization as a penalty for theft but not for embezzlement obviously treats one group of people worse than another.[53] But this differentially harsh treatment neither responds to nor reinforces cultural assumptions about thieves in contrast to embezzlers – unless, of course, the statute incorporates unarticulated class-based assumptions about the kinds of people who are likely to steal as opposed to those who are prone to embezzlement. If a licensing scheme assumes that optometrists are better qualified to examine eyes than are opticians, this kind of superiority is arguably justified on the basis of longer and better professional training. It hardly springs from culturally-rooted notions of intrinsic merit.

The striking fact about caste-reinforcing discrimination is that it is not arbitrary. It reflects and incorporates deeply-held local biases. The impetus for the differentiation lies in indigenous assumptions that, for reasons best known to the initiated, some people are intrinsically superior to others. Because one group is thought to be intrinsically superior, it deserves better treatment from the state.

When the state undertakes to distribute benefits and burdens for a particular purpose, it cannot award the benefits or impose the burdens on everyone. Therefore, it must design a system of categories for deciding the reach of its legislative program. This kind of line-drawing, which has nothing to do with ingrained cultural stereotypes, can give rise to claims of discrimination, and sometimes these claims prevail in the Supreme Court. Typical is the victory in *Morey v. Doud*,[54] which blew the whistle on a regulatory plan for currency transfers that had awarded a privileged position

---

53 See Skinner v. Oklahoma, 316 U.S. 535, 541-42 (1942) (holding that sentencing discrimination violates equal protection).

54 354 U.S. 457 (1957).

to American Express. The danger in legislative schemes allocating economic and social benefits is that they frequently have political sinecures built into them.[55] The Equal Protection Clause provides a good way for testing whether these legislative schemes for distributing benefits unfairly advantage or tax a particular group. The benefits and burdens are thought to be fair if they stand in an appropriate relationship, typically called a "rational" relationship to the legislative goal. "Rational" turns out to be the opposite of "arbitrary." If the legislation is rationally designed, it is not arbitrary and therefore not defective under the Equal Protection Clause.

Conventional "equal protection" doctrine recognizes the distinction I have in mind; the only differences are in the labeling and in the attitude toward judicial assessment. Cases of caste-reinforcing discrimination require the strict scrutiny of suspect classifications, while potentially arbitrary legislation requires only the minimal scrutiny of the rational basis test. The difference is supposedly only one of degree, and there can be various levels of scrutiny between the two extremes. Distinctions based on gender, for example, require only intermediate scrutiny.[56] The stricter the scrutiny, the stronger the state interest required to justify the apparent discrimination.[57]

The difference between the two categories of discrimination, however, runs deeper than suggested in the conventional doctrine. While the treatment for arbitrary legislation need not change, we should think differently about the practice of caste-reinforcing discrimination. In those cases where it makes sense to rely on the premise of human equality in the Declaration of Independence – namely, in cases of caste-reinforcing discrimination – the realization of equality under law should be treated as a categorical imperative.

---

55 Illustrative of these sinecures was the monopoly awarded to selected butchers in New Orleans after the Civil War. Litigation over this monopoly, which the privileged butchers won, set back the development of the Equal Protection Clause for generations. See The Slaughter-House Cases, 83 U.S. 36 (1872).

56 See Craig v. Boren, 429 U.S. 190, 204 (1976) (announcing the standard of intermediate scrutiny for gender discrimination); see also United States v. Virginia, 518 U.S. 515, 531-33 (1996).

57 See Lawrence H. Tribe, American Constitutional Law § 16-6, at 1453 (2d ed. 1988).

The courts are obligated in all cases to bring our legislation into conformity with our understanding of intrinsic human equality. No state interest can justify practices that both reflect and reinforce cultural assumptions about the intrinsic superiority of whites over blacks, men over women, "legitimate" over "illegitimate" children, or heterosexuals over homosexuals. This, at least, is the way our law of equal protection would look if the courts began to take human equality seriously.

IV

Kant secularized the image of God by capturing the idea in his notion of universal humanity, but even as he presented biblical ideas in a modern idiom, he remained close to the spirit of the biblical text. Establishing the common theme between Genesis and Kant emboldens me to adapt a Kantian principle to our understanding of equality: Realizing equality is a judicial imperative. It is a categorical obligation incumbent on the courts and on state institutions. Our dedication to the proposition "all persons are created equal" requires the elimination of all caste-reinforcing policies of the state. In this view of the matter, there is no room for the kind of reasoning that infects the current doctrine of strict scrutiny, which tolerates patent discrimination for the sake of compelling state interests.[58] To those who believe that it is all a matter of balancing the value of equality against the interests of the state in legislating on the basis of inequality, the appropriate response is to paraphrase the master: Woe unto him who searches in the winding paths of the theory of interest-balancing for some technique to uphold the debasing of human dignity.[59] And to bring the point home, we should recall a saying that Kant attributes to the rabbis: "If justice goes, there is no longer any value in men's

---

58 Washington courts, for instance, have upheld a state statute imposing more rigorous rules against aliens possessing guns than against citizens committing the same acts. See State v. Acosta-Perez, No. 20900-4-II, 1998 Wash. App. Lexis 102 (Wash. App. Ct. 1998); State v. Hernandez-Mercado, 879 P.2d 283 (Wash. 1994).

59 This is based on the passage in Immanuel Kant, The Metaphysics of Morals 141 (Mary Gregor trans., 1991).

living on the earth."[60]

It is helpful, in this context, to grasp the analogy between the German commitment to protect human dignity and the caste-reaffirming branch of equal protection law. The underlying value commitment of post-war German law, a commitment drawn from Kantian sources, emerges in the first article of the 1949 Basic Law: "Human dignity is inviolable. It is the duty of the state to protect and respect (human dignity)."[61] This proposition has a moral force analogous to "all men are created equal." In the same way that Lincoln revived and interpreted a phrase from the Declaration of Independence to redeem the nation from the sin of slavery, post-war German lawmakers drew on the Kantian tradition to refound a nation that had descended into the evils of National Socialism. The commitment to equality expressed the value precisely opposed to American slavery as human dignity, for the Germans, was the value most widely abused under the Third Reich. When a nation seeks to establish itself on the basis of a fundamental value, it hardly makes sense to treat that value as contingent and partial, subject to being overridden by competing interests of the state. It would be ludicrous for a German to claim that human dignity is "unassailable" and then proceed to reason that the state could sometimes subject people to demeaning treatment, violating their dignity, because this deviation was required by "compelling state interests." Similarly, in the equal protection cases where human dignity is an issue – namely, in the caste-reaffirming cases – we should regard the commitment to equality as an absolute. In those cases where it applies, the postulate "all men are created equal" brooks no exceptions.

The implication of treating equality as a judicial imperative is that supposed state interests cannot justify our toleration of caste-reinforcing discrimination. This conclusion flows for the suspect classes that we readily recognize – race, national origin, gender, birth out of wedlock, and alienage[62] (at least in the state courts). It means that there are no degrees of scrutiny – no way

---

60 Id.

61 Grundgesetz art. 1 (1) (author's translation).

62 On the special problem posed by federal jurisdiction over aliens, see Mathews v. Diaz, 426 U.S. 67 (1976).

to express a commitment to the equality of women for some purposes but not others. On this view, a military draft that takes only men or a law of statutory rape that punishes only men is clearly unconstitutional.[63] And if we ever did anything as silly as adopting the Russian rule on capital punishment, a rule that exempts women from the death penalty,[64] we would clearly run afoul of our dedication to the proposition that all persons are created equal. As Kant teaches us, we realize our equality not only in receiving benefits but also in accepting equal responsibility under the criminal law.[65]

As we have seen in our derivation of the commitment to equality, there is a close connection between punishment and the emergence of equality as a normative ideal.[66] This connection should help to better appreciate Kant's controversial theory of retributive punishment. As developed in his *Philosophy of Right* in 1797, the state must guarantee equality in two dimensions of criminal punishment. It must seek a sanction that restores equality between offender and victim, and it must respect equality among offenders.[67] Plea bargaining is prohibited, as it should be. All offenders must be held responsible, out of respect both for the law and for the offenders themselves.

This is the core of a liberal theory of law, one that adheres to strict equality among persons. And as Kant makes clear in the famous example of the duty to punish in the island society about to disband, the liberal theory of law has biblical roots. The problem

---

63 Unfortunately, the Supreme Court is willing to tolerate discrimination in these areas. See Rostker v. Goldberg, 453 U.S. 57, 64-65 (1981) (upholding an exemption for women from selective service); Michael M. v. Superior Court of Sonoma County, 450 U.S. 464 (1981) (upholding the application of statutory rape only to male defendants and female victims).

64 See UK RF (Russian Criminal Code) § 59. I wrote a detailed criticism of this provision while it was still in draft form. See George P. Fletcher, In Gorbachev's Courts, N.Y. Rev. Books, May 18, 1989, at 13.

65 Kant expresses contempt for the prisoner who would accept a punishment less than he deserves simply to further his self-interest. See Kant, supra note 43, at 142-43.

66 See supra notes 41-45 and accompanying text.

67 See Kant, supra note 43, at 142-45.

that inheres in failing to punish – the vice of failing to treat the equally-deserving equally – is that blood guilt for the crime will be on our hands.[68] By failing to punish, we become complicitous in the crime. This is the thinking that prevails in the contemporary approach toward war crimes and crimes against humanity. The effort to establish an International Criminal Court reflects the teachings of the Konigsberg philosopher. *Impunidad* – allowing war crimes and crimes against humanity to go unpunished – is itself a great evil. And in the Kantian view, the evil both of crime and of *impunidad* is that they violate our commitment to equality under law.[69]

Tolerating castes in a society supposedly dedicated to human equality is a form of *impunidad* – a failure to act that allows evil to triumph. The state cannot sit idly by as caste differentiations survive and flourish, and it cannot participate in any way in the perpetuation of these popular prejudices.

Of course, there are some difficulties when a legislative scheme has a caste-affirming impact. A good example of the problems at the frontier arose in *City of Cleburne v. Cleburne Living Center,*[70] where the legislative scheme at issue prohibited the building of homes for the mentally retarded without the kind of permit required to erect a prison near a residential neighborhood. The Court balked at treating the mentally retarded as a "suspect class" but struck down the zoning requirement, as a violation of the rational basis test.

The special cases involving the mentally retarded or the handicapped enable us to realize the relative simplicity of the affirmative action problem.[71] Legislation to help the disadvantaged

---

68 See Id. at 142.

69 See Preamble to the Rome Statute of International Criminal Court, U.N. Diplomatic Conference of Plenipotentiaries on the Establishment of an International Criminal Court, U.N. Doc. A/CONF.183/9 (1998) ("Determined to put an end to impunity for the perpetrators of these crimes ...").

70 473 U.S. 432 (1985).

71 Justice Stevens began the transformation of his thinking about affirmative action by reflecting on the propriety of special legislation benefiting the handicapped. See *City of Cleburne,* 473 U.S. at 454 (Stevens,

obviously has a tone and quality different from practices that stigmatize particular classes and reinforce their subordination. Affirmative action for historically disadvantaged groups should remain a matter of legislative judgment. The Canadian solution seems to be on the mark.[72] The Constitution should neither prohibit nor require historically contingent measures to overcome socially induced forms of domination.[73] As amended in 1994, the German Basic Law also recognizes affirmative action for women as compatible both with the principles of respecting human dignity and equality under law.[74]

If we take the elimination of castes as the aspiration of the Equal Protection Clause, then we must acknowledge and overcome the willful indifference of American jurisprudence to wealth discrimination, particularly to discriminatory patterns of education that contribute to the perpetuation of the class system.

The great culprit is *San Antonio Independent School District v. Rodriguez*,[75] which actually upholds a system of school financing in which people living in poor neighborhoods pay a significantly higher rate of tax and attend worse schools. That the state should participate in a system of education that gives greater opportunity

---

J., concurring). He later realized that the essential issue raised by benign discrimination was whether legislation furthered a caste system or was designed to counteract it: "There is no moral or constitutional equivalence between a policy that is designed to perpetuate a caste system and one that seeks to eradicate racial subordination." Adarand Constructors, Inc. v. Pena, 515 U.S. 200, 243 (1995) (Stevens, J., dissenting).

72 See Canadian Charter of Rights and Freedoms § 15(2) (allowing affirmative action programs).

73 John Ely developed this argument many years ago. See John Hart Ely, The Constitutionality of Reverse Racial Discrimination, 41 U. Chi. L. Rev. 723, 727-41 (1974). See also John C. Livingston, Fair Game? Inequality and Affirmative Action (1979). I am fully aware that the current Supreme Court has rejected the relevance of "benign discrimination." See *Adarand*, 515 U.S. at 200; see also City of Richmond v. J.A. Croson Co., 488 U.S. 469 (1989).

74 See Grundgesetz art. 3(2); see also id. at art. 3(3), which explicitly permits special assistance for the handicapped.

75 411 U.S. 1 (1973).

to the rich is an unspeakable injustice.

All children are created equal; they are entitled to an equal opportunity to escape the economic conditions into which they are born. A legal system that does not recognize that elementary truth could not possibly think of itself as a liberal system committed to equality under law. Fortunately, state supreme courts have ruled against *Rodriguez* on the basis of their state constitutions.[76]

If American judges and justices were not so insulated and parochial in their thinking, they would realize that a result like *Rodriguez* would be unthinkable in many European supreme courts. Even without appealing to the value of human dignity, German courts would summarily rule that avoidably unequal school financing violated the principle that, at the start of their lives, all children should enjoy an equal opportunity of personal development.[77]

In my view, it would not help much to adopt Justice Marshall's jurisprudence, set forth in his compelling dissent in

---

76 See, e.g., Serrano v. Priest, 487 P.2d 1241 (Cal. 1971) (holding that a public school financing system that relies heavily on local property taxes and causes substantial disparities among individual school districts in amount of revenue available per pupil violates the Equal Protection Clause).

77 See 1 Maunz-Dürig, Grundgesetz: Kommentar 3:44 (34th supp. 1998) ("The (German) Constitution is committed to equality of opportunity (Startgleichheit) in the context of education for children and young people, a presupposition for the later flourishing of their personalities."(author's translation)). Additional support comes from the prohibition against wealth discrimination as an expression of the Sozialstaat (state committed to social welfare). See Grundgesetz art. 20(1). These prohibitions have generated a detailed law on permissible line-drawing in the tax systems. See Bruno Schmit-Bleibtreu & Franz Klein, Kommentar zum Grundgesetz 186-95 (9th ed. 1999). Also note the perspicacious comparative comment by the leading German scholar on the theory of equality, Gerhard Leibholz, Die Gleichheit vor dem Gesetz und das Bonner Grundgesetz, 66 Deutsches Verwaltungsblatt 193, 197 (1951) (author's translation):

Or think, let's say, about the implications of classical liberalism: in the United States, the Supreme Court has taken a negative stand, in line with 19th century ideas, against protective legislation favoring socially-oppressed classes. We have come to regard this protective legislation as the true expression of ideas of equality and justice.

Rodriguez, endorsing a more flexible scale of graded "scrutiny" based on the classification and issue at stake.[78] The system of egalitarian justice that I am advocating disavows all scrutiny and interest balancing in cases that challenge caste-based inequalities. Closer to the mark is Justice Stevens, who regularly draws inspiration from the religious foundation of equal protection and quotes the principle that all persons are created equal.[79] The basis of egalitarian jurisprudence should not be the state and its interests but, rather, the intrinsic equality of all persons created in God's image. When the state tolerates ingrained social attitudes that violate the principle of human equality, it permits the evil to escape unchallenged. It becomes responsible for the *impunidad*.

The focus of egalitarian jurisprudence must not be the state and its interests but rather individuals and their dignity. Whether we ground our respect for human beings in the religious message of Genesis or in Kant's secularized version of the same teaching, we must begin in awe of a mystery of the human condition that we cannot completely explain. Though we are still searching for the grounds of our faith, we are dedicated to the proposition that all people are equal and are entitled to equal treatment under law.

---

78 Rodriguez, 411 U.S. at 98-110 (1973) (Marshall, J., dissenting).

79 See the views of Justice Stevens, supra notes 50 and 71.

CHAPTER TEN

God's Freedom

Arthur Jacobson[1]

George Fletcher's "In God's Image: The Religious Imperative of Equality under Law"[2] argues for enhancing the equal protection of law under the Fourteenth Amendment of the Constitution of the United States. For example, Fletcher argues for overruling *San Antonio Independent School District v. Rodriquez*,[3] in which the Supreme Court upheld a system of school financing in which people living in poor neighborhoods paid a significantly higher rate of tax and attended worse schools than people in rich neighborhoods.

Fletcher argues that for the state (to) participate in a system of education that gives greater opportunity to the rich is an unspeakable injustice. All children are created equal; they are entitled to an equal opportunity to escape the economic conditions into which they are born.[4]

But the exact enhancements Fletcher proposes do not

---

1 Max Freund Professor of Litigation & Advocacy, Benjamin N. Cardozo School of Law.

2 99 Columbia Law Review 1608 (1999).

3 411 U.S. 1 (1973).

4 Fletcher, supra note 2, at 1628.

concern me here. What does concern me is what Fletcher believes compels or commends the enhancements, what is at the very root of Fletcher's argument that the enhancements he proposes are in order.

Fletcher's argument for a more radical conception of equality under law than the one obtaining in contemporary Supreme Court jurisprudence depends upon the creation story in the book of Genesis. Or, more precisely, it depends upon the first creation story in Genesis, for there are two, and they are very different.

The first creation story is in Genesis 1. I quote Fletcher's precise and careful translation:

> And God said, we will make man (Adam) in our own image after our likeness: and they shall have dominion over the fish of the sea, and over the fowl of the heaven, and over the beasts, and over every creeping thing upon the earth. So God created the man in God's own image, in the image of God created God it; male and female created God them.[5]

Fletcher points out that the rich ambiguity of this passage, alternating freely as it does between the singular and the plural. "God created it – Adam. Yet 'male and female' God created them."[6] So did God create one being or two? Fletcher's "preferred reading of this passage is that a gender-neutral being called God created another gender-neutral being called Adam."[7]

Actually the description of Adam as "bi-gendered" – a description Fletcher uses on the very next page – is more accurate.[8] "Gender-neutral" does not quite capture the point, which is that this creature contained both male and female characteristics, that it was "bi-gendered." The case for Adam being a sexually plural being that is at the same time a single creature grows even

---

5 Fletcher, supra note 2, at 1615, translating Genesis 2:18-23.

6 Fletcher, supra note 2, at 1615.

7 Id.

8 Id.

stronger when one considers the Hebrew term always translated by the term "God." The Hebrew word is "*Elohim*," which is a plural word whose literal meaning is "Rulers." The text draws out this plural side of God by having God say "we will make man (Adam) in our image." Nevertheless, nothing in the first five books of the Bible can be plainer than that *Elohim* is singular, not plural. So God, like Adam, has both a singular and a plural nature, and by creating Adam in His image God must be imparting to Adam the combination of singularity and plurality that marks the nature of God. One can argue, of course, that when God refers to Himself as "we," He is really doing just what monarchs do, using the "royal we." But even that argument proves the point, for by using "we" to refer to himself or herself, the monarch is staking a claim to embody – to fuse into a single body – the multitude over which the monarch rules. The monarch *is* the multitude, both singular and plural all at once. Similarly God fuses into a single entity the multitude of forms of rule – rule by humans, rule by forces of nature, by passions, by logic, by mathematical forms. He is "Rulers" altogether.[9]

The support Fletcher draws from this creation story is that all men and all women, of all races and religions, of all nationalities – all have been created in the image of God. They can look and live differently; they can have different beliefs. All these differences can divide them. But at root they are united by one overwhelming, fundamental fact – they are all made in the image of God – and it is this fact that establishes their transcendent equality. "Though one could imagine other religious traditions supporting a conception of innate equality," writes Fletcher, "there is no doubt that the assumption of equality in the West has its most plausible source in the myth that we trace to Genesis 1."[10]

Fletcher finds nothing in the second creation story that provides any authority for the proposition that all men are created equal. Quite the contrary. The second creation story provides a text, he says, for the subjugation of women,[11] and that is surely

---

9 See Arthur J. Jacobson, The Idolatry of Rules: Writing Law According to Moses with Reference to Other Jurisprudences, 11 Cardozo Law Review 1079, 1081-1082 (1990).

10 Fletcher, supra note 2, at 1617.

11 Fletcher, supra note 2, 1616-1617.

true. But, as we shall see, the story establishes the conditions for a virtually limitless expansion of inequality. If one were, as Fletcher is, an advocate for equality over inequality, one would regard this consequence of the story as wholly negative – derogation from the good and an argument for evil. But it is crucially important to understand the source of inequality in the story: a virtue that advocates of equality, including Fletcher, would regard as an unalloyed good. But the fact is that the virtue displayed in the story is in unavoidable conflict with equality. This virtue and the argument for inequality must be approached step by step in a careful reading of the text.

The second creation story, in Genesis 2, reveals the Deity "fashioning" Adam from the dust. Fletcher points out that the Deity is not *creating* Adam, as in the first creation story, rather He is *fashioning* him, where it is understood that creation is *creatio ex nihilo*, as in the creation of the universe, whereas fashioning is a reworking of materials already present into a different form. But even more important is that the Deity that fashions Adam from the dust has two names, not just one. One of them, *Elohim* (Rulers) we already know from Genesis 1. The other name is four Hebrew letters – *Yud-hey-vav-hey*. This second name is sometimes referred to as the Tetragrammaton, because it is a word made up of four letters – the *yud*, the *hey*, the *vav*, and the *hey*. (These four letters are sometimes sounded out in English as Yahweh or Jehovah.) Rabbinic tradition holds that the word is made up of particles from the four tenses – past, present, future, and causative – of the verb "to be." So a suitable English translation would be particles drawn from "That which is, has been, will be, causes to be" or "Twhbwbctb." But let's just stick with the Tetragrammaton. Rambam equates the Tetragrammaton with the Greek term *ousia*, which means existence. So the Deity that fashions Adam from the dust is *Yud-hey-vav-hey Elohim* or Existence Rulers.[12]

---

12 The King James and every other translation of the Bible we know of translate *Yud-hey-vav-hey Elohim* by Lord God instead of Existence Rulers, using the term God for *Elohim* and Lord for the Tetragrammaton. The reason the translators chose essentially to mistranslate the Hebrew is twofold.

The first reason is simple and obvious: the Hebrew text must have a word for God. So of the many names for God in the Hebrew text choose one, and call it God. The second reason is subtler: use of the term Rulers obviously implicates the dangerous complexities of the dual plurality and unity of the one God, complexities the translators obviously wished to avoid. That is so even though the dual plurality and unity of the Jewish God recalls the dual plurality and unity of the Christian God. But it is a dangerous recollection, because it pits the endless multiplicity of every conceivable kind of ruling in the Jewish conception against a Christian conception that is dramatically limited both in number and in nature. The proper translation raises a host of difficult and distracting theological questions. Better just to bury the issue by translating *Elohim* with God.

The reason the translators used Lord for the Tetragrammaton and failed to follow Rambam's lead is also twofold. First, the translators of the King James Bible were unlikely to have known much if anything about Rambam. Second, when observant Jews come across the Tetragrammaton they refuse to say it in any way (such as, for example, Yahweh or Jehovah). The reason they refuse is that the only one allowed to say the Tetragrammaton was the High Priest of the Temple in Jerusalem, only on Yom Kippur and only out of the hearing of any of the worshipers. So to say something like Yahweh or Jehovah courts breaking the law. Instead, when an observant Jew comes across the Tetragrammaton in prayer, what he or she says is *Adonai*, which means my Lord. (*Adon* means sir; hence *Adonai* means my Sir, or Monseigneur or my Lord.) Thus the written English is a complete mistranslation of the written Hebrew: it is a translation of spoken, not written Hebrew and of Hebrew spoken in prayer. Closer to correct, but still wrong, would be the word the observant Jew speaks or writes when coming across the Tetragrammaton apart from prayer: *HaShem* – The Name. The reason for that practice will become clear shortly.

Fletcher follows English practice by referring to *Yud-hey-vav-hey Elohim* as *Adonai Elohim*. See Fletcher, supra note 2, at 1616. Curiously, he does so in a written transliteration of the Hebrew, where it is perfectly permissible to write out the Tetragrammaton.

He also follows the German school of biblical criticism, attributing the first creation story – the one with *Elohim* – to the "priestly tradition" of the E text, and the second to the "J tradition" (J standing for Jehovah – an imagined sounding out of the Tetragrammaton). But those "traditions" are all just so much speculation. They are interpretations of the text, and not very interesting ones at that. Instead of imagining or inventing two different traditions, why not ask, what possibly could be the significance of using the additional name *Yud-hey-vav-hey* to refer to *Elohim*? What does Existence add to Rulers, in the context of the two very different stories of the creation of man/woman?

Though it is not clear at first, it soon becomes clear in the text that the Adam of this second creation story has but a single sex – male – and that the word "Adam" does not refer generically to "man," as it did in the first creation story, but is the proper name of a single man. Because the Adam of the second creation is not bi-gendered, because he does not bear the burden of plurality, he can be and is strictly singular. This unalloyed singularity corresponds to the text's use of the term "fashioned" – molding from already existing materials – instead of the term "created" – *creatio ex nihilo*. Because when one "fashions" something one is necessarily fashioning "some thing," one by one. The singularity of the process is in the nature of fashioning. *Creatio ex nihilo*, in contrast, involves the creation of species of various sorts – elements of the periodic table, minerals, organic species and so forth. Certainly, the organic species have members, but the members have no individuality. Their individuality is completely subsumed by the species, or rather they do not exist in and for themselves, as do individuals; they exist only to perpetuate the species. The individuals, as individuals, have no "existence." As are the two halves of the original bi-gendered creature, they are completely bound by the demands involved in perpetuating the species. They have no names, no individuality. They are profoundly and completely unfree.

There is a larger significance to the lack of proper names, of individuality and freedom, in the first creation story. The first creation story is, of course, the culmination of the beginning of the creation of the universe. In the beginning of this process the earth was "*tohu v'bohu*" – "astonishingly empty" or "desolate and void" or "waste and wild." There are many ambiguities and complexities in parsing the very beginning of Genesis 1, but one thing is certain: The process involves moving from complete disorder to greater and greater conditions of order, and the order towards which the process is moving is an order created by lawfulness, the lawfulness of the laws of nature. So the process of creation, in which the creation of Adam is the very last part, is a process of the creation of lawfulness. The subject matter of creation is lawfulness itself.

And laws, whether the laws of nature or the laws of man, are no respecter of persons. When individuality does appear on the scene, in Genesis 2, it is precisely the ability of law to subsume individuality, to take individuality out of the scene, if but for a moment, that will be the great contribution of law to order, specifically in Genesis 2 and in the story of Cain and Abel in Genesis 4.

We are now in a position to appreciate the double name of the Deity in Genesis 2. In Genesis 1 the Deity has a single name only: Rulers. That is because Genesis 1 is about the creation of lawfulness in the universe. So the only aspect of the Deity that is relevant to the story is the Deity's lawfulness, His character of ruling. Or perhaps it would be more accurate to say that in Genesis 1 the Deity had not yet begun to "fashion;" He had been involved only in the process of creation. So the aspect of the Deity as fashioner had not yet come into existence. Individuality had not yet come into existence. Indeed, because individuality really is self-consciousness, self-consciousness is an absolute prerequisite for the apprehension of existence. Hence, only once God begins fashioning does existence comes into existence. Only then does Existence join Rulers in the name of God. That is why rabbinic tradition holds that the Tetragrammaton is the "personal" name of God: God begins to have self-consciousness only in relationship to His fashioning other individuals with whom He enters into relationships. Otherwise, He is just lawfulness itself.

And it is at this moment, when God fashions Adam, that because He now has a personal name, thus personality, that God becomes free. He ceases to be only lawfulness. He reflects the freedom Adam has as an individual and that Eve will have once God fashions her from Adam's flesh.[13] Before God has fashioned Adam He is unfree, because He is subject to the laws that have created the universe. It doesn't matter that He is the lawgiver; He is subject to His own laws.[14] Otherwise, they can't be laws. That is God's tragedy. He will be unfree so long as He doesn't fashion a

---

13 Genesis 2, 22.

14 Of course, God has the freedom possessed by any legislator – whether to legislate or not, i.e., whether to create the universe or not. He may also be free to choose what to legislate, though this sort of freedom must be constrained by the laws of mathematics and the fundamental structures of the material world. But the freedom of a legislator is freedom of a different order than the freedom conceived in interaction amongst personalities.

being into whose nostrils He breathes "the soul (or breath) of life,"[15] whom he makes self-conscious, so that God can be self-conscious in relation to the being He fashions.[16]

Even though it was Adam into whose nostrils God breathed "the soul of life" and therefore self-consciousness and freedom, it was not Adam who performed the first act of freedom; it was Eve, Adam's "helper."[17] Eve had two special characteristics distinguishing her from Adam and making her the likelier to be the first to perform an act of freedom.

First, God had fashioned Adam out of the same material He had fashioned all the other creatures, from the dust, though in the case of the other creatures the text says that they were to be "brought forth" from "the earth."[18] In contrast, God had fashioned Eve, not from the dust, but from Adam's flesh, from his "side" (often translated as "rib").[19] Thus the substance of Eve's body contained "the soul of life," hence individuality and freedom, whereas the substance of Adam's body was dead dust. Individuality and freedom are present in Adam, but they're not in the very substance of his being.

---

15 Genesis 8, 7.

16 It is worthwhile noting that God's release from strict lawfulness takes place over the whole spectrum of lawfulness. It is from this perspective that one may view God's ability to perform miracles. For what are miracles but God's departure from strict lawfulness?

17 "Hashem God said, 'It is not good that man be alone; I will make him a helper corresponding to him.'" Genesis 2, 19.

18 Genesis 1, 24. Interestingly, the text does not talk about "living creatures" being brought forth, but rather about "a living soul" being brought forth (and then says "after its kind" instead of "after their kind"). What God is calling to be brought forth is singular, not plural, and not a creature, but a soul. Nonetheless, no translation reports the literal Hebrew text, opting instead for "living creatures."

The obvious difference between the fashioning of Adam and the creation of these other creatures is that the creatures emerged alive from the earth, whereas God had to breath "the soul of life" into Adam's nostrils in order to transform the statue of Adam He had fashioned into the living Adam.

19 Genesis 2, 22.

Second, God ordered Adam not to eat of the tree of knowledge *before* He fashioned Eve.[20] This is significant for at least two reasons.

First, God directed the command to Adam. Eve wasn't present. Did God mean for the command to apply to Eve? We know that she knows about the command, because in response to the serpent's question whether perhaps God had said "You shall not eat of any tree of the garden?" Eve responds, "Of the fruit of any tree of the garden we may eat. But of the fruit of the tree which is in the center of the garden God had said: You shall neither eat of it nor touch it, lest you die."[21]

The first thing to notice about what Eve told the serpent is that it isn't accurate: she leaves out some things that God told Adam and adds some things He hadn't. For example, God told Adam that he may not eat of the tree of the knowledge of good and bad.[22] Eve reports the prohibition as including touching the tree. Also, she doesn't give the tree's name; she just reports that it's the tree at the center of the garden. She may be talking loosely to the serpent. Or, she may be repeating exactly what Adam told her. If so, the inaccuracies would be Adam's inaccuracies, his false report to Eve of what God had told him. In other words, Eve was dependent on Adam's report of what God told him, and *she knew she was dependent*. How reliable was Adam's report? Did God, in fact, issue the command Adam says he issued? It would not be surprising for a woman in Eve's position to have such questions.

Second, in order to conclude that the command applied to Eve Adam had to engage in legal interpretation. It may be a perfectly plausible interpretation, but it was an interpretation. Of course, he could have asked God whether the command applied to Eve, but the text doesn't report that he did. If Adam had indeed reported to Eve exactly what God said, then Eve would have known that Adam was engaging in interpretation and must have wondered whether Adam's interpretation was indeed the correct interpretation. Indeed, the omissions and additions in what she told the serpent may have been her interpretation of what Adam said to her.

---

20 Genesis 2, 17.

21 Genesis 3, 2-5.

22 Genesis 2, 17.

So Eve, who possesses individuality and freedom in her very bones, confronts a command that may or may not apply to her, that Adam may or may not be relating to her correctly, that may or may not have ever even been commanded, that is clearly the result of interpretation and Adam's interpretation, not necessarily hers – it is this woman whom the serpent approaches. The serpent did not speak to Adam. Did the serpent sense Eve's greater individuality and freedom? Rashi supposes that the serpent had seen Adam and Eve engaging in intercourse and consequently began to lust after Eve.[23] (Rashi bases his suggestion on the passage immediately preceding the serpent, "They were both naked, the man and his wife, and they were not ashamed."[24]) Rashi's suggestion has many virtues, but it must account for the particular action the serpent chose to take as a consequence of his lust. Why did he try to get Eve to disobey God's command? Was the serpent hoping that if he persuaded Eve to disobey that would create a rift between her and Adam? After all, the serpent was "cunning beyond any beast of the field,"[25] and he could easily have understood the inherent tensions between Adam and Eve created by Eve's not having been present when God commanded Adam. So Rashi's suggestion is consistent with the thought that there were indeed such tensions. Of course, the serpent's hopes (if he, in fact, entertained those hopes) were dashed when Adam simply ate the fruit Eve handed him.

Once Eve acts, that is to say, once Eve makes manifest her inherent freedom, God is free to act; He's no longer chained to strict lawfulness. God first speaks to the serpent: "Because you have done this, accursed are you beyond all the cattle and beyond all beasts of the field."[26] God's first act is to create an inequality between the serpent and the cattle and beasts of the field. Then he speaks to Eve: "He said, 'I will greatly increase your suffering and your childbearing; in pain shall you bear children. Yet your

23 Abraham ben Isaiah and Benjamin Sharfman (trans.), The Pentateuch and Rashi's Commentary: A Linear Translation into English, Genesis (Brooklyn, 1949), p. 27 (comment to 3, 1, Now the serpent was more subtle).

24 Genesis 2, 25.

25 Genesis 3, 1.

26 Genesis 3, 14.

craving shall be for your husband, and he shall rule over you.'"²⁷
One of the two punishments God inflicts upon Eve is subjecting her
to the rule of her husband. Eve's subjugation becomes the model
for the numerous subjugations to follow – the Egyptians over the
Israelites, the Israelites over Canaan and others.

God now turns to Adam, and ends his punishment of Adam
by saying: "By the sweat of your brow shall you eat bread until you
return to the ground, from which you were taken: For dust are
you, and to dust shall you return."²⁸ When God had warned Adam
not to eat fruit of the tree of the knowledge of good and bad, He
said: "for on the day you eat of it, you shall surely die." There is an
abundance of controversy in the rabbinic literature whether man
was originally an immortal being and God was, in effect, killing him
off, or was originally mortal and God was simply shortening his
lifespan. If the former, then God was, in effect, committing a kind
of homicide. God clearly treated Cain's killing of Able as homicide
(even though there were no laws against homicide at the time,
and the only model for killing was the one God had provided).
The only difference between the two is that God was doing to an
entire species what Cain did to just one man. Is God responsible
for homicide? By imposing the death penalty upon Adam and
his progeny (what about Eve?) or even just by shortening his life
(which is what Cain had done to Able) was God demonstrating a
freedom to be lawless. And there are many other episodes – killing
the Egyptian first-born, drowning Pharaoh's army, telling Joshua
to annihilate the Canaanites, and on and on. Were these killings
lawful, or was God expressing his freedom by behaving lawlessly?

Once God finishes his condemnatory speeches, the first
thing He does is to start playing favorites, treating the sacrifices
of the two brothers, Cain and Abel unequally:

> After a period of time, Cain brought an offering
> to Hashem of the fruit of the ground; and as for Abel, he
> also brought of the firstlings of his flock and from their
> choicest. Hashem turned to Abel and to his offering,

---

27 Genesis 3,16.

28 Genesis 3,19.

but to Cain and to his offering HE did not turn.[29]

The inequality in treatment had dreadful consequences – one brother dead, the other ostracized. It was not a harmless inequality. God's most consequential favorite, of course, is Israel, "the priesthood amongst the nations." But there are many others throughout the Bible.

God's freedom from lawfulness clearly permits him to perform what are arguably lawless acts and also to treat people unequally. God's freedom is an invitation to the rise of inequality. The second creation does contain a virtue, however, the virtue of freedom. The problem is that a consequence of the exercise of that virtue, either by man or by God, is an increase of inequality. The virtue of the second creation story is thus at odds with the virtue of the first. Most of us surely value both virtues to one degree or another. But we have to recognize that freedom's gain is equality's loss and vice versa. The two creation stories must be read together as a single statement of that perpetual dilemma.

---

29 Genesis 4, 3-5.

Contributors

George P. Fletcher

George P. Fletcher is the Cardozo Professor of Jurisprudence at Columbia Law School. Fletcher is regarded as one of the leading scholars in the United States in the fields of torts and criminal law, and, in particular, comparative and international criminal law. Fletcher is the only scholar, writing in English, to be cited by the International Criminal Court. In 2015, Fletcher received the Silvia Sandano Prize in Human Rights. The international prize was presented at a ceremony in the Rome Senate.

In 2009, Fletcher published two books, *The Bond* and also *Tort Liability for Human Rights Abuses*, which discusses tort liability in international cases. Another book he wrote, *Defending Humanity: When Force is Justified and Why*, explores the analogies between self-defense in domestic and international law. *The Grammar of Criminal Law: American, Comparative, and International* probes the basic structure and language of diverse systems in criminal punishment. In addition, he has published 10 other books and more than 150 law review articles.

Fletcher's most famous law review article is "Fairness and Utility in Tort Theory," which has been widely cited. In 2006, he wrote a brief in Hamdan v. Rumsfeld, which was adopted by Justice John Paul Stevens and the four-vote plurality. In 2004, Fletcher was elected to the American Academy of Arts & Sciences. Fletcher has lectured and conducted media spots in Russian, French, German, Hebrew, Spanish, Hungarian, and Italian. Fletcher has published dozens of op-ed pieces and longer articles in The New York Times,

The Washington Post, The New Republic, and The New York Review of Books.

Suzanne Last Stone

Suzanne Last Stone is professor of law at the Benjamin N. Cardozo School of Law of Yeshiva University and director of Cardozo's Center for Jewish Law and Contemporary Civilization. She has held the Gruss Visiting Chair in Talmudic Civil Law at the law schools of Harvard University and the University of Pennsylvania, and was a visiting scholar at Princeton and Columbia Law School. Professor Stone is also an affiliated visiting professor of Jewish law at Hebrew University Law and Tel Aviv University Law School.

Professor Stone writes and lectures on the intersection of Jewish legal thought and contemporary legal theory. Her publications include "In Pursuit of the Countertext: The Turn to the Jewish Legal Model in Contemporary American Legal Theory" (Harvard Law Review), "The Jewish Conception of Civil Society" (in Alternative Conceptions of Civil Society, Princeton University Press) and "Feminism and the Rabbinic Conception of Justice" (in Women and Gender in Jewish Philosophy, Indiana University).

Professor Stone is a graduate of Princeton University and Columbia University Law School and was a Danforth Fellow in 1974 in Jewish history and classical religions at Yale University. Before joining Cardozo, she clerked for Judge John Minor Wisdom of the Fifth Circuit Court of Appeals and then practiced litigation at Paul, Weiss, Rifkind, Wharton & Garrison.

In addition to teaching courses such as Jewish Law and Political Thought and Jewish Law and American Legal Theory, she currently teaches Federal Courts, Civil Procedure, and Law, Religion and the State.

Herbert Morris

Herbert Morris holds a joint appointment with the UCLA Department of Philosophy and recently has taught *Criminal Law I*, and *Law, Philosophy and Literature.* He is a nationally recognized philosopher of law. Professor Morris served as Dean of Humanities of UCLA's College of Letters and Science from 1983 to 1993, and Interim Provost of the College from 1992 to 1993. He chaired the Board of Governors of the University's Humanities Research Institute from 1988 to 1990. Professor Morris has lectured and written widely on moral and legal philosophy, including *On Guilt and Innocence: Essays in Legal Philosophy and Moral Psychology* (University of California Press, 1976). He is also the author of several works of literary criticism: *The Masked Citadel: The Significance of the Title of Stendhal's La Chartreuse de Parme* (University of California Press, 1961), and "What Emma Knew: The Outrage Suffered in Jorge Luis Borges's Emma Zunz" (*Indiana Journal of Hispanic Literatures*, 1997). He is editor of *On Guilt and Shame* (Wadsworth Publishing Company, 1971) and *Freedom and Responsibility: Readings in Philosophy and Law* (Stanford University Press, 1961).

Richard V. Meyer

Richard V. Meyer assumed the position of Director, Foreign LL.M. Programs for the Mississippi College School of Law in 2011 after retiring from a professor of law position at the United States Military Academy at West Point (U.S.M.A.). In 2011 he was appointed as a Senior Fellow for the West Point Center for the Rule of Law and has also been a member of the editorial committee of Oxford's Journal of International Criminal Justice since 2010. He received the rare honor of being appointed to the *Phi Kappa Phi* Honors Society as a faculty member for excellence in teaching at U.S.M.A. and at Columbia Law School. The Center for Teaching Excellence has certified him as a "Master Teacher."

Prior to entering academia, Professor Meyer was a Judge Advocate, Field Artillery Commander, and Military Intelligence Specialist for the United States Army from 1985 to 2007. He has served in a variety of positions around the country and the globe. A recognized military justice and trial advocacy expert, he has tried fully contested criminal cases in front of juries on three continents and trained some of the most respected trial advocates in the military. A frequently requested speaker in the United States and abroad, Professor Meyer has presented at the United Nations, Yale, Penn, Oxford, Columbia, as well as dozens law schools and conferences around the globe.

His primary areas of research and scholarship are military law, international criminal law, international humanitarian law, biblical jurisprudence, Catholicism & the Law, and intelligence law. At MC Law, he teaches or has taught International & Comparative Criminal Law, Biblical Jurisprudence, National Security Law, Torts, Contracts, and LL.M. courses in American Law and Legal Systems.

Joel Baden

Joel Baden is a specialist in the Pentateuch, Biblical Hebrew, and disability theory in biblical studies. He is the author of the books *J, E, and the Redaction of the Pentateuch* (Mohr Siebeck, 2009); *The Composition of the Pentateuch: Renewing the Documentary Hypothesis* (Yale University Press, 2012); *The Promise to the Patriarchs* (Oxford University Press, 2013); *The Historical David: The Real Life of an Invented Hero* (HarperOne, 2013); and the co-editor of the volume *The Strata of the Priestly Writings: Contemporary Debate and Future Directions* (TVZ, 2009).

Katharina de la Durantaye

Professor Doctor de la Durantaye, LL.M. (Yale) is the holder of an assistant professorship of civil law, in particular on Private International Law at the Humboldt University of Berlin. Previously, she was a visiting professor at Columbia Law School and Boston University School of Law and Assistant Professor of Law at St. John's University School of Law. She studied art history, law and modern German literature in Bologna, Passau, Berlin and New Haven, CT. She received her PhD has written to the Roman law. She has received a book of the year award and has over thirty publications.

Arthur J. Jacobson

Arthur Jacobson is the Max Freund Professor of Litigation & Advocacy at Cardozo Law. Professor Jacobson was an associate with the firm of Cleary, Gottlieb, Steen & Hamilton. He holds a Ph.D. in government; his thesis was on the political philosophy of Hegel. His scholarly work has focused on the idea of dynamic jurisprudence. In addition to his specialties, Professor Jacobson teaches classes in employment law and litigation.

Made in the USA
Middletown, DE
07 September 2021